THANKS FOR YOUR SUPPORT!

David N. Bossie

David Bossie
President, Citizens United

www.citizensunited.org

INTELLIGENCE
FAILURE

How Clinton's National Security Policy
Set the Stage for 9/11

DAVID N. BOSSIE

WND Books
A Division of Thomas Nelson Publishers
Since 1798

www.thomasnelson.com

Published by WorldNetDaily Books, a Thomas Nelson, Inc. Company, P.O. Box 141000, Nashville, Tennessee 37214.

Library of Congress Cataloging-in-Publication Data

Bossie, David N., 1965-
    Intelligence failure : how Clinton's national security policy set the stage for 9/11 / David N. Bossie.
        p. cm.
    Includes bibliographical references and index.
    ISBN 0-7852-6074-9
    1. Intelligence service—United States. 2. National security—United States. 3. September 11 Terrorist Attacks, 2001—Causes. 4. United States—Foreign relations—1993–2001. I. Title.
    JK468.I6B67 2004
    327.1273'09'049—dc22

                                                                    2004004975

Printed in the United States of America

04 05 06 07 08 QW 5 4 3

This book is dedicated to my beautiful and loving wife Susan,
whose encouragement during this difficult project
carried me to the finish line,
and to my darling children, Isabella and Griffin,
whose wonderful smiles and laughter make life worth living.

In memory of my friend Barbara Olson,
who was taken from us on 9/11.
If Barbara were alive today
I know she would have penned this book.

CONTENTS

CONTENTS

AUTHOR'S NOTE

A NOTE ABOUT MY SOURCES USED IN THIS BOOK. HAVING PARTICIPATED in all of the Clinton investigations from Whitewater to illegal foreign money contributions to the DNC and Clinton campaign to questionable dual-use technology transfers to China, I developed several reliable sources of information inside the federal government and Congress.

Throughout the process of writing this book I interviewed many senior members of the Bush and Clinton administrations as well as Congress who would only speak to me on the condition that I not reveal my sources.

I gave my word, and so throughout this book you will see unnamed sources mentioned. They are real, credible, and knew firsthand that 9/11 will always remain Bill Clinton's legacy.

FOREWORD

By Robert D. Novak

HISTORY IS WRITTEN BY THE HISTORIANS WHO, FOR MANY DECADES, have been mostly liberals. The writers of contemporary history rely on journalism, which in turn is even more thoroughly dominated by liberals.

Thus, the permanent worldview passed on to future generations is tilted to the reigning liberal conventional wisdom. The culpability of Franklin D. Roosevelt in the Pearl Harbor disaster was covered up by a series of investigations and is absolutely rejected in mainline history. Harry Truman is extolled as a hero of the Cold War, concealing his responsibility for the tragic no-win policy of the stalemated Korean War. The cautious policies of John F. Kennedy and Lyndon B. Johnson in dealing with the Soviet Union are applauded instead of blamed for being contrary to U.S. interests.

It is happening again. Bill Clinton's lassitude toward terrorism is covered up, and George W. Bush is blamed for failing to do in eight months prior to September 11, 2001, what his predecessor ignored in eight years. This process has been accelerated as Election Day 2004 nears to determine whether there will be a second Bush term.

Never has a corrective book been as badly needed as *Intelligence Failure*. This is must reading. It's also a shocker. David N. Bossie tells a story that cannot be found in mainstream newspapers, magazines, or books, but is all too true. It penetrates the cover-up of President Clinton's abysmal neglect of the terrorist menace, the blame for which is now transferred to President Bush.

Dave Bossie, to be sure, is no even-handed historian or middle-of-the-road journalist. He is a conservative advocate who fights hard for his views. But he is also a skilled and honest investigator who deals with facts, not urban legends spread by the Internet. As a journalist, I have dealt with Mr. Bossie over many years as the guiding force behind Citizens United before and after he served as chief investigator of the House Government Reform Committee probing the Clinton scandals. He is accurate and, indeed, meticulous in his handling of details.

Dave Bossie is always committed to the cause of a safe and strong America, but the passion behind *Intelligence Failure* is personal. He was a very close friend of Barbara Olson, who worked the Clinton investigations with him and was the most famous victim of the 9/11 terrorist attacks. Mr. Bossie has partially dedicated this book to the memory of Ms. Olson, who he says probably would have written it herself if she were still alive. So he does not want the Clinton culpability for the disaster to be erased by spin-doctors in the role of historians and journalists.

Mr. Bossie deals with documented facts, and that makes his story all the more appalling. He begins with the portrait of a president of the United States who refused any contact with his own CIA director, James Woolsey. A distinguished student of international affairs and a lifelong Democrat, Woolsey has endorsed the book in these words: "A thorough and powerful indictment, and a chronicle of all the ways that national security policy in the 90's helped lead to 9/11."

Such an assessment by a senior member of the Clinton national security team runs counter to the argument made by Richard Clarke, the counter-tearooms aide in the Clinton and, briefly, the Bush administrations. Clarke was the odd man out in the Clinton White House, a minority of one in advocating effective action against Osama bin Laden and Al Qaeda. Now, he has been transformed into Clinton's defender and Bush's scourge.

The Kean Commission, the so-called "independent" inquiry into 9/11, cannot be expected to be any more useful than were the numerous commissions on Pearl Harbor sixty years ago that covered up all responsibility by the White House.

Mr. Bossie strips away at the pretensions of a "fair and balanced" commission considering the background of its members. He writes: "The Democrats are, for the most part, a very political, ideological, and ruthless group of Clinton supporters, while the Republicans are, for the most part, tepid centrists that lack extensive foreign policy experience."

Jamie Gorelick, Clinton's deputy attorney general, supervised the FBI that has much to answer for, as is shown by this book. Former Congressman Timothy Roemer was chief counsel to Senator Dennis DeConcini, who is described in this book as leading the opposition to Woolsey's CIA budget requests. And also sitting on the commission is Washington super-lawyer Richard Ben-Veniste. Mr. Bossie knows him well from the Senate Whitewater investigation where Ben-Veniste was chief counsel for the Democrats and an ardent Clinton defender.

Dave Bossie's assessment does not mince words: "President Bill Clinton never effectively dealt with Osama bin Laden and Al Qaeda. Rather than acting in the interests of national security, his actions repeatedly jeopardized national security and encouraged Bin Laden and other terrorists to continue their openly declared war against the United States. Not only did he repeatedly fail to strike at Bin Laden and refuse to follow through after promising action, he oversaw the decay of both the FBI and the CIA."

This harsh verdict is fully justified by the long stream of evidence laid out in *Intelligence Failure*. It is a case that will not be found in mainstream journalism, in instant histories, and certainly not in the reports of investigating commissions. David Bossie has performed an invaluable service for America.

CAST OF CHARACTERS

YASSER ARAFAT:
Terrorist leader of the Palestine Liberation Organization.

MOHAMED ATTA:
September 11 hijacker, probably one of the pilots. Associated with the Al Qaeda cell in Hamburg, Germany.

ALI ATWA:
Terrorist involved in the hijacking of TWA Flight 847 in 1985.

SAMUEL R. "SANDY" BERGER:
Second national security adviser to President Clinton.

FERNANDO GARCIA BIELSA:
High-ranking Cuban communist associated with Fidel Castro's terrorism support.

JEAN-LOUIS BRUGUIÈRE:
French magistrate and world's foremost terrorism investigator.

RICHARD CLARKE:
National coordinator for counterterrorism under Bill Clinton.

DIANA DEAN:
U.S. Customs inspector in Port Angeles who saved the lives of many in Los Angeles when she stopped the "Millennium Bomber," Ahmed Ressam.

DENNIS DECONCINI:
Democratic senator from Arizona who opposed CIA Director James Woolsey and his requests for funds to hire Arabic translators. Tried to make the FBI responsible for counterintelligence.

JOHN DEUTCH:

Interim CIA director between James Woolsey and George Tenet. Clinton pardoned Deutch for national security felonies his last day in office.

LOUIS FREEH:

Controversial FBI director appointed by Clinton.

ENRIQUE GHIMENTI:

FBI legal attaché in Paris responsible for twenty-eight countries.

NAWAF AL-HAZMI:

September 11 terrorist, about whom the CIA knew but never told the FBI.

FRED HUMPHRIES:

Director of the Seattle office of the FBI, involved in the "Millennium Bomber" investigation.

KHALID AL-MIHDHAR:

September 11 terrorist, about whom the CIA knew but never told the FBI.

MANSOOR IJAZ:

Sudanese businessman and former Clinton campaign contributor. Tried unsuccessfully to get the U.S. government to deal with Sudan to get Osama bin Laden.

FATEH KAMEL:

French Islamic terrorist who moved to Montreal, helped recruit Ahmed Ressam.

MIR AIMAL KANSI:

Pakistani shootist who killed two CIA agents outside their headquarters in Langley, Virginia, on January 25, 1993.

OSAMA BIN LADEN:

Saudi Arabian born millionaire. Financier of terrorism and leader of the group known as Al Qaeda (spelled also al-Qai'da, etc).

TONY LAKE:

President Clinton's first national security adviser.

ZACARIAS MOUSSAOUI:

Would-be terrorist in Minnesota who was supposed to be involved in the attacks of September 11.

IMAD MUGNIYAH:
Terrorist leader involved in multiple attacks, a leader in terrorism before Osama bin Laden.

SHEIKH OMAR BAKRI MUHAMMAD:
Self-designated spokesman for Al Qaeda.

NIVULLDIN:
Terrorist involved in the hijacking of TWA Flight 847 in 1985.

JOHN O'NEILL:
FBI chief of the New York office who connected Fred Humphries and Jean-Louis Bruguière to put together a case against Ahmed Ressam. He ran into opposition from the State Department while trying to investigate the bombing of the U.S.S. *Cole* in Yemen.

KATE PFLAUMER:
U.S. Attorney in Washington state who prosecuted Ahmed Ressam with help from Jean-Louis Bruguière.

AHMED RESSAM:
Algerian residing in Montreal, the "Millennium Bomber."

NORA SLATKIN:
John Deutch's executive director over the CIA.

ROBERT DEAN STETHEM:
Navy diver murdered in 1985 during hijacking of TWA Flight 847. His killers included Nivulldin and Ali Atwa as well as terrorist leader *AQ*.

GEORGE TENET:
CIA director appointed by Clinton, who remained in place under George W. Bush. John Deutch's successor.

ROBERT TORRICELLI:
Democratic Senator from New Jersey who successfully pressured the CIA under John Deutch to adopt guidelines which made it more difficult for operatives to recruit people with a record for human-rights violations.

JAMES WOOLSEY:
First Clinton-appointed CIA director. He resigned in 1995 because Clinton never allowed any private communication.

RAMZI YOUSEF:
Explosives mastermind behind the bombing of the World Trade Center in 1993.

A NEAR MISS,
OR MISSED OPPORTUNITY?

The Millennium Bomber

GARY ROBERTS CAUTIOUSLY EYED THE MAN STANDING ACROSS from him. Benni Norris said he was crossing over to Port Angeles on a business trip to Seattle, but that was an unusually long way to go to get to Seattle. Norris would have to make several stops ferrying from the Canadian mainland to the island of Victoria, then to Port Angeles, and then drive to Seattle. Inspector Roberts was suspicious and asked Norris to open his trunk, but he didn't notice anything out of the ordinary. Finally, he let Norris drive his green Chrysler 300M sedan onto the waiting ferry to America.[1]

But Roberts had second thoughts about his decision. He picked up his phone in the U.S. Immigration Control office and attempted several times to call over to the U.S. side of the border; he wasn't able to get through.[2]

It was December 14, 1999, and Norris, a highly trained Al Qaeda terrorist on a deadly mission for Osama bin Laden, had just successfully left Canada on the last ferry of the day. He had escaped detection by Canadian intelligence, and United States law enforcement had no idea he was coming.

Something about the man in the green Chrysler 300M bothered Diana Dean, a U.S. Customs inspector working in the Port Angeles, Washington, terminal where the ferry arrived from British Columbia. She asked a couple of standard questions. His halting answers and sweaty nervousness raised her suspicions even higher.[3] She said later, "There was just something—something that wasn't quite right and something that needed a little closer look."[4]

Dean told Norris, a French Canadian, that she needed to look in his trunk. Unlike the customs inspector on the Canadian side of the border,

Dean's coworkers not only looked in the trunk but opened up the wheel well for the spare tire. There was no spare tire. Instead, they saw large bags.

Norris immediately fled the scene, leading customs agents, guns drawn, on an extended foot chase. They apprehended him after a short scuffle. Once they had him in the back of the police cruiser, the inspectors explored the content of the bags. Among other things, they found several bottles of an unidentified liquid. Customs Inspector Mark Johnson shook one of the bottles and watched the brown liquid slosh in the container. Norris saw what he did and immediately ducked down out of sight in the bottom of the police car.[5] Johnson had shaken a bottle of nitroglycerin. He could have easily killed himself and those close by had he shaken the bottle any harder.

None of the agents, however, had any idea of the danger they were in. They suspected that the man was smuggling drugs into the country. Inspector Johnson tested some powder found in the bags for heroin and other illicit drugs, but the tests were negative.[6] Not until he opened one of the small black boxes from the wheel well did he realize what kind of man Agent Dean had stopped. Inside was a Casio watch attached to a circuit board. "I looked at it, and I just felt the blood just go out of my body," he said later.[7] It was a timing device.

As it turned out, "Benni Norris" was actually Algerian terrorist Ahmed Ressam. In his trunk were 118 pounds of urea nitrate, two twenty-two-ounce jars of nitroglycerine, fourteen pounds of sulfate, and timing devices consisting of Casio watches, nine-volt batteries, and circuit boards.[8]

Most of the terrorist attacks covered in this book will review the response, or lack thereof, by the Clinton administration. In this case, however, the real story lies in what happened before the planned attack. Why did U.S. intelligence services fail to uncover this plot prior to its occurrence?

The "Millennium Bomb Plot," also known in the FBI case file as "border-bomb," is not widely considered a great intelligence failure under the Clinton administration because diligent U.S. Customs agents caught the terrorist before he committed mass murder. But that is an illusion. While it may be true that the intelligence community was alarmed by signs that Al Qaeda planned devastating attacks for New Year's Eve 1999, none of that had anything to do with how Ahmed Ressam was caught. If Diana Dean had been less alert at the end of her long shift, or if Ressam had acted more confident, a great many people would probably have died at Los Angeles International Airport, his intended target.

In their book *The Age of Sacred Terror*, former National Security Council members Daniel Benjamin and Steven Simon give the impression that a general alert from the intelligence communities had something to do with the interception of Ressam. These two Clinton supporters state that the foiling of a terrorist plot in Jordan "electrified intelligence and law-enforcement personnel around the world," and that the resulting "heightened alertness paid off" in Ressam being stopped.[9] But they cite no evidence that there was heightened security at Port Angeles, and all accounts of the Benni Norris arrest indicate that the customs agents were *not* expecting terrorists to cross the border. They initially thought they had caught a drug smuggler.

Of course, Benjamin and Simon are correct in saying that there was international "excitement" in the intelligence community over a horrendous plot in Jordan. An Al Qaeda cell planned to blow up the four-hundred-room Radisson hotel in Aqaba, which would be packed with Christians and Jews celebrating the New Year's season and millennial parties. The cell also had a stockpile of firearms to attack several Christian sites in the area.[10] Jordanian intelligence intercepted this go-ahead from Bin Laden's lieutenant in Pakistan—"The grooms are ready for the big wedding"—so they decided it was time to move.[11] In making their arrests and searches, the Jordanians discovered enough explosives to not only "flatten out the Radisson,"[12] but also to devastate the entire neighborhood.[13] Understandably, counterterrorism officials became rather nervous when Jordan informed the United States of what they had found.

There is no indication, however, that this "excitement" translated into increased vigilance against terrorists at U.S. border entry points or in any way resulted in the arrest of Ressam. In this case, we owe a debt of gratitude to an inquisitive customs agent who took her job seriously.

As the millennium approached, the intelligence and law-enforcement communities became increasingly fearful that there would be other attacks inside the United States. When none occurred, they were greatly relieved. What no one knew at the time was that Al Qaeda considered January 3 a much more important date. It was said to be the day that Allah gave the prophet Mohamed the Koran.[14] In celebration of that event, an Al Qaeda cell in Yemen, closely associated with the cell in Jordan, intended to send a suicide bomber against a Navy Destroyer, the U.S.S. *The Sullivans*, as it pulled into Aden Harbor. Luckily, the terrorists' twenty-foot skiff was so overloaded with explosives that it began to sink. The terrorists had to dump explosives and abort the mission.[15] Unfortunately, they were not seen and arrested. They later attacked the U.S.S. *Cole*, with tragic results.

The Canadian Network

While Diana Dean's attentiveness at the border saved many lives, north of the border authorities had received explicit warning. An Algerian member of the terrorist cell in Jordan had informed them of another cell in Montreal, Canada.[16] Canadian intelligence began to monitor the group more closely. They had, as we will see, already been told of the cell, but had not taken it seriously. Canadian intelligence missed their opportunity to stop the plot in its infancy. By that point, Ressam was already traveling under the alias Benni Norris.

Ahmed Ressam lived in Montreal from 1994 to 1998 after living in Paris, France, for two years. In 1998, he left Montreal to attend an Al Qaeda training camp in Afghanistan. He was recruited through a friend who attended the Assuna Annabawiyah mosque, under the leadership of Imam Bahaa el Batal. This mosque actively promoted terrorism as a career for young men.[17]

Also attending that mosque was Muhammadou Ould Slahi, from Mauritania, a small African nation on the southeastern border of Algeria.[18] Canadian intelligence knew Slahi worked with another of Ressam's associates who assisted in the Millennium Bomb plot.[19] After Ressam was arrested, Slahi fled to the mosque, then back to Mauritania.[20] Slahi was later named as an important leader in the Hamburg cell, which was based out of the mosque where two of the pilots involved in the 9/11 attacks originally drew up their plans. It was also a source of funding for Zacarias Moussaoui, currently being held by federal authorities for suspected involvement in the plot.[21] Although, according to *Newsweek*, federal prosecutors no longer consider Maoussaoui the twentieth hijacker, they still maintain that he was involved in a larger Al Qaeda plot surrounding 9/11. In addition to connecting Montreal to Germany, Slahi is also connected to Osama bin Laden. He is related by marriage to Khaled al-Shanquiti, "The Mauritanian," a key business associate of Bin Laden's in Khartoum, Sudan, who funneled Al Qaeda money to his relative to fund terrorism.[22]

In February 1999, after extensive terrorist training in weapons, explosives, and tactics, Ressam returned to Montreal in possession of a passport that identified him as Benni Norris. By this time, Canadian immigration officials were on the lookout for Ahmed Ressam, and his name was on the watch list to prevent him from getting back into the country. However, as Benni Norris, Ressam slipped back into Canada undetected.

After several months of planning, he departed, once again unnoticed, heading west in a rented Chrysler sedan. In a rented hotel room in Vancouver, he cooked up his deadly explosive concoction. He planned to take the ferry from Victoria, British Columbia, in an attempt to enter the United States.[23]

To show the reach and breadth of Al Qaeda's international network of terrorists, it is worth noting that when Ressam was caught, one of his Montreal accomplices, Hamid Aich, fled Canada for Dublin, Ireland. Aich then moved to Belfast, where he began working for an Islamic charity, Mercy International Relief Agency. The charity's director is known to have received calls from Bin Laden's satellite phone.[24]

Redemption

The sleeper cell in Montreal reveals something interesting about the nature of Islamic terrorism. Since 9/11, the news media has quite consistently portrayed these terrorists as devoutly religious zealots. No doubt some are. Osama bin Laden himself certainly talks that way. However, one element to the background of the Millennium Bomber story, as well as the Hamburg cell, that has been overlooked is that the members of these cells in France, Germany, and Montreal did not live like devout Islamic fundamentalists at all.

According to the *Seattle Times*, Ressam shared an apartment with Sahid Atmani in Place de la Malicorne. They also trained together in the Al Qaeda camp in Afghanistan.[25] Atmani was finally arrested by police in Bosnia, where he had been granted citizenship for fighting in the nation's civil war.[26] Yet, Atmani was also arrested for male prostitution while in Canada.[27] One of Ressam's known associates, an Algerian named Said Gasmi, actually tried to avoid deportation from Canada by claiming that he would face persecution at home because of his open homosexual activity. A court-appointed psychologist examined Gasmi and determined that he was being truthful about his sexual habits.[28] According to a knowledgeable source, Shadi Abdallah, a German-based jihadist who became one of Osama bin Laden's bodyguards and later a government informant, was also homosexual.

This lifestyle does not comport with the religion's zealotry and casts doubt on the idea that we can simply blame terrorism on Islamic fundamentalists. As we will see in the case of World Trade Center bomber Ramzi Yousef, whose "terrorist crusade appears to have been driven by a confluence of anti-American and anti-Israeli rage and a significant dose of ego rather than religious ideology,"[29] at least some of these terrorists are driven by things other than genuine religious devotion. Indeed, their own rhetoric of devotion may be, as some suspect was the case for Yousef, merely a means of manipulating and recruiting others.

In an odd way, Benjamin and Simon seem aware of this dynamic in *The Age of Sacred Terror*. They present terrorists as driven by religious devotion and perhaps by a desire to do penance for past sins. Yet they make allusions about Mohamed Atta, one of the hijackers of 9/11, and his close companion Marwan al-Shehhi, that imply repentance was far from their minds:

> For years before the hijackings, al-Shehhi and Muhammad [sic] Atta were inseparable. They met and lived together in Hamburg. While in the United States, they moved from one flight school to the next and one apartment to the next, and they were physically together virtually all the time. Rudy Dekkers, the owner of Huffman Aviation, the Florida school they attended the longest, said they were "joined at the hip" and like a "duck with little ones," Atta in front, al-Shehhi always behind him. Al-Shehhi was incapable of defying his master.[30]

It may well be that Islamic terrorists offer to such small-time criminals and "sinners," known as dead-enders, a means of redemption. This would be consistent with reports that some of the 9/11 terrorists were witnessed visiting strip clubs before their final suicide mission. If Atta and al-Shehhi weren't willing to change their ways to conform to Islamic norms, perhaps they saw another way to religious redemption. The pilots aboard the hijacked 9/11 flights were cut and bled to be "sacrificed," write Benjamin and Simon. And all the victims of September 11 in the planes and the buildings were "being rendered to the deity." The mass-killing, they explain, "was a sacrifice made for the most common reason: expiation, the removal of a sin through an act of giving."[31]

Ressam himself was nothing more than a common criminal. He was a petty shoplifter and thief who got hooked up with Islamic extremists in part because he could make money selling forged identity documents.[32] Additionally, he noticed that those who were known to have fought in Afghanistan were accorded more respect. Money, acceptance, and redemption seemed to be his mixed motives.

INTELLIGENCE FAILURES

Terror Networks Go Undetected

MORE IMPORTANT THAN POPULAR PRECONCEPTIONS ABOUT terrorists is the astonishing fact that American intelligence services were seemingly unaware of the Montreal terrorist cell. The very day that Ressam was preparing for his ferry ride to Washington State, President Clinton's State Department spokesperson assured the nation that "the information that we're sharing with the American public, the specific information that we have, is related to threats overseas and not to U.S. soil."[1]

Even as they kept the Montreal cell under surveillance, Canadian authorities failed to inform U.S. intelligence agencies that there were terrorists sixty miles from the U.S. border.

The French and German Cells

The presence of a terrorist cell in Montreal should have concerned, but not surprised, the intelligence community. It was a matter of record that Europe, specifically France, had a serious problem with Islamic terrorists dating back at least to 1995. Algerian terrorists initiated a bombing spree in the Paris Metro lasting from July to October of that year. Eight were killed and hundreds more were wounded. One victim had to have both legs amputated while still on a bombed out train. The explosives were loaded with screws to serve as shrapnel.[2] It was also a fact that Canada had very liberal immigration laws. Finally, it was known that Algerians had gone to Afghanistan to fight the Soviets, and that many had returned to Algeria as violent jihadists.

For French-speaking terrorists who wanted to target the United States, the transfer from France to French-speaking Canada provided a natural conduit.

These facts were of great concern to Jean-Louis Bruguière, one of four investigating magistrates in France. Vested with broad powers to arrest, detain, and question suspects, he focused exclusively on the pursuit of terrorists, especially Al Qaeda's operations in Europe and Canada.[3] A "larger-than-life figure, tall, heavyset, with carefully coiffed black hair and impeccably tailored suits," Bruguière has a record of fighting terrorism that goes back to the eighties, including the daring and creative capture of infamous killers like Carlos the Jackal.[4] One of the men he suspected of playing a part in the subway bombing was Fateh Kamel.[5] Kamel did not remain in France, however. He somehow slipped away.

Soon after the terrorist bombing campaign there was a new crime spree. From January to March 1996, there was a series of tremendously violent robberies in Roubaix, France, involving masked men armed with machine guns and rocket launchers.[6] The attacks culminated with an attempted car bombing near the G7 summit meeting in Lille, France.

Fortunately, the police discovered and defused the bomb before it exploded. They were then able to track the bombers to their house. In the gun battle that ensued, the house was burned to the ground. Nevertheless, two terrorists got away, including their leader, Christopher Caze. Caze had traveled internationally, serving as a medic in Bosnia. It was in Bosnia that he embraced Islamic terrorist ideology, even though he had been raised a Roman Catholic.[7]

Caze's escape was short-lived. He was shot dead the next day as he tried to drive through a police roadblock. In Caze's electronic organizer, Bruguière found addresses of his contacts. One of the contacts was Fateh Kamel who was then living in Montreal, his place of residence on and off since 1988, where he was friends with Ahmed Ressam.[8]

Fateh Kamel was only one of many names found after searching Caze's belongings. Two other important names surfaced, including Imam Abu Hamza al-Masra and Mohammed bin Nasser Belfas. Having these three names linked together, Bruguière had insight into an international web from Canada to France, London to Hamburg, Bosnia to Silver Spring, Maryland,

and beyond. It was the beginning of a global network that would produce the September 11 attacks.

ABU HAMZA AL-MASRI

Abu Hamza al-Masri, known as "the Egyptian," is the Imam of the Finsbury Park mosque in London. He has only one eye and hooks for hands, due to an explosion in Afghanistan.[9] His mosque was frequented by the likes of Richard Reid, the so-called "shoe bomber," who tried to blow up a plane over the Atlantic in December 2001, and by Zacharias Moussaoui, believed to have plotted with the other September 11 terrorists.[10] The Egyptian-born cleric had contact with Osama bin Laden through Abu Zubaydah, Bin Laden's director of operations.[11] When police raided the Finsbury Park mosque in January 2003, they found suits designed to protect against chemical warfare.[12]

It turns out Hamza was also working with James Ujaama, an Islamic militant from Seattle who tried to set up a terrorist training camp in Oregon in 1999. Ujaama designed and helped operate Hamza's Web site called "Supporters of Sharia." On April 14, 2003, Ujaama entered into a plea agreement with federal authorities, under which he pleaded guilty to conspiring to provide goods and services to the Taliban. The plea agreement stipulates that in late 2000, at the direction of "co-conspirator #1," Ujamma traveled with "co-conspirator #2" from London to Pakistan, then facilitated co-conspirator #2's travel to jihad training camps in Afghanistan. *Newsweek* has identified co-conspirator #1 as Hamza, and co-conspirator #2 as Feroz Abassi, a student from south London who is being held by U.S. forces at the antiterrorism detention camp in Guantanamo Bay, Cuba, following his capture in Afghanistan.[13]

MOHAMMED BIN NASSER BELFAS

Mohammed bin Nasser Belfas was a leader of the Hamburg cell and is still on the loose.[14] He visited the United States in 2000 with the help of Agus Budiman, who gave him a false driver's license.[15] They also did reconnaissance of Washington, D.C. When German police raided Belfas's Hamburg apartment after September 11, they found photographs of the two men in front of the U.S. Capitol and in front of the Pentagon.[16] The pictures were taken before the suicide attacks of 9/11 on the Pentagon. Belfas was also friends with Mohamed Atta, one of the pilots and the leader of the 9/11 hijackers.[17]

Failure To Connect the Dots

September 11, 2001, was still years away when Bruguière gathered the information linking some of these men to the Paris subway bombings. All the threads were visible, just waiting for the right intelligence team to unravel them. But Bruguière was less than successful in getting other countries to take these terrorists seriously.

In 1998, Fateh Kamel successfully recruited Ressam to commit himself to Bin Laden's jihad and sent him to the Kalden training camp in Afghanistan. Because of pressure from Bruguière, by this time Canadian intelligence was keeping Ressam and others under observation. They did not perceive Ressam and his friends as a dangerous terrorist cell, however, referring to them in their reports as a "bunch of guys" and the "Tupperware Terrorists."[18] The Canadians considered Bruguière somewhat eccentric in his concerns. By the time the Jordanians confirmed Bruguière's concerns, it was too late to stop Ressam. The Canadian intelligence services missed their opportunity.

Due to Bruguière's diligence, Kamel was eventually arrested in Jordan and extradited to France to stand trial. But Ressam was back from Afghanistan, now a trained terrorist. Canadian intelligence was never able to locate him again, even though he was to be stopped if he attempted to return to the country. Not only had Ressam learned new and deadly skills, but with the arrest of his friends, he fell into the role of leader and recruiter rather than mere follower.[19] The Canadians thought Bruguière was absurd to think Ressam and his friends were dangerous, but Bruguière was now incensed that Ressam had slipped through his grasp.

Yet in all of this, apparently no one in France or Canada informed U.S. intelligence that a man who had been trained in an Al Qaeda camp in Afghanistan was living near the American border. Nor, as far as we know, did U.S. intelligence agencies, alerted by the terrorist attacks in France, ask any questions of the French intelligence agencies to learn what they knew about the terrorist networks.

In its joint inquiry into intelligence community activities before and after the terrorist attacks of September 11, 2001, Congress heard testimony from CIA Director George Tenet on things held in common by Mohamed Atta, Marwan al-Shehhi, and Ziad Jarrah, the three hijackers who piloted the jets on September 11. "Of particular note, the three were part of a group of young Muslim men in Hamburg, Germany, who came from different countries and backgrounds but attended the same mosques, shared acquaintances, and were drawn together by Islamist views and disenchantment with the West."

Ressam had also met with Al Qaeda operatives in Germany.[20] More significantly, in 1999, German intelligence had the Al-Quds mosque under surveillance because of its known association with Al Qaeda, at a time when American intelligence officials were desperately trying to figure out where Al Qaeda was going to strike.[21] The Germans also monitored Atta's apartment.[22] Yet, American intelligence was never alerted to these facts. For reasons unknown, German intelligence never thought to tell their American counterparts, and the Central Intelligence Agency never acquired the information on its own. As it turned out, it was probably around this time that Atta and his terrorist colleagues came up with the plan for their September 11, 2001, attack.[23] The one lead we know German officials did give us was dropped by the Clinton administration. In March 1999, German intelligence alerted the CIA to the identity of al-Shehhi, gave U.S. officials his first name and phone number, and requested that the U.S. government keep an eye on him. They didn't.[24]

While it is amazing that our allies did not offer more assistance, the fact remains that the CIA, FBI, and others should have asked questions, should have followed up on the leads they received. Our intelligence agencies failed to gather any information on their own. This neglect was a glaring sin of omission, bordering on incompetence. There are no good excuses for not following the leads that came out of the 1995 Paris subway bombing case.

In 1993, terrorists detonated a bomb at the World Trade Center, the first terrorist incident on American soil. Al Qaeda attacked our interests in other countries repeatedly after that. Then in December 1999, when Ressam tried to blow up LAX, we simply prosecuted him and cut a deal to prosecute a few others, leaving the network intact. Clearly, no one tried to learn more about it.

Putting the Puzzle Together

Perhaps saying "we" is rather unfair. Two major players are involved in dealing with terrorism—the FBI and the CIA—but they have different missions, and obstacles were put in place to keep them from working together too closely. As former Director of Central Intelligence James Woolsey said, "The system was set up that way on purpose so that the FBI and the CIA would have different missions and protect the American public from an out-of-control government." As a law enforcement agency, the FBI is concerned most with convicting criminals in a court of law. Foreseeing and preventing attacks from overseas is the CIA's mission. There are barriers that prevent either agency from sharing intelligence or secret grand jury testimony in ongoing investigations with the other.

On New Year's Eve 1999, John O'Neill was serving as the head of the FBI's National Security Division in New York. He had organized thousands of federal agents and police in a massive attempt to prevent or be able to respond quickly to a terrorist attack. When New Year's Day had come and gone, he might have thought he could afford to relax.

But he didn't. Instead he phoned Fred Humphries, the head of the FBI's Millennium Bomber case in Seattle and told him that he knew someone who could help with the Ressam case.[25] O'Neill arranged for Judge Bruguière to meet with the two of them in New York City. Among other things, Humphries was stunned to learn that Bruguière had warned Canadian Intelligence, prompting them to monitor the Montreal cell for four years. Why hadn't the U.S. been made aware of this dangerous threat? A few weeks later, he traveled to Paris with Kate Pflaumer, the U.S. attorney for Seattle, to take a crash course in "Terrorism 101," with Bruguière as professor. With almost twenty years of experience, Bruguière was able to explain the intricate web of connections between the Montreal cell and Al Qaeda's worldwide network.[26]

Humphries traveled the world in pursuit of evidence that could convict Ressam. In Canada, he found pants with holes matching burns on Ressam's legs where he had accidentally spilled chemicals on himself. He also found something the Canadian authorities had missed—a map of Los Angeles with a circle drawn around the three Los Angeles-area airports.[27]

The trial began on March 13, 2001.[28] Just two days prior, Canadian officials ordered Canadian intelligence personnel not to testify against Ressam for fear of compromising their intelligence secrets. It required immense pressure from the Bush Justice Department to get them to change their minds.

After he was convicted, Ressam cooperated as an informant. In addition to revealing much about Al Qaeda terrorist camps, in the words of the *Seattle Times*, Ressam "confirmed one of the greatest fears of the CIA, FBI and other intelligence agencies: The camps had trained thousands of men in chemical warfare."[29]

Ressam's testimony was clearly valuable to the intelligence community, but where was the CIA in all of this? Even if the FBI didn't disclose anything to the agency, why couldn't someone have picked up a newspaper in January 2000 and started following the connections? It is hard to believe that Humphries had traveled to France, Algeria, and England to gather evidence against Ressam, and the CIA knew absolutely nothing about it or chose to do nothing about it.

After all, if the news media could write about the extensive network associated with Ressam, then one would expect that the CIA could find this information as well. The *L.A. Times* wrote a Sunday special in July 2001 about the Algerian terrorist network and quoted Jean-Louis Bruguière saying he was "surprised by the low level of public awareness compared to the high level of the threat" that our nation faces from the Algerian cells.[30] By then, it was probably too late to piece together the plot in time to stop Al Qaeda. Nevertheless, there was nothing in that story about the international network in Canada, France, Afghanistan, and many other countries, that could not have been written in January 2000. Did the CIA have intelligence analysts capable of putting this puzzle together? Even as late as April 2001, when Bruguière was in L.A. offering to testify against Ressam, there would still have been enough time to disrupt the September 11 attacks.

CIA analysts who bothered to read the papers knew what was going on in France in 1995 and 1996. Analysts should have been in France working with Bruguière and his team, arranging for cooperation and shared intelligence. As Director Woolsey said, "The summer and fall of 1995 was crucial because we were just able to see the trial documents from the first World Trade Center bombing, and the Riyadh bombing had just taken place. By the end of 1995, then-CIA Director Deutch should have been burrowing in on this, and his people should have seen a pattern developing. The National Security Council adviser to Clinton and others should have been looking at this and asking, 'Are we facing something different and new? Who is involved, and is it state sponsored?'"

The FBI had a legal attaché in Paris headed by Enrique Ghimenti, former chief of an FBI counterterrorism unit with over twenty years' experience tracking down terrorists.[31] But again, the FBI is not responsible for tracking down and rolling up foreign terrorist cells. For one thing, they have daunting legal hurdles to clear in order to take action.

Consider, for example, the case of Zacarias Moussaoui, a French national of Moroccan descent, who when questioned on August 15, 2001, refused to cooperate. He came under scrutiny because he frightened flight instructors when he asked how to steer a jumbo jet without wanting to know about takeoffs or landings. Ghimenti asked French officials if they knew about him. It turned out they knew quite a lot. They gave him a huge dossier on Moussaoui, the result of surveillance since 1995. It established that Moussaoui had been to Afghanistan more than once and had definite terrorist connections.

What followed was a struggle between Ghimenti, along with FBI agents in Minnesota, and the counterterrorism unit in Washington, which repeatedly claimed that there were no grounds for a warrant. According to the *Seattle Times*, "Ghimenti was disappointed but, with FBI responsibilities in 28 countries, he had plenty else to do."[32] Naturally, on September 11, the Minneapolis FBI called Ghimenti back for help with the warrant, and this time it was approved.

With those sorts of difficulties facing the FBI, whether real or perceived, and with their different focus and mission, it is hard to believe that the CIA could reasonably assume that the bureau would deal with all the complex issues related to Ressam. They should have been investigating on their own, developing sources and comparing notes with French and German intelligence. The administration should have pressured other governments, not simply to allow their agents to testify at trial, but to cooperate with U.S. intelligence in rolling up Al Qaeda cells in Montreal, France, and Germany, as well as in places such as London and Ireland.

After 9/11, Germany rounded up some of the remaining terrorists. That was when Shadi Abdallah confessed to working for Al Qaeda. He has subsequently testified against other terrorists.[33] This doesn't change the fact, however, that German, French, Canadian, and American intelligence services did not communicate and did not share vital information that could have stopped the September 11 attacks from happening at all. The German cell, as well as those in France and Montreal, should have been dealt with long before they became operational.

Missed Opportunity

In 2000, everyone claimed victory because Ressam was caught before he executed his plan. But as revealed in this book, terrorism, which required good intelligence work to combat, was treated as a law enforcement problem throughout the Clinton administration. Law enforcement, however, was not accustomed to unraveling international conspiracies. The Justice Department wanted to prosecute Ressam and a few others that may have helped him, but no one looked at the bigger picture. Even at a time when there was increasing knowledge of Al Qaeda, there seems to be a disconnect on the intelligence-gathering side of the CIA, and a failure on the analytical side to recognize these dangers when they surfaced.

We avoided disaster at the Los Angeles International Airport thanks to an observant and competent customs agent. We weren't able to avoid it on September 11. Was investigating mosques on the suspicion of promoting terrorism too politically incorrect? Was the president so disinterested in intelligence matters that our capabilities degraded to the point where we were simply unable to connect the dots? Were our agents so demoralized that they were afraid to show initiative, opting instead to play it safe in order to advance the intelligence community?

The following chapters set forth the argument that the Millennium Bomber case is indicative of the effect that President Clinton had on both our nation's law enforcement and intelligence agencies. It is also *the* story of the missed opportunity that we were given to learn about Al Qaeda's plan and consequently stop the September 11 hijackings. The fact that we didn't will remain Bill Clinton's legacy.

WHAT YOU DON'T KNOW WILL KILL YOU

Clinton's Low Intelligence Priority

WHEN BILL CLINTON CAME TO OFFICE IN 1993, INTELLIGENCE became oriented more toward economic security than national security, in keeping with that administration's concept of a new world order and globalization in the post-Cold War environment. This shift in priorities gutted U.S. intelligence capabilities, making it incapable of meeting the new asymmetrical threats of the approaching millennium.

There have been "dozens" of U.S. intelligence failures, acknowledges Richard Haver, who served as special assistant on intelligence to Defense Secretary Donald Rumsfeld. In a May 2003 speech before the Institute for World Politics, Haver pointed out that U.S. intelligence officials don't like to speak of intelligence failures. He explained that lapses are rarely, if ever, acknowledged, and when they are acknowledged, they are played down.[1]

Haver spoke of the problem of avoiding intelligence surprises, such as Pearl Harbor and 9/11. "Our job related to surprise is to either eliminate it or to mitigate it; to reduce the probability of surprise . . . when surprise would have strategic effect," Haver said. "Intelligence failures are rarely caused by immediate problems. If there are difficulties in intelligence, they probably stem back five to ten years."

President Bush's administration is "paying the price for decisions made in the middle 1990s," Haver added. "I've been asked to go back and review dozens, literally dozens, of major intelligence failures, and when you get down to the nub, you always find the same problem: A lack of analytic rigor that didn't understand what were the missing pieces."

In a *Washington Times* op-ed from August 7, 2003, Peter Huessy, senior defense associate at the National Defense University Foundation, asserted that the Clinton administration was "clueless" as to the potential threat from terrorism. It imposed a set of policies and legal restrictions on U.S. counterterrorism and counter proliferation that made it, "while not impossible, extraordinarily difficult in the near-term to stop terrorism, either at home or abroad."[2]

Dick Morris, once a top political adviser to President Clinton, wrote of the former president's complete lack of interest in dealing with Al Qaeda, Iraq, Iran, or Afghanistan in his most recent book, *Off with Their Heads: Traitors, Crooks & Obstructionists in American Politics, Media & Business*: "Clinton left us naked and unprepared for the peril of terrorism."[3] Morris pointed to Clinton's benign neglect toward state-harbored and state-sponsored terrorism. He further asserts that the 1993 World Trade Center attack, the bombing of the U.S. embassies in Africa, the attack on the U.S.S. *Cole*, and the attack on Khobar Towers were treated as disparate actions of deranged individuals with no connection to any state-sponsored terrorist groups.

Bill Clinton's antimilitary, anti-intelligence community philosophy set the tone of intelligence gathering throughout the 1990s. Mansoor Ijaz, a Pakistani American businessman and former Clinton campaign contributor, wrote that a deal to extradite Osama bin Laden was completely fumbled by Clinton. "Clinton's failure to grasp the opportunity to unravel increasingly organized extremists, coupled with [National Security Adviser Sandy] Berger's assessments of their potential to directly threaten the U.S., represents one of the most serious foreign policy failures in American history."[4] Sudan had given the United States the opportunity to round up Bin Laden before it "invited" the Al Qaeda leader to leave the country. Bin Laden simply moved his operation to Afghanistan, where he set up terrorist training camps.

Throughout the Clinton years, the CIA suspended its former practice of initiating analysis on complicated issues that might have an adverse impact on national security. Instead, the agency waited for inquiries from policymakers to determine what intelligence to collect or analyze. Due to a lack of interest in intelligence matters, sparse resources made the collection and assessment of new threats to the United States all but impossible. As a consequence, briefings to policymakers were shallow, especially for the incoming Bush administration. Sparse human intelligence meant that most information was based on analysis derived from the thinnest of information.

When asked during his Senate confirmation hearings in mid-January 2001 what was the one thing that "kept him up at night" more than any other specific threat, terror, or trouble the Pentagon confronts, Donald Rumsfeld responded, "Intelligence."[5] After the hearing, columnist Austin Bay wrote, "Rumsfeld's response fingered what is the major American foreign policy and defense weakness, even in this era of extraordinary American economic, political and military strength . . . America's 'intelligence vulnerability' is intricate, detailed and complex."[6] He would know. From 1989 to 1993, Austin Bay served as a special consultant in war-gaming in the office of the secretary of defense.

In what was a prophetic comment, Bay added, "The penalty for intelligence failure, however, is often cruelly simple. In the defense business, what you don't know will kill you. To draw an even finer bead, what you know but understand poorly, or what you know well but fail to use decisively, will also cost you in blood, money and political capital."[7] The worst terrorist attack on the United States occurred seven months later on September 11, 2001.

The massive intelligence failure leading up to the events of that terrible day was the consequence of decisions made in the 1990s. Even now, with holdovers from the Clinton administration still in place in many critical positions of national security and intelligence, President Bush must guard against future intelligence failures.

Demoralizing the CIA

When Bill Clinton ran for office, many wondered what would happen to national security if he were elected president of the United States. A serious review of the Clinton-era record proves those concerns were well-founded.

With Bill Clinton's election, national intelligence suffered two great blows. One was a result of chance: the discovery of a high-level Soviet spy in the Central Intelligence Agency.[8] The second was a president who was indifferent to the CIA's agenda. Michael Ledeen, former member of the National Security staff, counselor to the secretary of state during the Reagan administration, and an expert on terrorism stated, "There are two things that demoralize the intelligence community: penetration by its enemies and the disinterest of its leadership." While the Clinton administration was not responsible for the first of these—the spies had worked their way into the CIA long before Bill Clinton's watch—the second was the personal responsibility of the president. Bill Clinton virtually exiled his handpicked CIA director.

> At the same time that the intelligence community was reeling from the discovery it had been penetrated at very high levels, it soon became evident that Clinton had no interest in intelligence matters. His first DCI [Director of Central Intelligence], James Woolsey, was a man of high intellect and impeccable character. But Woolsey was permitted no personal relationship with the president, and was no doubt astonished to discover that the president didn't want to talk to him. In two years on the job at Langley, Woolsey managed exactly two private conversations, a record for futility. CIA career officers were quick to realize they'd been cut out of the action.[9]

Ledeen explains this succinctly: the CIA needs a client. Congress isn't it; the president is. "The CIA needs a great relationship with the president, because if they don't, they don't have a client." By pointedly avoiding and ignoring Woolsey, "Clinton hamstrung the CIA," Ledeen said.

Former senior CIA official Dewey Clarridge stated his view: "A close relationship is vital for the CIA Director and the president. It's essential. Jimmy Carter didn't give the time of day to Stansfield Turner. I see Clinton didn't give his director of Central Intelligence much time either."

James Woolsey stated in an interview what he thought of Clinton's treatment of him and the Central Intelligence Agency. "I met Bill Clinton at a dinner party at Pamela Harriman's house in 1991, as a guest of Sandy Berger. I later signed a letter to the *New York Times* endorsing Clinton over Bush as a conservative Democrat."

In September of 1992, Woolsey spent a few hours with Clinton, Tony Lake, and other campaign staffers, discussing foreign and defense policy. After Clinton won the election, Warren Christopher, head of Clinton's transition team, invited him to Little Rock in December of 1992. At Christopher's request, Woolsey flew out that same day and met with President-elect Clinton for about an hour, "discussing Arkansas and Oklahoma, where I'm from," Woolsey said. "During the meeting Clinton never asked me if I wanted a job in the administration."

The next day, a Clinton staffer called and instructed him to see Webster Hubbell at the Rose law firm, the man responsible for vetting possible Clinton appointees. Woolsey met with Hubbell, and it appeared that Hubble already had a file on him. They discussed Woolsey's investments and law firm clients to determine if there were any problems. Later, another staffer called Woolsey to tell him to attend a press conference with President-elect Clinton—he still had not been asked to take any job, nor had he accepted one.

> I called Warren Christopher and asked him if the president-elect wanted me to be CIA director, because everyone told me he did and there was a press conference scheduled, but he hadn't asked me yet. Christopher put the phone down after he said he was going to ask Clinton and came back and said, "Yes, he wants you to be CIA director."
>
> I arrived for the press conference, and the staff was gaming the press questions they thought we'd get. George Stephanopoulos said the press was going to say this group looks like a group of Carter retreads, and Dee Dee Myers agreed. I stated that they could say I served in the Bush administration as an ambassador. Meyers thanked me and addressed me as Admiral. I corrected her and informed her that I never served in the uniformed Navy, just as undersecretary of the Navy. She said in response, "We'd better correct your bio [that] we're about to put out [to] the press, because it calls you Admiral."

Thus began Woolsey's two-year tenure as CIA Director.

The president, Woolsey said, simply would not see him. "I never felt like a confidant of Bill Clinton's. . . . During my tenure at the CIA I had only two substantive meetings that were semiprivate with President Clinton." Although he did attend the National Security Council meetings that occurred two to three times per month, he could not discuss certain classified material in those larger meetings because the people attending didn't have the proper clearance.

This wasn't just a matter of not getting an invitation or a phone call. Woolsey began his career with the CIA being proactive with the White House, only to be scorned. During the first two to three weeks in office, he went with the CIA daily briefing from Langley to the White House. Calls were always made in advance of these visits to Tony Lake, Clinton's national security adviser. It didn't matter. The president never invited him in to discuss the briefing material and would sometimes send the briefing paper back with scribbled notes or questions on it. Clinton preferred allowing his CIA director to sit outside his office and read the daily briefing rather than discuss important issues of national security face-to-face.

After several weeks of this routine, Woolsey stopped going to the White House. "I said to myself, 'They'll call me if they need me.'" They never did. "Tony Lake and I got along real well, I saw him every week and we would go through a lot of substantive matters. I saw Secretary of State Christopher all of the time, as well as the secretary of defense. I saw the vice president a lot as well. I just didn't see the president."

Woolsey's lack of access was so bad, and so *obviously* bad to others, that it became a source of humor at the White House. In the fall of 1994, a small plane crashed on the lawn of the White House. "Tony Lake called me," Woolsey said, "and told me there was a rumor around the White House that they thought it was me trying to get in to see the president. It was an ongoing joke."

What was the reason for Clinton's strange and irresponsible behavior toward James Woolsey? One might conclude that Clinton's narrow focus on domestic concerns resulted in his complete neglect of intelligence and national security. That is true, but possibly something else was going on as well. After all, Clinton himself picked James Woolsey for the job. It is hard to imagine why someone would neglect his own director of Central Intelligence.

One possible explanation is found in *Losing Bin Laden: How Bill Clinton's Failures Unleashed Global Terror*. Investigative reporter Richard Miniter writes, "In February 1993, Director of Presidential Personnel Bruce Lindsey approached Woolsey and said he had a candidate for the CIA's general counsel post."[10] Woolsey liked his present general counsel and said he wasn't interested. He missed a heavy hint that this new suggestion was President Clinton's—more than a simple suggestion—and went on his way. Only weeks later, after being refused time and time again, did it dawn on him what may have happened.[11] "The White House may have treated me this way because I cut off a request from President Clinton's top adviser Bruce Lindsey to place a 'Clinton person' in as my general counsel," offered Woolsey, "but I told Lindsey I already had a general counsel and did not want to replace that person. I never heard about it again, but that could have had something to do with it."

Woolsey has another "frost theory." He attributed the treatment he received to another kind of politics. "It was over Haiti," he said. "The White House loved Aristide. The CIA had big problems with Aristide. He was a necklacer and a murderer. He had someone murdered during a coup attempt. Our position at the CIA was, go in with your eyes open, we could have some serious problems with this guy. He is a mentally disturbed guy. You don't know what he could do if he goes off his medication."

The White House culture under Clinton was not willing to hear this. They simply didn't trust what their intelligence agency told them. According to Woolsey, this even affected CIA directors who had a closer relationship to Clinton than did he. Bosnia also caused tension. The White House simply assumed, he said, that Director Deutch ought to side with the guerillas in Guatemala. Bosnia also caused tension. "In Bosnia, there were no huge issues of who the good guys and who the bad guys were. It was consistently the view that there were atrocities being conducted on all sides. The Muslim and Croatian numbers were small, but the Serbs were huge under Milosevic."

Woolsey summarized the administration's attitude toward the agency: "The White House thought we were just a bunch of crazy right-wingers who just wanted to cozy up to Papa Doc and Baby Doc." When the national intelligence officer for Latin America wrote an assessment on Aristide, some at the White House wanted Woolsey to move him aside or fire him. Instead, Woolsey backed him up. As bad as one might feel for James Woolsey personally, the frightening question is, Did the Clinton administration penalize Woolsey to the detriment of American intelligence and national security?

The Consequences of Neglect or Contempt

Whatever the exact cause for Clinton's behavior, the results were tragic: Ledeen, for example, observed that the twin attacks on the CIA's integrity—the discovery of spies in their midst and the utter denial of presidential access to the director—caused the agency to waste resources by concentrating "its energies on internal damage assessment." This manifested in the CIA an inordinate fear of taking risks:

> The CIA became so risk-averse that it shut its doors to Soviet-bloc defectors in Clinton's first year, thereby closing down one of the most useful sources of information on the terror masters. Thus, the Clinton administration failed to accept what the FBI later proclaimed "the most complete and extensive intelligence ever obtained from any source."[12]

The scope of what happened to James Woolsey, and thus to the CIA, became clear in an unexpected way when he was interviewed by Katie Couric for NBC in July of 2003. This was during the initial uproar over President Bush's statement regarding Iraq's search for uranium in Niger. Katie wanted to get Woolsey to compare himself working for Clinton to George Tenet working for Bush. Media Research Center's Brent Bozell commented:

> Bush is being punished by the liberal media for strategic boldness and a quick military victory on the ground. Neither of these was a strength of the Clinton presidency. This became evident last week when NBC's Katie Couric tried to press former Clinton CIA Director James Woolsey over how CIA Director George Tenet should have looked over the dreaded Saddam-seeks-uranium sentence. Didn't you vet Clinton addresses, she asked? Woolsey coolly replied that Clinton didn't speak about intelligence in his first two January addresses to Congress. Furthermore, when Clinton launched the strike on Iraq in retaliation for Saddam's attempt to kill former president Bush in the summer of 1993, "not only did I not vet the statement, I did not know the strike was going to occur until it was in the process of occurring. We hadn't been invited into the meetings to make the assessments."[13]

So Woolsey was kept completely out of the loop in planning a major military operation. Furthermore, in his first two years in office, even after the 1993 bombing of the World Trade Center, the first foreign terrorist attack on U.S. soil, President Clinton didn't find any reason to say anything about intelligence in his State of the Union Addresses.

This outrage was summed up in the *Washington Times:*

> It had been the habit of previous presidents to welcome the CIA director into the Oval Office for the briefings so that complex issues could be clarified and advice given. Mr. Clinton, however, left Mr. Woolsey cooling his heels outside in the hall each time. The humiliating treatment of the nation's top intelligence expert reflected Mr. Clinton's cavalier lack of respect for the dangers facing the world's only superpower. The impertinence of the White House toward Mr. Woolsey reached the level of casting the CIA director as an object of ridicule.[14]

THE CIA AND FBI IN OPEN CONFLICT

Not having the support or interest of the White House really hurt the CIA right when it needed increased support for the war on terror. Woolsey found himself in a turf war with another Clinton appointee and a Democrat Senator, with no political support of his own. "Senator [Dennis] DeConcini [D-Arizona] and [FBI Director Louis] Freeh imbedded in legislation to give the FBI purview over overseas counterintelligence work, but I fought it, and they didn't get it."

Woolsey's problems with Freeh seem to have originated in the Aldrich Ames case. In our interview, Woolsey referred to an article by Andrew Cockburn entitled, "The Radicalization of James Woolsey."[15] Cockburn portrays Woolsey as fascinated with spy work but naïve about it as he came into the CIA. He had analyzed classified data for a long time, but he had not worked in the agency. Cockburn writes that, "Woolsey was quickly exposed to the murkier side of life at the CIA."[16] After he came aboard as director, he was told of Ames's crime, selling out our spies to the Russians. "The fact that Ames, a drunken incompetent, had not stood out among his peers was a damning indictment of the institution."[17] But Woolsey considered it his job to defend the agency from attackers, once the news about Ames broke.

Before that point, while working on the Ames case, the FBI had been a help to Woolsey. "When Freeh came in, we had a good working relationship for the first year, especially on the Aldrich Ames case."

Everything began to change when it was time to go public. "After the Ames arrest, we were supposed to have a joint press conference to discuss the case and take questions." However, for reasons still unknown, on the day it was to occur, the FBI cancelled it and held their own instead, during which they stated that the CIA had not done enough to catch Ames. "From that point on," Woolsey said, "Freeh and I had a cool relationship, and it got cooler over the next year." The war on terrorism was a casualty of that feud. With terrorism treated primarily as a law-enforcement function, the FBI became more international, which created problems for the CIA.

CONGRESS ATTACKS THE CIA

Woolsey's struggle with Senator DeConcini was another ongoing battle without administration support. After defeating the attempt to hand over a majority of overseas counterintelligence work to the FBI, the struggle continued. "DeConcini attacked me at every turn. I privately met with him and asked him to stop saying things that can blow our sources and methods."

After that, Deconcini moved to cut translators, satellite programs, and supercomputers. "In 1994, Congress was in session 195 days," Woolsey said, "and I had 205 appointments on the Hill with members of the House and Senate. Two thirds of those were to undo things that Senator DeConcini did."

The Clinton budget was another issue on which Woolsey needed to interact face-to-face with the president. "I came into the office in February 1993, and the budget for that year was already in," he said. "I did try to get reconnaissance satellite budget money increased during '93. However, in the only meetings I attended with the president to be able to discuss these issues, people were in the room . . . that didn't have the proper security clearances to hear that discussion, so I couldn't raise the issues, and I couldn't get in to see the president to discuss it appropriately. I called vice president Gore to help me on budget issues and help run interference for me. He spoke to quite a few members of Congress for me and was a lot more engaged on national security issues than Clinton was."

Bill Clinton's lack of support severely undercut the CIA's ability to deal with the rise of Islamic terrorism. "DeConcini tried to stop everything we attempted to do. He even went so far as to quash a few million dollars, which is not a lot of money in the overall budget picture, for Arabic and Farsi translators." Budget conflicts like these can easily be resolved by a little pressure from the White House. However, the Clinton administration simply looked the other way while DeConcini gutted the CIA.

Quiet Dissension Slow-Rolls Woolsey

A knowledgeable Defense Department source told me of another aspect of the fallout, bringing to my attention Reuel Marc Gerecht's article, "The Counterterrorist Myth" in *Atlantic Monthly*. Gerecht, a former case officer in the CIA's Directorate of Operations (DO), pointed to the urgent need in the early 1990s to develop human intelligence and to offer incentives to case officers to recruit such candidates.[18]

He pointed to DO managers offering three-thousand-dollar bonuses and bottles of champagne for "scalps" provided by case officers who generated the most intelligence reports. The race was on to increase numbers, the quality or allegiance of those being recruited notwithstanding. According to Gerecht, all of the CIA's Cuban agents had probably been double agents. "The competition realized long ago how desperate America's case officers are for scalps. They have been happy to provide them."

Gerecht said that in 1993, CIA Director Woolsey sent a cable to all stations encouraging case officers to push for quality, not quantity in their recruitment and intelligence production. Ignoring this instruction, the DO continued to press for numbers. "Woolsey never knew that the DO had betrayed his good intentions," Gerecht said.

A senior Defense Department source told me, "This was not surprising. The CIA DO sought from the very beginning to undermine Woolsey's efforts at CIA reform, knowing that he did not have the ear of the White House. If he [had] that ear, the outcome may have been different. Basically, the CIA DO slow-rolled Woolsey through internal DO inertia until Woolsey became ineffective."

Bill Clinton never knew of the battles or that his own top intelligence appointees were in conflict with each other, with a senior Democrat senator, or with their own agency. He was simply oblivious to major intelligence problems in his administration. These battles did not help the CIA do its job, nor did they encourage those who worked for the CIA.

As far as Woolsey is concerned, national security and intelligence were not part of Clinton's focus. "The focus of the administration was the domestic agenda: Hillary's health care reform, the economy, taxes, NAFTA, and the budget. Remember, 'It's the economy stupid.' These were the priorities, not foreign policy. The Cold War was over and the Defense Department and intelligence communities were taking budget cuts to reflect his priorities."

The problem was, the entire nation was being led to a false sense of ease when what was needed was strong leadership to meet the developing crisis of terrorism. "The country wanted a beach party after the Berlin Wall fell, and so did Clinton. President Clinton would have had to move decisively away from the beach party mentality to build up defense and the intelligence community." That never happened.

Clinton's aversion to dealing seriously with the growing threats, according to Woolsey, was illustrated in his handling of the Oklahoma City bombing. "In the spring of 1995, Clinton announced 'no foreign involvement' in the bombing of the Murrah Building," said Woolsey. "I believe he was premature to knock off attention to foreign involvement. There could have been a John Doe #2, and he could have had connections to a foreign government like Iraq or a terrorist organization like Al Qaeda. It's possible, and now we will never know."[19]

By that time, though, Woolsey was no longer the Director of Central Intelligence.

In October or November of 1994, Woolsey made a decision based on his "terrible relationship with Clinton. . . . Really no relationship." He resigned. Since he didn't speak to President Clinton, he called Vice President Al Gore to ask him if the president wanted him to resign. Gore called Clinton and then called him back: "Clinton wants you to stay."

A few weeks later, though, shortly after Christmas 1994, Woolsey wrote a letter of resignation to Clinton, effective early January 1995.

After leaving this post, Woolsey closely followed the goings on at the CIA. He was surprised to learn that the president had similar relationships with officials other than himself. "Bill Clinton rarely spoke to the attorney general or the FBI director," according to a former White House Counsel, who wished to remain anonymous. How was the nation's chief law-enforcement officer and commander in chief doing his job?

The former director of the Central Intelligence Agency thought out loud: "What the hell was happening over there?"

4

DEUTCH TREAT

A New Director Guts Intelligence Collection

ONCE WOOLSEY WAS OUT OF THE PICTURE, HIS SUCCESSOR, JOHN Deutch, had better access to the White House. But a change in access did not mean a change in focus for President Clinton. He continued to focus on domestic concerns at the expense of national security and a growing terrorism concern. Clinton's politically correct agenda got foisted on an agency that we rely on for national security.

Writing for the *New York Times Review of Books*, Thomas Powers interviewed several dissident former CIA operatives and summed up their consensus:

> They have differing career histories and views but on some things they agree. The Clinton years, in their view, saw a crippling erosion of the agency's position in Washington. Its leadership is now timid and its staff demoralized. Top officials, they say, worry more about the vigilantes of political correctness than the hard work of collecting intelligence in the field.[1]

As a result of this pressure, the line drawn between analysts and operatives was erased. "Henceforth, a year in some country where it was dangerous to drink the water would get you no farther up the ladder than a year pushing paper in Langley." Thus, after these changes, it was possible for Deborah Morris, an agent with no field experience, to be appointed deputy chief for the Near East for the director of operations, simply because she climbed the bureaucratic ladder. As one dissident told Powers, "She worked her way up in Langley. I don't think she's ever been in the Near East. She's never run an agent, she doesn't know what the Khyber Pass looks like, but she's supposed to be directing operations—telling the operators if some pitch [plan] is a good idea."[2]

Deutch worked to push the CIA into a politically correct mold.[3] Everyone near the top of the bureaucracy had to submit to AIDS awareness and sensitivity training. Quotas were imposed to ensure a diversity that allegedly represented the American people.

The effect of these changes was worse than one might think. Once talent and initiative are no longer rewarded, incompetent people are given responsibilities they can't handle and are rewarded when they shouldn't be. Competent, talented people are pushed out of the agency or decide to look for work somewhere else. The talent pool left at the agency got smaller as the challenges got larger. Thus, the "dissidents" spoke up.

The criticisms didn't come from think tanks or rival bureaucracies. Instead, they came from an outspoken group of former intelligence officers—mostly young field officers from the Directorate of Operations. These highly respected officers, all of whom had promising careers ahead, strongly believed that the CIA was in steep decline.[4]

One of these dissidents is Robert Baer, a dedicated agent of twenty years assigned in the early nineties to organize opposition to Saddam Hussein in Iraq. He quit because, as he told Powers, "When your own outfit is trying to put you in jail, it's time to go."[5] In 1995, Baer was, by order of President Clinton's national security adviser, made the object of an FBI criminal investigation for "the crime of plotting the assassination of Saddam Hussein."[6]

With the dissidents gone, what was left (despite the presence of many dedicated and hard-working agents who insisted on remaining) was and is much more likely to put American security at risk. Powers writes that the exodus of competent agents from the Directorate of Operations caused the assignment of station chiefs to particular countries to become even more irrational and dangerous to gathering real intelligence. In one case, Nora Slatkin, Deutch's executive director, chose a station chief for Beijing who was unable to speak or understand Chinese.[7]

This sort of problem struck outside the CIA as well. Because the National Security Agency had only a single Pashto speaker, when they intercepted communications, the transcripts were sent to the Pakistani intelligence agency for translation, even though that group is known to have been involved with the Taliban and Osama bin Laden. Some current and former agents believe that it was Pakistani agents who got word to Bin Laden after the attacks on the East African embassies, giving him time to flee Khost before American cruise missiles hit their targets in August 1998.[8]

According to a former CIA operative, "Tenet's briefer, a desk analyst who didn't speak Arabic, became chief of station in Saudi Arabia. He called himself George Tenet's ambassador to Saudi Arabia. They weren't recruiting informants because it was too risky."

Intelligence Scrub

In 1995, the problems at the CIA became much worse. According to a senior Defense Department source, "From the mid 1990s, the Clinton administration capped the decimation of U.S. intelligence with a human rights scrub that prevented the CIA from recruiting assets with a tainted past. This further insult to an already crippled intelligence-gathering system came on top of the priority the Clinton administration gave to intelligence at the end of the Cold War for collection on economic rather than national security threats."

CIA Director John Deutch and his handpicked executive director, Nora Slatkin, effectively shut down operations for six months to a year, following public assertions by Senator Robert Torricelli (D-New Jersey) that the agency had recruited an asset who had allegedly killed an American citizen in Guatemala. Torricelli, who was later forced to retire from the Senate over serious public corruption charges, publicized the CIA's sources and methods in making his revelation.

Indeed, shortly after becoming the CIA's executive director, Slatkin chaired a panel to review an inspector general's report charging two dozen operatives with failure to reveal links between a Guatemalan colonel on the CIA payroll and the murders of an American innkeeper and a rebel married to an American. "Once the panel decided to sanction half of those implicated, Slatkin called the operatives personally to tell them of the penalties, which forced a number of them to retire. The sanctions sent a serious ripple of retribution into the circle of operatives who felt that the

1995 disclosure standards were being applied to actions that had taken place many years earlier."

A former senior CIA operative told me, "There was a saying at Langley in the nineties: 'Big operations, big problems; little operations, little problems; no operations, no problems.'"

"Deutch and Slatkin handed down the now-infamous Deutch guidelines, which outlined that any human-intelligence source had to be certified by Langley as being clean of human-rights violations," according to a Defense Department source. "The effect made it impossible to have sources who may be terrorists, criminals, or other assets in a position to provide valuable, verifiable information that could enhance U.S. national-security interests."

National security scholar Michael Ledeen agrees that the guidelines were terrible for the intelligence service. He also contends that the scandal that caused the guidelines to be written should never have been a cause for alarm: the agency had not broken the law and was "engaged in proper activities that were necessary to advance our national security."[9] Ledeen is confident, however, that the Democrat senator should not bear all the blame for what happened. Torricelli could not have done serious damage had the administration resisted his crusade.

Any Director of Central Intelligence worthy of the name would have challenged Torricelli, because the congressman's accusations went to the very heart of the agency's proper mission, especially in the war against terrorism. The question is whether our intelligence agencies should associate with unsavory characters, and the answer is, hell yes; that's why we have intelligence agencies in the first place. We have diplomats to deal with nice people, and spies and case officers for the others. If the CIA isn't permitted to recruit agents among the world's killers, it will inevitably fail to obtain firsthand information on the terror masters, all of whom are serial murderers.

But the Clinton administration gave up on intelligence to look good on human rights. CIA Director Deutch admitted guilt where none existed, case officers were reprimanded, and new guidelines were drafted that tightened the restrictions on recruiting agents with dubious human rights records. While it was still theoretically possible to do it—the usual legalese stipulated that in exceptionally important cases, if you got formal approval from on high, you could chance such a recruitment—no case officer in his right mind would continue to pursue that kind of soiled-hands target.[10]

While it is true that the CIA director could have resisted the pressure to develop these guidelines, the problem seems to be much worse. The new rules did nothing to enhance our national security, but career officers did not fight their imposition. Rather, the agency's senior staff defended the guidelines in response to bipartisan criticism.

For example, the CIA's leadership was highly critical of the report issued by the National Commission on Terrorism, which was established in 1999 by Congress as an independent body charged with finding ways to improve how we deal with terrorism. The commission's report took strong issue with the Deutch guidelines. James Woolsey, who served on the commission, told the press, "One cannot prowl the back streets of states where terrorist incidents occur and recruit only nice people in order to inform on terrorist groups."[11]

CIA officials "immediately"[12] took issue with the commission's findings, claiming that the restrictions didn't hamper intelligence operations against terrorism in any way. "It's time to put the myths aside,' one senior agency official said. 'The transparency that we ask for at headquarters protects our officers. . . . It does not slow us down.'"[13] Another denied that the restrictions had caused any agent to refrain from recruiting an informant. Several insisted "the guidelines both protect and embolden case officers in the field by making senior operations officials at headquarters buy into decisions about recruiting terrorists and other criminals."[14]

Several retired senior CIA officials disagreed.

Woolsey stated forcefully, "The guidelines deterred CIA people from getting sources and the informants they needed. Recruitment became a big problem. You could not recruit people with violence in their past. Those are just the type of people we need to have as sources."

Woolsey explained that it didn't matter that it was still theoretically possible to recruit violent spies. "People in the agency felt like they would be hung out to dry if an operation went wrong. They knew that they would not get any backup, so it's easier to not do anything, than to take a risk."

A former senior CIA operative told me that agents were repeatedly told they would be left holding the bag. During operational briefings, shooters received warnings from lawyers that if someone got killed other than the intended target as a result of their operation, they might be handed over to the local authorities for prosecution. It made everyone very adverse to risk. "In 1998, the chief of station in Amman, Jordan, went to King Hussein and asked permission to recruit some people to help against Iraq. He wanted to be able to threaten them with physical harm, assured of the Jordanians, help. The King approved his tactics, and the operative proceeded to recruit sources. When the operative reported his activities to Langley, he was ordered back to the States. He later resigned."

According to Ledeen and others, this situation was not simply the result of events that took place under the Clinton administration. The CIA and FBI desperately needed to be released from restrictions placed on them in the wake of Watergate. Instead of correcting the problem in response to increasing terrorism, however, the administration allowed even more burdens to be placed on the intelligence community. "The Levy guidelines were outrageous!" Ledeen told me, referring to guidelines placed on the FBI during the Carter administration, through the Church and Pike Commissions (named after Senator Frank Church and Representative Otis Pike). "Congress held investigations, and tighter and tighter guidelines came out of the hearings. Congress created a situation where on September 10, 2001, the FBI could not review open-source information. They couldn't even read the newspapers."

Also affecting the agency during this time was the fallout from the Iran-Contra affair under Reagan. "The CIA devoured their own during this congressional investigation. Everybody learned from these issues. The administration was not going to protect them, and all operations had to be approved with the Good Housekeeping Seal of Approval. Lawyers are involved in every operational decision now."

Former CIA operative Dewey Clarridge agreed that the agency has become extremely averse to taking risks. In 1999, he and some associates learned that Robert Dean Stethem's killers were in West Beirut. Stethem was the Navy diver who was murdered during the hijacking of TWA Flight 847 in 1988. They made an offer to the CIA to outsource the operation and bring the terrorists back to the U.S. Clarridge spoke to the deputy director of operations at CIA and the head of counterterrorism at the FBI. After getting the runaround, they were turned down by both. They met with the congressman who represented Stethem's Maryland district, looking for support to convince the administration to allow the operation. He also rejected them, evidently afraid of stirring the pot in Beirut. The State Department didn't want to go into Lebanon, and the U.S. Ambassador opposed the operation, all because they wanted to avoid any sort of risk.

"We offered to outsource the operation in return for the $2 million reward," Clarridge explained. "It was quite simply magnificent malfeasance on their part not to allow us to move forward and grab these guys. It was a complete lack of willingness to do anything. We had fantastic human intelligence on the ground in West Beirut. General Downing developed contacts on the ground, and we had good surveillance on them. We had great intelligence that Nivulldin and Ali Atwa, the two terrorists on board the plane with Imad Mugniyah, who killed Stethem, were there and we could have attempted to grab them."

Oliver "Buck" Revell, former executive assistant director of the FBI, is a living legend in the bureau. He served for thirty years, rising as high as possible in career government service before retiring in 1995. Revell stated, "Because of the Church Commission's and Senator Torrecelli's activities, there was a chilling effect, it created a chilling atmosphere for legitimate intelligence collection. The agents inside the CIA and FBI were afraid to take aggressive action because they were afraid it would come back to haunt them. The Deutch guidelines handcuffed even further the agency's ability to gather intelligence on the bad guys. Not being able to put bad people on the payroll to get good solid intelligence was ridiculous. How do you think we investigated the mob? We put other mobsters on the payroll."

This left the nation severely unprotected. Revell went on to tell me that the FBI was not in a position to make up for what was lacking in the CIA. "The FBI had ridiculous rules to live by. The policymakers in Washington, D.C., the president, and Congress are responsible for the FBI not being able to review, collect, collate, and store open-source information. We could not read the newspaper and keep articles on bad guys in a file."

Between the CIA's human-rights scrub and the FBI's own restrictions, neither agency could really protect national security the way it was supposed to. "Because of the failures of the Congress and the president, the CIA was unable to infiltrate the Hezbollah, Hamas, and other terrorist groups like Islamic Jihad, because the handcuffs were on the CIA, and the FBI could only gather intelligence with the tools they were given and by the rules they had to play by."

Why did the CIA try so hard to defend the Deutch guidelines when the agency could have operated more freely without them? Keep in mind that the National Commission on Terrorism recommendation to rescind the Deutch guidelines stated, "The Director of Central Intelligence should issue a directive that the 1995 guidelines will no longer apply to recruiting terrorist informants. That directive should notify officers in the field that the pre-existing process of assessing such informants will apply." This statement came out well *before* the September 11 attacks. Simply put, the agency's refusal to rescind the Deutch guidelines was a clear intelligence failure.

Perhaps there was an assumption that without the guidelines the CIA would get embroiled in another scandal. The Association of Former Intelligence Officers (AFIO) commented in their *Weekly Intelligence Notes*:

> The case for the use of "polluted" informants and agents rather than Choir boy types is plain enough, justified by the cause of pursuing U.S. policies and campaigns against terrorism, etc. Thus the report is no surprise and on the face of it, valid. This is a case where both media-fanned political human rights hysteria *and bureaucratic CYA efforts* impact on clandestine operations. One trusts that common sense prevails and our capability is not damaged.[15]

For common sense to prevail, however, we need CIA officials to defend their vital mission aggressively, rather than meekly submit to agendas that have nothing to do with keeping America safe. That simply didn't happen once Clinton took office. The rules didn't change until thousands of Americans were murdered.

A Culture of Disdain

The extent to which John Deutch imposed a culture of disdain about security was revealed upon his retirement from the CIA on December 15, 1995. After he left, it was discovered that he had illegally put thousands of pages of classified documents on unsecured CIA computers at his home. According to the *New York Times*, Deutch "declined" to have a secure computer installed in his Maryland home, and he also refused to have CIA security officers assigned to his home. Citing the CIA inspector general's report, the *New York Times* reports, "One job of officers assigned to the home of a director is the securing of classified material the director has brought from work."[16]

According to a source in the Department of Defense, CIA General Counsel Tom O'Neill and Nora Slatkin were among the first to be advised of this breach of security. Slatkin reportedly advised newly appointed DCI George Tenet. In January 1997, CIA security officials complained to Slatkin that O'Neill was dragging his feet on the Deutch investigation, but Slatkin took no action. During the internal CIA investigation, Deutch refused to be interviewed by CIA security staff. By the summer of that year, the CIA security staff had completed its report on Deutch, but it languished, awaiting action.

In the fall of 1997, at Deutch's request, DCI Tenet granted Deutch new security clearances, claiming ignorance of the security office's investigation. In October, Slatkin left the CIA and joined the board at Citigroup. Deutch had joined Citigroup's board only a few months earlier, during the height of the security breach investigation. By December, the one-year statute of limitations lapsed because the Justice Department had not received a criminal referral from the CIA.

In February of 2000, Attorney General Janet Reno secretly reopened the criminal investigation of John Deutch by the Justice Department, following a news report of the CIA inspector general's report on Deutch's conduct. Reno's Justice Department had declined to prosecute Deutch by April 1999, even though it had jailed Los Alamos nuclear scientist Wen Ho Lee for similar violations.

During the waning days of the Clinton presidency, a lingering concern centered on the prospect that incoming Attorney General John Ashcroft would aggressively pursue criminal charges against Deutch. So, on January 20, 2001, his last day in office, President Clinton pardoned John Deutch.

The conclusion of the Deutch investigation was not simply a case of the CIA protecting its own—the sort of institutional cover-up that a bureaucracy might perpetrate under any administration—it was a cover-up orchestrated by the White House. The president's action sent a message of approval to those who had impeded the investigation.

There was a great deal at stake not only for Deutch but for Citibank. "For years," say Defense Department sources, "Citibank was known to have funneled Chinese funds to pay for U.S. high technology that was diverted to the Chinese military. Such money-laundering activity was encouraged by the Clinton administration's policy to export high-end militarily related technology to China that inevitably would be diverted to the Chinese military. Citibank also was directly involved with drug and criminal money laundering, which Deutch would have had to know about."[17]

In addition to the laundering of money on behalf of the Chinese military and organized criminal elements worldwide, Citibank had a relationship with Peruvian CIA-backed strongman Vladimiro Montesinos. There is some belief that Slatkin's hiring at Citibank in October 1997 was a quid pro quo for stalling the CIA security office investigation of Deutch's transfer of classified information onto his home computer. There is further concern that the timing of her hiring at Citibank facilitated her ability to act as a liaison with the CIA, using Citibank to open approved channels for money laundering.

"Curiously, Citibank in New York also was used to launder Al Qaeda money for various terrorist activities over the years," according to information contained in a U.S. government evidentiary proffer in *U.S.A. v. Enaam.*

Given this type of financial trafficking through Citibank under the watchful eye of Slatkin, and indirectly the CIA, what information and analysis did the CIA conduct in reviewing such financial flows? Given its access to the Financial Crimes Enforcement Network (finCEN) and information from the National Security Agency, CIA analysts—including those at Treasury—should have had some insight into terrorist financial activities.

"But then," the Defense Department source told me, "it was CIA during the Clinton administration that helped fund and support in Bosnia the Mujahideen belonging to Al Qaeda and Iran."

More PC, Less Intel

The drive for political correctness affected the agency in ways other than the Deutch guidelines. Under the direction of George Tenet, Deutch's deputy who was promoted by Bill Clinton, the CIA devoted time and resources to continuing and extending Deutch's "heavy layer of political correctness."[18] J. Michael Waller, writing for *Insight*, gives us a glimpse as to just how little the nation could afford such questionable priorities. Three days after Mohamed Atta was spotted in Prague on his way to the United States to take part in the attacks on the World Trade Center, George Tenet convened a special meeting.

"About 60 CIA employees and a group of like-minded National Security Agency (NSA) cryptographers, linguists and electronic-intelligence experts brought in by bus from Fort Meade, Maryland, gathered in the Awards Suite to hear him."[19] Tenet introduced Massachusetts Congressman Barney Frank to an applauding audience, in celebration of the agency's first official recognition of Gay and Lesbian Pride Month.

Congressman Frank joked about the fact that he had been trying to both cut and reveal the CIA's secret budget. "Let me be clear," Frank said to the assembled agents, "I've not only been trying to cut your budget, I've been trying to out your budget."[20] He told the *Washington Post* that the fact that he had been invited to such an event by the CIA was "a sign of real progress."[21]

Progress to what? According to one source, Tenet assured Frank that the CIA was "recruiting very actively" from the homosexual community.[22]

While Tenet wasted valuable time making politically correct innovations and defending the Deutch guidelines, which actually hampered his ability to recruit spies, Al Qaeda was getting ready to implement the largest terrorist attack that has ever occurred on American soil. Waller writes of how Tenet was fixated on expanding political correctness, to the point that he even named a special assistant for diversity plans and programs. And that was just the beginning. He also instituted a Directorate Diversity Office in every important section of the agency, and an agency Diversity Council was established to oversee programs. Finally, he also started a Community Diversity Issues Board to coördinate various issues that might come up in the intelligence community—a community of thirteen agencies.

This quest to make the CIA more politically correct under the guise of diversity did not just happen. Agents in the CIA's reputedly conservative bureaucracy did not just wake up one day and decide to celebrate Gay and Lesbian Pride Month. It was imposed from above. One former CIA operative stated, "CIA employees would go out to Arizona for bonding sessions, hiking, and rappelling together. Staff from different departments at CIA would do this to bond, so that we are all in touch with our feelings."[23]

One anonymous official told Waller, "The management wasted countless thousands of hours by making all of us sit through workshops to make politically correct diversity quilts." Cloth patches were given to agents who were then instructed to paste, draw, or write things that reflected the theme of diversity. Intelligence personnel were "re-educated" in a battery of sensitivity-training seminars and diversity classes, some taught by outside consultants with professional ties to activist advocacy groups. CIA spokespersons later denied the existence of the quilts.[24]

Whatever the story on the quilts, George Tenet made it clear that people under him must conform to his politically correct dictates. "I regard diversity as a precious resource, and I expect all supervisors and managers to do the same. The higher your rank, the more accountable you will be for ensuring that this agency and community are inclusive institutions." It also seems clear that one cannot expect to get promoted based solely on one's merits, but rather on the basis of one's race or gender. "Minorities, women, and people with disabilities still are underrepresented in the agency's mid-level and senior-officer positions," he told his underlings. "I challenge each and every one of you to join me in increasing and nurturing diversity within our agency and community. Each and every one of us—staff, contractors, detailees, and students alike—can find ways to help make our offices vibrant places where diversity is welcome."[25]

Of course, everyone knows the CIA needs a diverse set of operatives, as James Woolsey's fruitless attempt to get Arabic translators demonstrates. They should be supported in recruiting whoever is necessary for protecting the country's national security. But it is hardly true that promoting and hiring people based on race, gender, or sexual orientation is in the best interests of the agency's mission or the American people.

> Almost none of the more than 20 employees and officials that Insight surveyed in the national-security and intelligence communities—including the CIA, DIA, FBI and departments of Defense, Energy and State—see any real value to the sensitivity-training courses and diversity programs that became so important under Bill Clinton, except where the specific hiring of, say, a native speaker of Pashto would further U.S. objectives to collect intelligence or conduct operations.[26]

On the contrary, it is a recipe for driving real talent and focused ambition out of the CIA, as promotion will depend more and more on other factors. A former CIA operative gave me an example: "You got ahead by kissing up to Nora Slatkin. One guy, an Asian-American, got promoted from a GS-13 to a Senior Executive Service-2 (SIS-2) in just two or three years. He got promoted because he was a minority and picked up Slatkin's laundry. He was her butt-boy." The alternative to kissing up was to be sanctioned. An agent in the Mideast complained about the bureaucracy, saying that the agency was being run like Washington, D.C. After this comment was overheard, "the agent got pulled out of his overseas assignment and returned to Langley for a reprimand because they thought it was a racial slur."

Tenet knew how to spin his agenda in order to make it appear to be in the best interests of national security. He rationalized that diverse human intelligence was needed to investigate and stop terrorism. The legitimate need for information from a diversity of sources was used as an excuse for politically correct mandates that not only didn't do anything to better intelligence, but actually hampered it. As one longtime intelligence watcher put it, "He simply mixed up the concepts of recruiting a wide variety of HUMINT [human-intelligence] experts with the PC goo-goo with which he was moving to condition CIA employees to behave like so many clones of Eleanor Roosevelt."[27]

Tenet's push for diversity was different than the normal desire for wide recruitment, however, because it involved pressure to disregard national security concerns. As the Association of Foreign Intelligence Officers pointed out, "not mentioned is what used to be a concern in regard to hiring 'ethnics.' That is, might they be more loyal to their motherland than to their new country? Probably not, but concerns about 'racial profiling' make it politically incorrect to ask or even consider such questions."[28]

Historically, there had been serious security-clearance issues and concerns about homosexuals in the intelligence community, concerns based on legitimate rationales. Unfortunately, in the Clinton administration, we didn't see any serious study of the issue. Rather, Clinton's ideology, and his need to pay back the homosexual community, forced the CIA to change, regardless of the effect on national security.

Where will this end? It is hard to say. The Agency Network of Gay and Lesbian Employees (ANGLE) was established after Tenet became director, and it was officially recognized in 1999 by the CIA Office of Equal Employment Opportunity once Tenet's diversity guidelines were put in place.[29] That same year, the National Security Agency also recognized a chapter of gays and lesbians. Homosexual activists have since successfully lobbied the State Department to fund their partners' living expenses overseas, as if they were spouses.

In a recent presentation to Congress, Tenet reported on "CIA conducted Heritage/History Month programs for the following special emphasis groups: Hispanic, American Indian, Black, Asian & Pacific Islander, Deaf & Hard of Hearing, People with Disabilities, and Women."[30] The CIA has gone so far as to hire two outside companies to assist the CIA in ensuring and celebrating "diversity."

How this helps the CIA's mission, not to mention the morale of the rank-and-file, remains a mystery. Many different types of people go to the CIA in order to serve their country, not to have their values judged. A forced participant in this propaganda campaign commented, "It was all very condescending and insulting."

Signals Intelligence v. Human Intelligence

With PC distractions so prevalent, having nothing to do with the agency's mission, intelligence gathering suffered. Concentrating on irrelevant matters and degrading the CIA's capacity to recruit sources of human intelligence had forced the agency to make do largely with signal technology, the term used for all electronic methods of gathering intelligence. A Department of Defense source complained, "The CIA relied almost 98 percent on signal intelligence for its information on weapons of mass destruction." Given the nature of signal intelligence, it often comprised one-time hits of information, bringing into question its long-term reliability as an avenue of intelligence for serious policymaking. Signals intelligence from the National Security Agency became the predominant source of intelligence, to the exclusion of developing human intelligence or open-source information in order to detect intelligence gaps and create new collection requirements.

A former senior CIA agent confirmed that human intelligence was allowed to dwindle: "At one point in the mid and late 1990s there were zero Arab press assets. No ability to publish material in the Arab press. It's a vital part of any intelligence operation and easy to get, the CIA just didn't have any. It's an important arrow in your quiver." The CIA had no assets in the southern tier of the former Soviet Union and no agents in Eastern Europe. "There are no agents in those areas today either, as far as I know. During the Clinton years the places were shut down, and no one gave a s—. The CIA is incapable of running operations in most of these countries today."

According to Michael Ledeen, the political climate actually encourages the CIA not to worry too much about these shortcomings. "The CIA does not want to know certain things. Policymakers get mad at the CIA when the CIA brings forward information. Policymakers get angry and careers get hurt. The CIA became risk averse to bring information to policymakers, because then they either need to do something or be held accountable if something bad happens."

The lack of interest in open-source information had dire consequences, according to a senior Defense Department source. As an example, literally days before the September 11 attacks, DOD personnel sought unsuccessfully to bring a Milan newspaper's interview with Sheik Omar Bakri Muhammad, a self-designated spokesman for Al Qaeda, to the attention of the FBI. In the interview, he bragged about the organization recruiting "kamikaze bombers ready to die for Palestine" and boasted of training them in Afghanistan. In the same time frame, the FBI had information concerning Middle Easterners receiving pilot training in the United States. There was no effort to bring together these vital pieces of information that comprised an elaborate puzzle.

"DOD sought to present its information, given the increased 'chatter,' of a possible attack in the United States just days before it happened. The earliest the FBI would see the DOD people who had the information was on September 12, 2001"—the day after what was to be the worst foreign terrorist attack on the domestic soil.

Ledeen believes that even in the wake of 9/11, we have not solved the problems with our intelligence gathering. "The CIA has some of the same problems under Bush as they did under Clinton because Tenet is still in charge." For example, Ledeen cites a friend in Geneva involved in the oil business. "He called me one day before the war to offer up hundreds of documents he had to the CIA. These documents had information related to the location and amounts of billions of dollars that Saddam Hussein has hidden. They also covered [Saddam's] oil and gun deals."

After being told about this treasure trove of information, the CIA failed to contact him until months later, after the war had already started. The businessman offered agents the opportunity to read the documents in his office in Geneva. The agent sent to review the material asked for permission to make copies for the CIA's use. He said, "Yes, as long as you return them, because I want to help but I need them for my business." The CIA took the documents and never returned them.

SYSTEMIC FAILURES

The Intelligence Community
Incapable of Reforming Itself

WAS THE CIA'S DEFENSE OF THE NOW TOTALLY DISCREDITED DEUTCH guidelines representative of the agency's inertia? Could the agency reconsider what was going on without any motivating interest from the president? Many months prior to 9/11, President Bush requested that Director of Central Intelligence George Tenet undertake a full-scale review of the intelligence community. "The problem with asking Tenet, who oversaw persistent intelligence failures during the second Clinton administration, is that he cannot think outside the box and make recommendations that would change fundamentally the intelligence system or help identify intelligence needs in a post–Cold War era," said a senior Department of Defense official. "To make the sea change in intelligence, there would have to be a fundamental systemic change in the intelligence community to provide policymakers with the necessary information about possible strategic threats of terrorism, proliferation, and other asymmetrical threats facing the United States."

The recommendations from the Bremer study in 2000[1] and the Gilmore Commission in 2002 were in response to systemic failures in the CIA that persisted on Clinton-appointed Tenet's watch over the intelligence community.

"Even though Bremer's National Commission on Terrorism Report was issued on June 5, 2000, *none* of the recommendations had been implemented by September 11, 2001—a full 15 months—when terrorists attacked the United States" (emphasis added).

Bremer Commission Unheeded

The Bremer study came in the aftermath of the terrorist attacks on the U.S. embassies in East Africa. Congress had commissioned the nearly $2 million study which, among other things, called for many of the same FBI intelligence sharing and gathering reforms proposed in the 2002 Gilmore Commission study.

"The guidelines the CIA changed [after September 11] are ones we said should have been changed and revised two years ago," former CIA Director James Woolsey said.[2] Woolsey was a member of the Bremer Commission.

As early as 1998, Tenet recognized that Osama bin Laden was the root cause of increased terrorist activities around the world. Nevertheless, Tenet failed a major leadership test. He moved terrorism up to a "0" priority along with everything else at the CIA. No reallocation of resources took place. He failed to move or prioritize the collection of critical intelligence relating to terrorism, or use readily available avenues to disrupt terrorist activities and their private sources of support, as the Bremer report recommended.

Tenet has also been reluctant to undertake serious efforts to curtail America's reliance on suspect sources, or to convince his counterparts among America's allies to cut ties with dubious sources. Instead of recruiting its own sources, the CIA frequently looks to Syrian Intelligence for information regarding Al Qaeda and other Islamic extremists. Germany actually maintains a formal intelligence agreement with Syria and has even sought to cultivate warmer relations with Iran. Both countries are on the U.S. list of supporters of terrorist groups, including Hamas, Hezbollah, the Palestinian Islamic Jihad, the Popular Front for the Liberation of Palestine, and the more radical PFLP-General Council. The U.S. cannot afford to rely solely on these suspect sources.

Even though the Bremer report called on the U.S. intelligence and law enforcement communities to "use the full scope of their authority to collect intelligence regarding terrorist plans and methods," the CIA never removed the guidelines adopted by former Director John Deutch in 1995 restricting recruitment of unsavory sources. The Bremer report stated that the Deutch guidelines "should not apply when recruiting counterterrorism sources" and urged the CIA to aggressively recruit informants "with unique access to terrorists' plans. That sometimes requires recruiting those who have committed terrorist acts or related crimes, just as domestic law enforcement agencies routinely recruit criminal informants in order to pursue major criminal figures."

According to a knowledgeable source, "Up until the September 11, 2001, terrorist attacks and more than three years after the bombing of the U.S. embassies in Africa, Tenet still had not undertaken any aggressive recruitment of human intelligence sources on terrorism. Nor had Tenet issued a directive to state that the 1995 Deutch guidelines would no longer apply to recruiting terrorist informants."

The source continued: "Bill Clinton never directed the Attorney General to insure that the FBI exercise 'fully its authority for investigating suspected terrorist groups or individuals,' as the Bremer report directed. Bremer felt that the structure of the U.S. intelligence system had to be looked at, since many of the Middle East attackers had been living in the United States for months and in some cases for years."

Noting that the divided U.S. system has the CIA collecting intelligence internationally and the FBI focusing within U.S. borders, Bremer said this division of authority is "one we keep for bureaucratic reasons, but it's not one that terrorists keep. And it's clear that you need to have a more seamless interaction of the intelligence that is collected." Bremer added: "We don't have enough analysts. We don't have enough linguists to deal with this tremendous flow of information we're getting."[3]

The Bremer Commission's recommendation with regard to the sharing of information between the FBI and CIA should not have been necessary. Under Bill Clinton, the counterterrorist elements of the CIA and FBI were supposedly working together at the Counterterrorism Center at CIA headquarters in Langley, Virginia. Thus, when the Bremer Commission issued its report in June 2000, the CIA and FBI were already sitting together in the same office. Unfortunately, as the Bremer Commission concluded, the two agencies were still not sharing crucial information.

While it has been popular to blame this lack of cooperation on the FBI, one former CIA agent felt that there was blame on the part of the agency as well. "Nothing changed for the better at the CIA in the '90s. The agency is still not truly cooperating with the FBI even today."

Evidence that the CIA and FBI had poor coordination is found in the fact that the CIA failed to share vital information they possessed with the FBI that could have averted some or all of the 9/11 attacks. The CIA learned about Khalid al-Mihdhar and Nawaf al-Hazmi, two of the 9/11 hijackers, and their connections to Al Qaeda in early 2000, when the two attended an Al Qaeda leadership meeting in Malaysia. This important meeting got the attention of CIA operatives, but the intelligence gathered from it lay dormant. The CIA failed to place these two dangerous terrorists on the watch list that would have denied them entry at our borders. According to "The Joint Inquiry into Intelligence Community Activities before and after the Terrorist Attacks of September 11, 2001," Khalid al-Mihdhar and Nawaf al-Hazmi later came to the U.S. and had repeated contacts with a counterterrorism informant working with the San Diego FBI field office. Hani Hanjour, a third hijacker, also had a degree of contact with the same informant. However, the CIA never informed the FBI of the three men's connection to Al Qaeda before September 11, 2001. Had the FBI had possessed this intelligence, they could have had the informant gather details about the 9/11 attacks.

FBI Obstacles

Despite the Bremer recommendations, Senate Judiciary Committee Chairman Patrick Leahy remained an obstacle to intelligence reform. In 2000 he blocked FBI and other reforms that might have prevented the 9/11 terrorist attacks. Leahy and other Democrats had "bristled at many of the key proposals of the Bremer report, claiming that they were too intrusive and discriminatory toward foreigners."[4] For example, Leahy objected to making it easier for the FBI to obtain warrants to search suspected terrorists' computers and look at their e-mails.

Ironically, it was e-mail exchanges between the terrorists that gave the FBI their first hint in 1993 that they were planning another attack on the World Trade Center. Because of guidelines still in effect from the days of the Carter administration, however, the e-mails and dozens of boxes of evidence collected could not be used to open an investigation. FBI agents never ana-lyzed any reference to a possible terrorist attack until it was too late.

The evidence held valuable clues to Al Qaeda's network and operations. Some forty boxes of material left over from the first World Trade Center bombing investigation, which lasted through the late 1990s, "were never gone through," one FBI agent said. Another seven to eight boxes of evidence from the Manila, Philippines, investigation also were never reviewed. The information included data concerning Khalid Sheika Mohammed and his nephew Ramzi Yousef, both of whom lived in Manila in 1995.

At the time, the pair were suspected of plotting to blow up several trans-Pacific airliners headed for the United States. As will be told in more detail in a later chapter, Yousef was a dangerous terrorist. He blew up a pas-senger and damaged an airplane while conducting an experiment into how his explosives would perform. His apartment held evidence indicating that he planned to assassinate the Pope on his visit to Manila. It is also believed that Yousef planned to blow up multiple airliners at the same time and to crash a plane into CIA headquarters. Despite this information, Democrats in control of the Senate and the Clinton administration did not take the Bremer recommendations seriously.

The Bremer study took the FBI to task for throwing "bureaucratic and cultural obstacles" in the way of field agents trying to open probes of ter-rorist suspects, and urged the bureau to "direct agents in the field to inves-tigate terrorist activity vigorously, using the full extent of their authority." In the aftermath of 9/11, the Gilmore Commission would point out that the FBI actually had more power than it used. The Gilmore report noted, "A full investigation may be opened where there is a reasonable indication of a criminal violation, which is described as a standard 'substantially lower than probable cause.'"

With the Bremer recommendations implemented, the FBI could have used its existing authority more effectively. The circumstances surrounding the arrest of Zacarias Moussaoui prior to 9/11 demonstrate how things might have been different had this been done. Moussaoui was arrested on August 17, 2001, on a passport violation charge. In the weeks prior to 9/11, supervisors at FBI headquarters blocked Minneapolis agents seeking a war-rant to search Moussaoui's apartment and computer. Headquarters felt there was not enough "cause" to obtain a warrant, even though the field agents cited two criminal violations in the request. The agents also made mistakes in their application for a FISA court order. (FISA is the acronym for Foreign Intelligence Surveillance Act of 1978. The law sets forth the procedure for FBI surveillance of a non-U.S. citizen. After 9/11, FISA was amended to permit surveillance of suspected "lone-wolf" terrorists who lack a known connection to a foreign state.) The Gilmore report suggests the field agents had ample cause to obtain the search warrants. Thus, even under the old FISA rules, had a warrant been pursued properly, it likely would have been issued.

The Bremer report also referred to the confusing and contradictory process within the FBI for obtaining terrorism information. Guidelines in existence, even after revision following the Oklahoma City bombing in 1995, still had not clarified rules with regard to international terrorism investigations. In dealing with these investigations, the FBI had two sets of guidelines from the attorney general. One was for Foreign Intelligence Collection and Foreign Counterintelligence Investigations (FI guidelines). This guideline applied to investigations of terrorism occurring outside the U.S. Domestic terrorism, on the other hand, was governed by the attorney general guidelines on general crimes, racketeering enterprise, and domestic security/terrorism investigations. The domestic guidelines applied to an investigation into a foreign terrorist group's activities in the U.S. when the FBI didn't have sufficient information to make the international connection required.

Each set of guidelines set forth standards to be met before the FBI could open a preliminary inquiry or full investigation. Domestic guidelines authorized a preliminary inquiry where there is information or an allegation indicating possible criminal activity. A full investigation could be opened when there was reasonable indication of a criminal violation. Even though the domestic and foreign intelligence guidelines provided the FBI with sufficient legal authority to conduct its investigations, the Bremer study pointed out that agents remained unsure as to whether the circumstances of a particular case allowed that authority to be invoked. "This lack of clarity contributes to a risk-averse culture that causes some agents to refrain from taking prompt action against suspected terrorists," the study said.

Despite these significant problems, the Clinton administration never attempted to clarify the application of both sets of guidelines. Clinton's politics also undercut a unified war on terrorism. According to a knowl-edgeable Defense Department source, "In addition to the need to clarify FBI guidelines to deal with terrorism, the Clinton administration also had 'de-emphasized' fighting Arab-led international terrorism to focus on domestic terrorism, particularly white right-wing militia groups. "The effect led the FBI to ignore Arab nationals signing up for U.S. flight schools," according to veteran FBI agents.

"In 1998, domestic terrorism was the number-one priority," according to retired FBI agent Ivian C. Smith, former head of the analysis, budget, and training section of the FBI's National Security Division. "This priority pre-vailed as well on September 11, 2001."[5]

The Clinton administration emphasis was political. It underscored the limited instances of domestic terrorism to bolster its efforts to draw paral-lels between the antigovernment extremists that brought about the bomb-ing of Oklahoma City in 1995 and the anti-big-government ideology of Republicans in control of Congress.

Events at Oklahoma City and the Atlanta Olympics, along with the Unabomber, were the full extent of domestic terrorism, but foreign attacks were on the rise. Attacks of foreign origin during the Clinton administra-tion included the shooting at the CIA building in January 1993, the World Trade Center bombing in February 1993, two attacks on U.S. military installations in Saudi Arabia in 1995 and 1996, the simultaneous U.S. embassy bombings in Africa in 1998, and the attack on the U.S.S. *Cole* in 2000.

Funding and the War on Terror

On February 2, 1993, James Woolsey gained early notoriety by refusing to endorse Clinton's budget cuts for intelligence. "Yes, we have slain a large dragon," he said to the Senate Intelligence Committee, referring to the former Soviet Union. "But we live now in a jungle filled with a bewilder-ing variety of poisonous snakes. And in many ways, the dragon was easier to keep track of."[6]

This point was also emphasized by the outgoing administration. The *New York Times* reported,

As they left office last month, both former President George Bush and the departing Director of Central Intelligence, Robert M. Gates, warned bluntly that such an effort would lead to disaster. But President Clinton's calls for sharp cuts across the military budget has led to expectations that he would impose a similar levy on intelligence accounts.

Other Republicans agreed:

> As Mr. DeConcini and some other Democrats made plain that they intended to pursue deeper cuts, Senator Malcolm Wallop, Republican of Wyoming, took issue with the chairman's contention that intelligence agencies might have to accept less than state-of-the-art technology. "If we're not ahead of the curve, we're going to be behind it," Mr. Wallop said. "If we're not on the cutting edge, we're going to be under it."[7]

When the Republican revolution captured a majority in Congress, new leadership increased the intelligence and defense budgets. Former Appropriations Chairman Bob Livingston stated,

> Newt Gingrich is the reason we have a capable intelligence system today. It was Newt's initiative to request significant increases in the intelligence, counterterrorism, CIA, and NSC budgets. In 1997, Gingrich proposed a 20 percent increase over and above what President Clinton requested in his budget submission. Newt and a very few others had a major hand in making sure the intelligence agencies had what they needed. It still was not enough, but we would have been even worse off today if Newt hadn't carried their water. Since the 1994 Republican takeover of the Congress, it has been the goal of the Republicans to beef up the Defense department and cut most everything else and the Democrats goal to cut Defense and increase spending on every social program that comes down the pike.

James Woolsey confirmed Livingston's observation regarding Gingrich's vital role in security funding for the CIA and NSA. But as a former member of House leadership said, "It just wasn't enough." All too often, additional funding was limited to short-term issues. "The morning after the millennium celebration was over, the money was taken away by the Office of Management and Budget and by the Congress, and it went back down to a lower level of spending," said Woolsey.[8]

The report of the U.S. Senate Select Committee on Intelligence and U.S. House Permanent Select Committee on Intelligence released an evaluation of what the intelligence agencies did and did not do before and after 9/11 ("Joint Inquiry into Intelligence Community Activities before and after the Terrorist Attacks of September 11, 2001"). The section titled "Counterterrorism and the Competition for Scarce Resources" reveals the following about the agencies' scramble for funds dealing with terrorism:

> Because intelligence budgets were shrinking while counterterrorism resources were steadily growing, senior policy and intelligence officials were reluctant to make the additional cuts in other programs that would have been necessary to augment counterterrorism programs further. This would have jeopardized their ability to satisfy other collection priorities within the Intelligence Community.

The report also stated that "the Intelligence Community, for a variety of reasons, did not bring together and fully appreciate a range of information that could have greatly enhanced its chances of uncovering and preventing Osama bin Ladin's plan to attack these United States on September 11, 2001."[9]

There are two things to bear in mind here. First, a president has a great deal of power to get the various intelligence agencies to respond to his priorities and concerns. As the chief executive, he is able to order these entities to prioritize their budgets according to what he perceives to be the national interest. Second, the president has immense power over the entire budget. If he believes the budget of a certain agency needs to be increased, he can exercise considerable influence.

In both cases, of course, Congress is far from powerless. The president is able to lobby for his budget priorities, but Congress doesn't necessarily have to go along. The debate over spending is no secret, especially with different political parties controlling the presidency and Congress. The Congressional record provides evidence of the president pressuring Congress to go along with his wishes, but there is no evidence that Clinton wrestled with Congress to increase these budgets. Tenet suggests that Clinton had other foreign-policy priorities.

Consider the CIA director's testimony:

> As I "declared war" against Al Qaeda in 1998—in the aftermath of the East Africa embassy bombings—we were in our fifth year of round-the-clock support to Operation Southern Watch in Iraq. Just three months earlier, we were embroiled in answering questions on the India and Pakistan nuclear tests and trying to determine how we could surge more people to understanding and countering weapons of mass destruction proliferation. In early 1999, we surged more than 800 analysts and redirected collection assets from across the Intelligence Community to support the NATO bombing campaign against the Federal Republic of Yugoslavia.[10]

This is not the only time that Kosovo was a distraction from the war on terror. Nor is it the only area in which the Clinton administration was rudderless, leaving others to deal with a variety of problems without presidential priorities. The same lack of focus beset the NSA's budget, according to Director Hayden.[11]

Of course, in its attempt at bipartisan evenhandedness, the joint inquiry report goes on to implicate Attorney General Ashcroft for failure to deal with terrorism before 9/11 on the word of an unnamed "FBI budget official."[12] The new Attorney General had lunch with Janet Reno on February 8 to discuss Justice Department priorities, shortly after he was confirmed in a contentious Senate hearing. According to a senior Ashcroft aide, "Terrorism was not on her list of priorities."

Whatever Ashcroft's priorities, it is simply irrational to compare the first eight months of the Bush administration with the previous eight *years* of the Clinton administration, as if they both impacted our national security equally. For the CIA, the budget was so tight under Clinton that despite "some attempts to protect counterterrorism" after Tenet's "Declaration of War," the agency was not able to do much of anything to focus on Al Qaeda. In fact, "By the late 1990s, intelligence community coverage of many issues was exceptionally slim, and staffing was skeletal."[13]

The joint committee report continues on this issue, reporting how the various agencies did not have the resources to make counterterrorism a higher priority. Former National Coordinator for Security, Infrastructure, and Counterterrorism Richard Clarke was especially critical of the FBI and the intelligence community for

> not putting aside other priorities to ensure that al-Qa'ida received sufficient coverage. Mr. Clarke explained in a briefing that only a small part of CIA's counterterrorism expenditures was devoted to al-Qa'ida, even though "[w]e in the NSC and we in the OMB asked CIA repeatedly to find programs of lesser priority, either in the CIA budget or the Intelligence Community budget, to increase the size of these activities, and they claimed there was no program anywhere in the intelligence budget where they could get any funding to reprogram." Former OMB officials corroborate Clarke's argument that the Intelligence Community was reluctant to reprogram money to pay for efforts against al-Qa'ida or otherwise re-align overall spending.[14]

Investigations and committees can evaluate and assign blame to different agencies, but the buck stops with Bill Clinton. Agency heads are *appointed* by him to do a job and follow his priorities. If Bill Clinton had for one minute seriously focused on counterterrorism, others would have focused on it as well.

> Mr. Clarke has testified that, when the Clinton administration came into office, "the furthest thing from [its] mind in terms of the policy agenda was terrorism." This quickly ended with Mir Amal Kansi's murder of two CIA employees outside agency Headquarters shortly after President Clinton's inauguration. That event, plus the Iraqi attempt to assassinate former President Bush in 1993 and the February 1993 bombing of the World Trade Center, "catapulted" terrorism onto the administration's agenda, according to Mr. Berger. He also noted that these events led to the president becoming personally focused on terrorism.[15]

Others close to Clinton tell a far different story. But despite Clarke's testimony, it is not believable that a master politician like Bill Clinton would sit back and watch the intelligence community and the FBI scramble for money had he deemed an increase in the budget necessary. President Clinton never paid attention to or cared about the trivial matters of national security.

6

DEGRADING THE FBI

Inadequate FBI Funding to Fight Terrorism

BILL CLINTON'S APPROACH TO FIGHTING TERRORISM ENTAILED primarily shifting responsibility from the hands of the CIA and the military to the hands of the FBI as a matter of law enforcement. But the FBI's only tool for fighting terrorists is to bring indictments against those individuals involved in specific attacks. As illustrated in Chapter Thirteen, such indictments are typically worthless when the suspected terrorists live on foreign soil. So the question needs to be asked: Is using the FBI to obtain indictments against terrorists a suitable response to an act of war?

Former Attorney General William Barr believes the answer is no. "I strongly oppose using law enforcement and the criminal justice process in terrorism situations. The criminal justice system has proven itself to be ineffective."[1]

Barr may be overstating his case. Louis Freeh is quite aware of the limitations of pursuing terrorists solely through the FBI. Freeh stated to the Joint Intelligence Committee, "The FBI's criminal investigation of the 1993 World Trade Center bombing led directly to the discovery and prosecution of a terrorist plot to blow up New York City tunnels, buildings, and infrastructure which would have killed thousands of innocent people."[2]

So pursuing terrorists and putting them in jail, when successful, can prevent other terrorist attacks that could have been instigated by those individuals. But Freeh also pointed out that neither the FBI nor the CIA can be successful unless other resources are brought to bear. In 1988, the Justice Department indicted General Manuel Noriega, the leader of Panama, for running drugs into our country. But prosecution was successful only because the U.S. military went into Panama and forcibly "extradited" him. As Freeh told the Joint Intelligence Committee, "I certainly don't equate Noriega and Osama Bin Laden in terms of their destructiveness and evil. However, the comparison makes an obvious but often overlooked point that our response to terrorism must be expansive, unmistakable, and unwavering across all levels of the United States Government."

But, as shown in the Khobar Towers attack, it was not Clinton's practice to use "other resources" outside the FBI's mandate to enforce indictments the FBI was able to formulate. In fact, most indictments against terrorists in foreign countries serve only as symbolic victories and certainly do not deter those who can easily escape the FBI's limited reach. Furthermore, though Bill Clinton used law enforcement as the first line of defense in the war on terror, he failed to provide them with the necessary support.

Why would the president neglect the FBI when he depended on the bureau so heavily? As the former attorney general of Arkansas, Clinton seems to have thought of the criminal justice system, by default, as the way to deal with terrorism, rather than the military or the intelligence community. However, his various scandals placed him at odds with any conscientious member of the law-enforcement community, especially his own appointee, FBI Director Louis Freeh.

Fighting Freeh

It is hard to understand why the president would turn to the FBI to investigate terrorism cases when Clinton did not trust Freeh. In order to understand the complicated, dysfunctional relationship between President Clinton and FBI Director Freeh, it is important to remember the events that shaped it. As the *Washington Post* wrote, "Within a year, the relationship would become troubled. And within a few years, according to many associates of both men, it would turn downright rancid."[3] Occasionally, this hostility broke out into the open. In 1999, for instance, in response to questions from a reporter about his many fundraising scandals, Clinton blurted out, "Yeah, the FBI wants you to write about that rather than write about Waco."[4] According to Harvard Law School professor Philip Heymann, a former senior Justice Department official in the Clinton administration,

"There is obviously a very large amount of hostility and suspicion between them."

Clinton's scandals, of course, were the root cause of his division with Freeh. Clinton thought that Freeh should be loyal and, if not approve of his behavior, at least do his best to cover for him. Freeh not only refused to protect Clinton, he openly declared his opinions about what was going on. It began early on with the Filegate scandal, when the White House "accidentally" collected and kept the FBI's background information on Clinton's Republican opposition. Later, during a 1997 House hearing on illegal funding of the Clinton campaign from foreign sources, Committee Chairman Dan Burton asked Freeh whether he had ever seen a case where so many witnesses had invoked the Fifth Amendment or fled the country. Director Freeh responded plainly, "Actually, I have . . . I spent about sixteen years doing organized-crime cases in New York City, and many people were frequently unavailable." Clearly, President Clinton could not have taken kindly to being compared to the New York Mafia. From that point on, the relationship only worsened. Freeh was horrified by Bill Clinton's clemency for Puerto Rican terrorists and openly voiced his concerns.[5]

According to Connecticut Senator Joseph Lieberman, the highest-ranking Democrat on the Senate Judiciary Committee, the failure of the Justice Department and the FBI to cooperate with one another, was "impeding the successful prosecution of serious crimes."[6] The reason for this lack of cooperation was that Janet Reno defended the president, while Freeh was outraged by the idea that anyone was above the law.

"In 1997, friends recalled Clinton sputtering in a profane rage when he and White House national security adviser Samuel R. 'Sandy' Berger read in the newspaper that the FBI was investigating suspicions that China may have been using surreptitious political contributions to buy influence and facilitate espionage in Washington. . . . It soon became clear that the FBI—which is part of the Justice Department—had briefed members of Congress, but not the White House, on the incendiary case."[7] If a congressman had come under suspicion, would Bill Clinton have expected Freeh to brief him before proceeding with the investigation?

Of course, Clinton could have fired Freeh. But Clinton knew that his own scandals were so bad, firing Freeh would have raised a great many questions.[8] "That Clinton was unwilling to exercise his most basic presidential power again demonstrates how his character affected his governance," observes *National Review* editor Richard Lowry. "His scandals made it politically risky to fire the director of the FBI and his innate caution meant it was impossible. Says a former FBI official, 'He didn't have the guts to do it.'"[9]

Clinton Fails To Support His Own Initiative

Despite Clinton's efforts to shift antiterror responsibilities to the FBI, he effectively undercut his own initiative by failing to secure the funding needed for the FBI's expanded role.

FBI Director Louis Freeh had overseen several different programs, operations, and investigations relating to counterterrorism.[10] For example, with help from Congress, the bureau positioned agents around the globe in legal attachés (legats) to assist in the fight against terrorism. Without those FBI legats, the advances made post-September 11 could never have taken place so quickly. The FBI tripled the number of joint terrorism task forces (JTTFs) around the United States. This allowed the bureau to better coordinate intelligence and counterterrorism operations with its federal, state, and local law enforcement partners. Thirty-four of these JTTFs were in operation by the end of 2001. Furthermore, the FBI mobilized five rapid deployment teams to respond to terrorist threats around the globe.

As part of its obligation to coordinate protection of the United States critical infrastructure, the bureau created the National Infrastructure Protection Center (NIPC) and the Strategic Information Operations Center (SIOC). The NIPC was tasked with critical responsibilities regarding terrorist threats and cyber attacks. The SIOC was to coordinate plans for dealing with several major and simultaneous terrorist threats or attacks. The FBI was also assigned the responsibility of setting up the National Domestic Preparedness Office to counter terrorist threats and enhance homeland security.

To manage its new counterterrorist responsibilities, Freeh created a new FBI Counterterrorism Division in November 1999. This was Freeh's idea; no one in the executive branch or the Congress had suggested that the bureau take this important step. He then proposed the creation of an Investigative

Services Division to support the new Counterterrorism Division. The Investigative Services Division would be responsible for coordinating the FBI's analytical and support assets in order to better prevent terrorism and enhance our intelligence bases with the resources available. Nine months later, this reorganization was approved. Freeh created these divisions because he firmly believed they were necessary to expand and enhance the FBI's counterterrorism capability.

Despite the new responsibilities, the bureau was denied the crucial resources needed to carry out its new mission. According to Freeh, the number of FBI special agents peaked in 1999 at 11,516. Between then and September 11, 2001, the bureau lost 165 of these agents. Freeh says he sought to increase the number of agents by 1,895, but the money just wasn't there. "The 2000, 2001, and 2002 (pre-September 11, 2001) budgets fell far short of the counterterrorism resources we knew were necessary to do the best job."[11]

For example, for fiscal year 2000, Freeh requested 864 additional counterterrorism people at a cost of $380.8 million. He got five people funded for $7.4 million. "Thus," as he told the Joint Intelligence Committee, "at the most critical time, the available resources for counterterrorism did not address the known critical needs."[12]

As in the case of the military, wages for the bureau's agents languished in relation to the dire need for trained specialists. Pointing out that the bureau had fewer agents than the Chicago police department had sworn officers, Freeh urged the Joint Committee to recommend significant increases in the personnel of the FBI and to favorably consider pending legislation that would more fairly compensate them for the "life-saving work they do every day."

In the wake of 9/11, Freeh's plea was finally heeded. For fiscal year 2002, Congress appropriated an emergency supplement of $745 million to fund 823 new positions.

Information Technology

The difficulty in obtaining funds to upgrade its computer technologies further illustrates the FBI's low priority in the Clinton administration. In 1992, the FBI developed a a five-year IT upgrade plan called the Information Sharing Initiative (ISI). The initiative was designed to allow the FBI to replace outdated desktop computers; upgrade network capacity to permit the exchange of images and other large files; provide improved analytical capabilities; and permit information sharing with other law enforcement, prosecutorial, and intelligence agencies. The FBI estimated the cost of the ISI at approximately $432 million.

All of this was highly important. As Freeh testified a decade later:

> I can't underscore how important IT is to the ability of the FBI to combat terrorism, in particular, and in performing all aspects of its national security, criminal investigative, and law enforcement assistance missions. The FBI's problem with acquiring necessary information technology has a long history. We didn't just wake up one day and realize that our IT systems were unable to perform even basic functions, such as e-mail and electronic files that were available in other government agencies and the private sector.[13]

It took six years for Freeh to even get the Clinton administration's clearance to submit the ISI budget to Congress. Freeh asked for $70 million for fiscal year 1999, but due to lackluster support from the administration, Congress appropriated only $22 million, conditioned upon the FBI submitting a comprehensive implementation plan. This game was repeated for fiscal year 2000, when the FBI asked for a total of $58.8 million for ISI—their funds were again delayed.

To prepare for fiscal year 2001, Freeh recruited Bob Dies, who had recently retired from IBM. He came into the bureau in early 2000, reworked the proposal, and in September of that year submitted a revised plan that called for a reduction in spending from the original proposal by some $52 million.

Congress approved the plan that same month. The bureau finally had permission to spend $100.7 million for the first year, which included the 2001 appropriations plus the balance of requested funds from 1999 and 2000. Following the bidding process, contracts were awarded in May and June 2001. Thus, a project that was proposed in the early nineties and could have been implemented by the end of the decade did not get off the ground until three months before September 11.

In contrast to the Clinton years, when Freeh presented a proposed budget for the 2002 fiscal year that included a request for $67.7 million for IT upgrades, Congress immediately granted the FBI everything it asked for.

According to the FBI's Oliver "Buck" Revell, there was a great deal of alienation between Clinton and law-abiding bureau agents. "You couldn't respect Bill Clinton if you were in a position to know these cases, like Whitewater and campaign finance, you couldn't respect his actions," he said in an interview. "That's even before the Monica Lewinsky scandal surfaced. He demanded no respect from people at the agencies or in the field."

More Problems in the Name of Political Correctness

Why did Clinton allow the FBI's basic staffing and technology needs to languish? Did his lack of interest in intelligence matters bleed into a lack of concern for the bureau as well? Or was something else at work?

According to Revell, political correctness had a great deal to do with some of the missed opportunities to stop 9/11. Revell cited the famous Phoenix Memo. According to a joint report by the House and Senate intelligence committees, the FBI in Phoenix never acted on a memo that warned of foreigners taking flying lessons and named someone now known to have been working with Al Qaeda.

"The Phoenix memo was bulls—! The agents were doing their job, and they did a fine job. However, they didn't open a case because of political correctness. They had explicit orders not to racially profile, and if they had opened a case because a bunch of 'Arab students' were taking flying lessons, they would have been shut down immediately and their careers would have been hurt. The Arab community would have been in an uproar. Before 9/11 there was no ability to look at a segment of the population and target it for investigation as there is now."

In general, terrorism cases were not attractive to the FBI, Revell told me. "It's because the agents didn't have a good atmosphere to work on terrorism cases. The feeling was that no risk was good. The chilling effect created a situation where the FBI field offices had to be ordered to open terrorism investigations. They wanted to work mob case or bank robberies and kidnapping cases. Cases that had public support and no downside for the agent's career."

Naturally, Clinton was unwilling to free the restrictions placed on the FBI. His record of neglect and hostility did not help the bureau's efforts in the war on terror. Instead, it caused problems to go unfixed and created new ones.

The Clinton administration's policy that shifted antiterrorist responsibilities to the FBI was compounded by the president's failure to secure funds for essential upgrades, leaving Director Freeh to secure his own funding. It also imposed politically correct policies that had direct consequences on our nation's ability to stop the events of 9/11. Eight years of Clinton degrading our intelligence capabilities could not be undone in the eight months between the Bush administration taking office and September 11, 2001.

7

DEGRADING THE MILITARY

Off Mission and Off Target

And that is where I am now, writing to you because you have been good to me and have a right to know what I think and feel. I am writing too in the hope that my telling this one story will help you to understand more clearly how so many fine people have come to find themselves still loving their country but loathing the military, to which you and other good men have devoted years, lifetimes, of the best service you could give. To many of us, it is no longer clear what is service and what is disservice, or if it is clear, the conclusion is likely to be illegal.

—BILL CLINTON,
December 3, 1969

THIS CLOSING STATEMENT TO A LETTER WRITTEN BY CLINTON IN 1969 is quite revealing. It does not reveal simply that he loathed the military, but that he would lie barefaced to avoid the draft.

Clinton was writing to Col. Eugene J. Holmes, Commandant of the ROTC program at the University of Arkansas, to tell him that he had gotten away with lying. Claiming high regard for the victim of his deception, he wrote, "In retrospect, it seems that the admiration might not have been mutual had you known a little more about me, about my political beliefs and activities. At least you might have thought me more fit for the draft than for ROTC."

The claim that Clinton knew this "in retrospect" was another lie. He knew from the beginning what would happen if he told the truth, so he didn't. As Holmes wrote in a notarized public letter in 1992,

I was not "saving" him from serving his country, as he erroneously thanked me for in his letter from England. I was making it possible for a Rhodes scholar to serve in the military as an officer. In retrospect, I see that Mr. Clinton had no intention of following through with his agreement to join the Army ROTC program at the University of Arkansas or to attend the University of Arkansas Law School. I had explained to him the necessity of enrolling at the University of Arkansas as a student in order to be eligible to take the ROTC program at the University. He never enrolled at the University of Arkansas, but instead enrolled at Yale after attending Oxford. I believe that he purposely deceived me, using the possibility of joining the ROTC as a ploy to work with the draft board to delay his induction and get a new draft classification.

The scandal here was not simply that "a man who was not merely unwilling to serve his country, but actually protested against its military, should ever be in the position of commander-in-chief of our Armed Forces," as Col. Holmes pointed out. It was also that he would inevitably have an effect on the morale of the United States armed forces. Every soldier knew about Clinton's lying to avoid the draft and his statement that he loathed the military. Yet they were supposed to trust him as their leader?

That Clinton continued to loathe the military was revealed as soon as he took office and attempted to overhaul military policies, such as allowing homosexuals to serve with the new "don't ask, don't tell" policy and forcing our soldiers to wear the UN insignia instead of a U.S. flag on their uniforms.[1] The military was not something to respect; it was something to tolerate.

Surely, no one is going to deny that defense spending was a major point of contention between the Clinton administration and Republicans in Congress during the nineties. The goal of Congressional Republicans was to increase defense spending. Clinton's goal was to cut funds to the military and spend them instead on any social program he could find.

More particularly, Republicans never trusted Clinton to support the military. A former House Republican leader said, "Clinton evaded the draft and told the world that he loathed the military, and therefore he didn't want to put anyone else in harm's way."

Opposing SDI

The terrifying thought of nuclear weapons being launched against the United States had not entered the American consciousness—until the events in North Korea that began the summer of 2003. Then people were forced to contemplate the possibility as never before. If, in fact, a missile was launched at a West Coast city from either North Korea or some other terrorist state, nothing could be done to protect the American people.

President Clinton's attitude toward Reagan's attempt to develop a missile defense shield destroyed any hope for technological advancements aimed at protecting the American people. Said Senate Appropriations Chairman Bob Livingston in a Heritage Foundation lecture:

> In today's post-Cold War world, the danger to guard against isn't any longer a massive nuclear attack aimed at destroying our own capability to respond in kind. Instead, the danger is of a rogue nation, ruled by one of the several madmen on the world stage, which could use its limited nuclear capability in a sort of atomic Tet Offensive aimed at destroying America's morale by inflicting unspeakable horrors on one of our great cities. A single missile could do the job. . . . Protecting missiles and missile sites does no good if tens of thousands of people die. Yet ongoing liberal opposition continues to prevent deployment of any viable protection for civilians.[2]

Had we aggressively pursued the Reagan administration's Strategic Defense Initiative program during the eight years Bill Clinton lived in the White House, perhaps we would not be as threatened by North Korea or other rogue states as we are today. But that didn't happen. The failure of the Clinton administration to use forward-thinking, asymmetrical-threat analysis put America at risk. We are still defenseless today against a lone missile attack.

The Military Budget

Clinton's budget strategy was to propose spending that simply did not meet our known military commitments. This was never admitted, of course, but it is nevertheless what occurred.

Take, for instance, the administration's defense budget request for fiscal years 1998 through 2002. "While the amount requested for defense is $19 billion higher in budget authority than sought last year," reported Baker Spring of the Heritage Foundation, "it is still inadequate to fund the current defense policy, which was established after the Pentagon's now-discredited 1993 Bottom-Up Review. President Clinton's new budget falls about $105 billion short of fully funding the forces that this Administration's review identified as necessary to defend American security and freedom."[3]

This budget demanded specific trade-offs, Spring noted. If it was to meet its commitments, the Clinton budget restrictions would force the military to either institute troop reductions, shrink spending on combat readiness, or reduce the money spent to modernize equipment. But none of these options was tolerable. Clinton's own former secretary of defense William Perry admitted before leaving office that the size of the military at that time "is about the minimum required to allow the United States to be able to maintain its role as a global power."[4] A reduction in readiness was also not an option.

So the Clinton administration decided to stop new weapon procurement and equipment modernization. Said Spring, the White House's defense budget slashed spending on new weapons and equipment to roughly one third of the amount spent in fiscal 1985. "The current budget defers the start of needed annual increases to the procurement budget for another year," which in turn would mean that America would "continue to lose the technological lead which is a key to low-casualty victories on the battlefield."[5]

The bottom line is that the president knew the military budget was unworkable, but he sought to avoid the problem by simply projecting his budget onto the next administration. As Spring put it, "After four years of refusing to come to terms with the problem of national defense, the Clinton administration has chosen once again to kick the can down the road, leaving the coming defense budget crunch to be solved at some later time."[6]

The accuracy of Baker Spring's analysis was confirmed two years later by former defense policy analyst James Anderson:

The declining readiness of U.S. military forces has become so acute that even President Clinton has been forced to acknowledge it. Last September, in the waning days of the 105th Congress, the chiefs of the armed services testified during a contentious hearing of the Senate Armed Services Committee on the steadily deteriorating state of the armed forces. During this widely reported hearing, Senators took the Pentagon and the administration to task for starving the armed forces of the resources needed to carry out the unprecedented demands being placed on them, including the open-ended Bosnia mission that devours approximately $2 billion in scarce defense dollars each year. Under verbal fire from worried Senators, the chiefs agreed that their soldiers, sailors, airmen, and Marines could no longer be asked "to do more with less."[7]

Anderson also noted that in Clinton's 1999 State of the Union address, the president spoke of "urgent national needs in education and defense." He also admitted, "It is time to reverse the decline in defense spending that began in 1985" and pointed out he was setting aside new money for modernization.[8] Clinton had the audacity to blame Ronald Reagan for the defense budget slashing that occurred during his own two terms in office.

Regardless of its motive, the president's call to address these "urgent national needs" meant the military had to launch a new program involving a lot of hard work, only to see it totally ignored. Clinton commissioned the Quadrennial Defense Review (QDR), a Pentagon program to determine America's long-term defense needs, to do a Bottom-Up Review (BUR). Due to be completed by the end of 1997, the QDR was to provide the president with defense budget priorities for the next several years. Before the review was completed, however, the president submitted a defense budget outlining spending through 2002, thus undermining much of the QDR's purpose.

Congress had established the QDR for the very purpose of informing policymakers of defense priorities. According to the law, the QDR "shall include a comprehensive examination of defense strategy, force structure, force modernization plans, infrastructure, budget plan, and other elements of the defense program and policies with a view toward determining and expressing the defense strategy of the United States and establishing a revised defense program through the year 2005."[9] Congress imposed the

QDR because prior initiatives, including the Bottom-Up Review, had been ignored. They did not want to see that error repeated.

Bottom-Up Review

President Clinton promised in February 1993, "The men and women who serve under the American flag will be the best trained, best equipped, best prepared fighting force in the world, so long as I am president."[10] Clinton's first secretary of defense, Les Aspin, reminded everyone of this pledge when he finally released his report, "The Bottom-Up Review: Forces for a New Era." The Heritage Foundation took special interest in this report, because it seemed familiar.

> After harnessing the efforts of thousands of Pentagon bureaucrats and military planners, Secretary Aspin presented a force structure that bears a striking resemblance to that which was outlined in *A Safe and Prosperous America: A U.S. Foreign and Defense Policy Blueprint*, published by the Heritage Foundation last May. (Kim R. Holmes, ed., *A Safe and Prosperous America: A U.S. Foreign and Defense Policy Blueprint* [Washington, D.C.: The Heritage Foundation, 1993]). For each military service, the Bottom-Up Review proposes force levels nearly identical to those described in the Heritage publication. This is surprising given that *the defense budget proposed by President Clinton in April will pay for only a far smaller force*, which then-House Armed Services Committee Chairman Aspin presented last year and referred to as Option B.[11]

Lawrence T. DiRita, Baker Spring, and John Luddy conducted a thorough analysis and found several major shortcomings in the BUR. As previously mentioned, the conclusions were unaffordable. The Clinton budget didn't even allow for the minimal force proposed by Aspin. The previous year, he had floated a proposal for a force that "would cost somewhat more than the $270 billion per year proposed by Clinton for the fiscal period of 1993 through 1997."[12] But the next year, the administration cut back further so that "the Clinton budget reduced defense spending to $246 billion by fiscal 1997."[13]

A lack of funding was not the only problem. Aspin also overstated the military's capabilities. He admitted in a statement that the U.S. military must have sufficient resources to victoriously wage two wars "nearly simultaneously." He also stated that "we need to avoid a situation in which the United States . . . makes simultaneous wars more likely by leaving an opening for potential aggressors," allowing them to "take advantage of the commitment of forces to other conflicts." Aspin tried in this way to leave the impression that his proposed force could meet that sort of challenge, thereby causing potential enemies to be cautious in the face of our military resources.[14]

This point turned out to be rather important. While we had never engaged in two regional conflicts under Clinton's presidency, the administration did have to make decisions about responding to the war on terror while military resources were engaged in Bosnia and elsewhere. The military was already averse to taking the risks necessary to get Osama bin Laden, and a lack of resources would solidify this position.

Further, Aspin's numbers didn't work. He declared that the U.S. would need a hundred bombers per regional conflict, "yet in the projected force structure for 1999, the Air Force is assigned 'up to 184 bombers,' not including those that would be assigned to the strategic nuclear forces."[15] The number of aircraft carriers also stretched military forces quite thin. The stated objectives could not be met by Aspin's plan.

The problem was even worse in light of the defense secretary's own admission that his "collection of general purpose force" must not only cover the wars in two regions, but also provide for "peace enforcement and intervention operations." So from these forces, Aspin claimed he would withhold "up to two Army divisions, one Marine brigade, two aircraft carrier battle groups, and two Air Force wings."[16] As DiRita, Spring, and Luddy observed, this meant that under the Clinton administration's own plan, our military was massively overcommitted.

Win, Hold, Win?

Aspin may have realized that his stated objective of winning two simultaneous regional conflicts was simply unrealistic. He attempted to come up with a more feasible goal. In June of 1993, he floated a "Win, Hold, Win" strategy, in which only one region received the full attention of the U.S. military, while the other was held at bay awaiting our quick victory elsewhere. We could then devote our attention to the second conflict.

But this, too, was a completely unworkable plan. Livingston pointed out, in words that now seem darkly prophetic, "The whole idea came under intense ridicule from people who pointed out that a nuclear North Korea, for instance, would hardly consent to being held at bay while we tidied up a problem in the Persian Gulf."[17] A four-star general renamed the plan "win-lose-lose."[18]

Aspin rightly scrapped the idea and, two weeks later, announced that we would plan to win two regional conflicts simultaneously. But he simply announced a new objective without making any adjustments in his plan, showing the complete lack of serious regard for the military within the Clinton administration. Just two weeks after admitting that the military was at least $20 billion shy of the funds needed to sustain a "win-hold" strategy in one region, Aspin recanted and said that we could, in fact, win two victories after all. Explaining why he had not increased his estimate of the needed size and resources for this military force, he claimed to have reassessed the impact of "new technologies."[19] Plainly, this was spin to justify the White House's inadequate spending.

Apparently, in two short weeks, Secretary Aspin learned of new technologies that increased our capabilities so drastically that we could now win in two regions simultaneously. These new technologies must have also come at bargain-basement prices, since he didn't see a need to increase the defense budget to cover their cost.

When criticizing Aspin's plan, there is little evidence to suggest that he simply made mistakes in the process of creating a workable plan. The earlier trial balloons indicate that the ability to win two ground wars simultaneously was not the administration's priority, but winning the public relations war was. Aspin, who was always respected in Washington for a sizable intellect, could not reasonably have gone, within two weeks' time, from thinking our military capable of winning one conflict at a time to suddenly thinking we could win two.

The bottom line was that Clinton was committed to deep cuts in the military and the job of the administration was to find a way to make these cuts look manageable. "In all, if the proposed Clinton defense cuts are computed just like the rest of the federal budget, under a 'current services' baseline, they total some $241 billion in cuts over five years."[20] What was amazing about this was that the Bush administration had *already* planned a massive reduction in defense spending. Yet this was not enough for Clinton, who proposed another $127 billion removed from defense on top of what was already being cut.[21]

Other Problems with BUR

There were still other problems with Aspin's BUR plan. Like Clinton's later budget proposals in 1997, Aspin also put off modernization. "The 1994 defense budget imposes a 17 percent real reduction in procurement spending from the previous year."[22] Future conflicts were going to be fought without the advanced weapons systems the military had once had. In addition to neglecting modernization, maintenance of the current equipment was also to be reduced. "Because of maintenance budget cuts," it was recognized "the Marines will go from no backlog in depot maintenance orders in 1992 to more than $160 million worth of backlog by 1994."[23]

Despite the massive cuts, Aspin planned not only to maintain overseas commitments, but also to take on more responsibilities. How could this be done with less money, less maintenance, and less modernization? The only answer was to make soldiers bear more of the burden with longer deployments, doing their best with reduced numbers and resources. This was how the president kept his promise to maintain "the best trained, best equipped, best prepared fighting force in the world." The actual result was a precipitous dip in troop morale. As Livingston pointed out in a September 1993 speech, "The morale of our sailors, soldiers, Marines, and airmen is essential to an effective fighting force. Yet by not diminishing the calls on our service people, while at the same time reducing the size of our forces, we directly threaten that morale by insuring longer and more frequent deployment of a smaller number of ships, planes, and armament."[24]

The falloff in troop morale would have further consequences for our military defense. Not only would troops with low morale fail to function as effectively as they should, they would leave military service altogether.

> Re-enlistment of trained personnel suffers as a result. For example, in 1979, at the height of the "hollow force" period, only 50.5 percent of enlisted personnel re-enlisted after their first tour of duty; in 1991, after a decade of robust defense spending, retention in the military stood at an impressive 73.4 percent. (Department of Defense, Directorate for Information, Operations and Reports, Selected Manpower Statistics, Fiscal Year 1991, pp. 10, 103.)[25]

Clinton's irresponsible defense-budget policy unnecessarily risked casualties for service men and women in future war zones—casualties that could be avoided. As we will see when we review what happened in Somalia, a lack of will and advanced technological support for troops in a war zone did, in fact, lead to unnecessary loss.

The cuts in procurement also meant that Clinton's supposed commitment to high-tech warfare was never meant to be fulfilled. Aspin had scheduled the retirement of the Navy's all-weather bomber, the A-6 Intruder, as well as the A/FX and F/A-18 C/D *Hornet* fighter jets. The Air Force was scheduled to lose its multi-role fighter and F-16 *Falcon*. None of these was scheduled to be replaced. DiRita, Spring, and Luddy point out that the retirement of the A-6 Intruder left the Navy without a way of reliably providing air support for ground troops. More generally, though, this policy meant that, across the board, technological support for the armed forces would drastically decline.

> Aspin is thus relying on modernizations to existing weapons to sustain America's air power until a new generation of combat aircraft can be conceived, designed, tested, and produced. Had Ronald Reagan adopted this type of planning, many of the magnificent systems that performed with such impact during the Persian Gulf War—the Stealth bomber, the Tomahawk cruise missile, satellite communications systems—would never have been fielded.[26]

Other support structures for troops were also weakened. In addition to providing aircraft protection, protecting troops from incoming missile assaults is a vitally important mission. Baker Spring described this U.S. security need in 1993:

> As the Scud-Patriot duels of Operation Desert Storm demonstrated, anti-missile defenses are a critical element of regional warfare. The Army should operate ground-based elements of U.S. defenses against short- and intermediate-range (theater) ballistic missiles, as it did with the Patriots in the Persian Gulf. Unlike during the Persian Gulf War, however, new systems must be designed to protect a wide area, and not just limited military positions. This is required to obtain the cooperation of U.S. allies, whose civilian population would be vulnerable to missile attack. The Army's contribution to the role of anti-missile defense should be coordinated with those of the other services. These include the Air Force space-based anti-missile defense and space-based sensor and command and control systems, plus the Navy's shipboard anti-missile systems.[27]

Thankfully, this hasn't been an issue in the last decade; but in 1993, when the Clinton administration cut the budget, they had no way of knowing. Yet, according to DiRita, Spring, and Luddy, Aspin cut the budget for missile defense to the point that actual deployment of such a defense system was unlikely. Research and development would be all the military could afford. But the problem went further than the budget cuts.

> Aspin further damaged the prospects for early deployment of theater missile defenses by declaring that all theater programs should comply with the nearly obsolete 1972 Anti-Ballistic Missile (ABM) Treaty. Although this treaty was never intended to impose restrictions on theater systems, the administration is now prepared to reverse the traditional interpretation of the treaty.[28]

Again, this was a strange policy for the administration of a president who wants his troops to be "the best trained, best equipped, best prepared fighting force in the world."

The gap between public relations ploys and actual proposals was all the more visible in the case of aircraft carriers. The stated Department of Defense mission, remember, was to be able to deal with two simultaneous major regional conflicts and, at the same time, meet other general requirements of an international presence to protect our interests.

Aspin's plan called for eleven carriers in service with a twelfth used for training. Even twelve full-service carriers, however, would be insufficient to deal with two simultaneous conflicts, if we were to keep our presence in the world and meet our obligations to the peacekeeping missions contemplated under the plan. Citing a Congressional Research Service study, DiRitia, Spring, and Luddy concluded that "every permanently deployed carrier presence requires at least four additional carriers to allow for crew training, transit time, maintenance, and other deployment preparations."[29] To reiterate this point, even with the availability of regional airbases for our planes, Operation Desert Storm *still* required six aircraft carriers.[30]

Furthermore, Aspin's assertion that the remaining aircraft carrier could be put into full service when necessary was unrealistic.

> This carrier will be manned with only 80 percent active duty personnel; the rest will be reservists. A carrier manned with a 100 percent active duty crew normally takes eighteen months to prepare for an extended overseas assignment. Aspin does not say how long it will take to prepare a carrier for a six-month deployment in which one in five crew members have trained onboard for only one weekend a month.[31]

Naturally, this sort of policy decision needed to somehow be reconciled with Clinton's stated goal not to jeopardize America's defenses, so Aspin rationalized the Clinton budget cuts: Stimulating the economy was key to national security. This allowed the administration to claim that taking money from defense and using it to allegedly stimulate the economy was an expenditure *for* the defense of the United States. Clinton's plan cut defense spending by 176 billion dollars from 1993 to 1997. He hoped to spend sixteen billion of that on economic stimulus in 1993.

The fallacy of such reasoning is obvious when you consider the difference in scale between defense spending and the U.S. economy. The U.S.

economy in the nineties involved $30 trillion in goods and services every year. Clinton's entire proposed cut for 1993 to 1997 represented a 15 percent reduction of the $1.2 trillion defense budget—a tangible amount.[32] But even if it were all poured into the U.S. economy, the impact would be insignificant. The $16 billion Clinton wanted for 1993 would likewise have had no appreciable effect on the economy, but that same sum could go a long way for defense.

> [T]hat same $16 billion could buy three aircraft carriers or dozens of sealift ships. These could help guarantee America's security and prosperity by maintaining access to foreign resources. They also could place military muscle in the way of a potential crisis and help avert a long, expensive conflict. The Clinton defense cuts guarantee that new technology will not be developed, weapons programs will be terminated, older systems will be phased out without replacement, spare parts will become unavailable, and military pay will lag behind civilian pay.[33]

DiRita, Spring, and Luddy remind us that in 1990, Kuwait had an extremely healthy economy but not much national security. Clinton's defense cuts left America more vulnerable, even if they stimulated the economy.

The Clinton Complex

Following the Republican triumph in the 1994 Congressional elections, President Clinton sought political cover by moving to undo some of his earlier defense cuts. On December 1, 1994, Clinton announced that he needed to find new funding for the military.[34] He wanted two billion more dollars for 1995 to supplement the defense budget and give the military more resources for the occupation of Haiti and similar operations. He also proposed an additional $25 billion from 1996 to 2001. Was this a turnaround?

> Clinton's announcement is a good first step toward correcting the decline in military readiness that has occurred during his tenure, but it does not go far enough. Outside estimates of the shortfall in defense spending range from The Heritage Foundation's $100 billion to the General Accounting

Office's $150 billion. Military pay has fallen behind comparable civilian pay by as much as 12 percent. Funds needed for day-to-day operations and maintenance are now being used to pay for unexpected and unfunded peacekeeping operations like the one in Haiti. Future force modernization is threatened both by a drastic decline in procurement spending and by a significant reduction in research and development spending. And the size and organization of the armed forces are inadequate to meet the administration's official goal of being able to fight and win two major regional conflicts "nearly simultaneously."[35]

With all of these problems, Clinton only addressed the pay in the military. The rest had yet to be acknowledged. In their paper, DiRita, Spring, and Luddy advised Congress on how to make up for the administration's shortcomings. Given Clinton's campaign promises for fiscal responsibility as a "new Democrat" some of their suggestions are revealing:

Remove non-defense spending from the Pentagon's budget. The Congressional Research Service has identified $5.8 billion in the 1995 defense authorization bill for "items that may not be directly related to traditional military capabilities." This includes $10 million for "U.S.-Japan Management Training" and nearly $300 million for AIDS, prostate, and breast cancer research. When environmental clean-up and research programs are included, this figure rises to more than $11 billion.[36]

An additional budget problem, however, was Bill Clinton's acquiescence to United Nations missions around the world. This fact had already become evident midway through the president's first term.

At last report, there were more than 73,000 U.S. troops acting in support of various United Nations "peacekeeping" missions worldwide. Cambodia; the Middle East; the Western Sahara; Macedonia; Somalia; Korea; Croatia; Yugoslavia; Iraq and Kuwait, where some people have been called on for three or four separate tours of duty. We even have 1,000 troops in the Sinai.[37]

With so many obligations, Clinton was not only slashing budgets but was also freezing soldiers' pay, even as he began promoting a new mission for

U.S. troops to support Haiti's leftist former President Jean-Bertrand Aristide.[38]

In Bob Livingston's view, the president suffered from a "flawed world view,"[39] which placed our troops at the beck and call of the UN. The "Clinton complex" (Livingston's term) was driven by guilt. Rather than being the "last remaining superpower" with an obligation to protect national interests, in the Clintonian perspective, "we are merely large and overweight and available any time that Secretary General Boutros Boutros-Ghali of the United Nations might call on us—much like a sumo wrestler hired to contain an angry mob."[40] Was this a perspective that would take the war on terrorism seriously, let alone wage it effectively?

An ominous indication of the answer to this question was seen as early as 1993, when Clinton tried to appoint Morton Halperin to the office of Assistant Defense Secretary for Human Rights and Democracy. Halperin was openly sympathetic to the communists in Central America in the 1980s. He had actively opposed United States policy to protect free elections in El Salvador against the disruptive tactics of FMLN communist guerillas—an interesting resumé for a candidate being considered for a job protecting and promoting democracy. But most important for the war on terrorism and Bill Clinton's legacy, Halperin had called for an end to all covert operations. This was recognized by many as an enormous policy problem, but not by Clinton. In the wake of September 11, we now recognize that we needed more covert operations, not less.[41]

The Decade of Decline

In February of 1999, many Republicans in the Senate were outraged that these trends, having begun in 1993, were still at work. The Clinton administration did not seem to be against using the armed forces, only against paying for them. Troops had been deployed forty-six times, defense spending had fallen 25 percent, while other spending had increased by 16 percent.[42] The discrepancy led to several problems. Troops were being kept overseas in back-to-back deployments. This would be demoralizing under any conditions, but other factors made it worse. Aging equipment that had not been modernized was a frustration and a danger. Aircraft were being stripped for spare parts to repair other aircraft.[43] As a result, "top military leaders have testified repeatedly about recruitment goals not being met and about a large number of critical personnel leaving the military early."[44]

Clinton's response to the situation was rather revealing. The military identified $148 billion in "hard military requirements."[45] The Clinton administration earmarked $90 billion to meet them. And while it claimed that it would increase defense spending by $12.6 billion that year, only a third of that was revenue actually given to defense. The rest was supposed to come "from uncertain funding sources and budget gimmicks: low oil prices, low inflation, and foreign currency exchange rates."[46]

In short, Clinton's policies for the military demonstrate an unmistakable attitude of apathy or even contempt for the U.S. military and our national defense.

What Bob Livingston said in 1993 remained true in 1999: "Clinton has turned on its head the old Teddy Roosevelt maxim to 'speak softly and carry a big stick.' Instead, President Clinton speaks interminably while brandishing a toothpick."[47]

On January 26, 2001, President Bush spoke at the swearing-in ceremony of Donald Rumsfeld as secretary of defense. He promised three things: to give the military the equipment and respect they ought to have, to work at defending the U.S. and allies from new growing threats, and to create "the military of the future" by providing new technologies.[48] But he had to make up for eight years of degrading the American military and its readiness capabilities. To increase military preparedness and reinvigorate our once-proud military would be an enormous challenge.

8

A PATTERN OF FAILURE

Paving the Way for 9/11

MANY SCHOLARS AND INTELLIGENCE EXPERTS ACKNOWLEDGE THAT
the Clinton administration had a poor track record with terrorism in general and with Al Qaeda and Osama bin Laden in particular. Clinton's
defenders typically claim that each incident involved circumstances beyond
the administration's control. The White House can't be blamed, they posit,
for turning down Sudan's offers to give us Bin Laden time and again,
because they weren't sure they could trust the Sudanese government. The
Clinton team claimed not to know who blew up the U.S.S. *Cole* until
Clinton's term was almost over.

The fact is, Clinton has no credibility as someone serious about fighting
terrorism. Indeed, his entire approach to terrorism was not in the United
States' best interest. Byron York, White House correspondent for *National
Review*, interviewed Clinton's top political strategist, Dick Morris.
According to Morris, Clinton was well aware of how important terrorism
was, both to his legacy and to the safety of Americans, but his response was
far from adequate:

> Even though Morris's polling showed the poll-sensitive president that the
> American people supported tough action, Clinton demurred. Why? "He
> had almost an allergy to using people in uniform," Morris explains. "He
> was terrified of incurring casualties; the lessons of Vietnam were ingrained
> far too deeply in him. He lacked a faith that it would work, and I think he
> was constantly fearful of reprisals." But there was more to it than that. "On
> another level, I just don't think it was his thing," Morris says. "You could
> talk to him about income redistribution and he would talk to you for hours

and hours. Talk to him about terrorism, and all you'd get was a series of grunts."[1]

Many others agree. The *Boston Globe* is hardly known as a conservative newspaper; yet it ran a commentary entitled "While Clinton Slept" by Scot Lehigh. While admitting that hindsight is 20/20, Lehigh suggests that even if we accept former presidential adviser George Stephanopoulos's assessment that the first World Trade Center attack didn't push the administration to greater action because it "wasn't a successful bombing," it doesn't explain the muted response to the bombing of the United States embassies in Kenya and Tanzania, which killed 224 in addition to the thousands injured. And why did Clinton resist the advice of his political adviser to promote an antiterrorist agenda? Morris told Clinton the public would support "federalizing airport security and taking military action against terrorist installations in foreign countries," but even after the bombings in Africa, the White House did not lead an aggressive plan to deal with the attacks. "While it is hardly fair to say the administration did nothing, it is completely fair to say that the response fell far short of the peril."[2]

Lehigh attempts to share the blame with those who thought that perjury, the gross abuse of authority, and violations of ethics were things to be concerned about. In other words, he makes the typical noises about the "partisan atmosphere," which he blames on then-House Speaker Newt Gingrich and the rest of the Republicans who expressed outrage at one Clinton scandal after another. But he has to admit the obvious: No one was more destructive to President Clinton's legacy than President Clinton. "The root cause of that politically debilitating scandal was the mind-numbing lack of self-discipline" which allowed Clinton to get sexually involved with a young girl.[3] He also notes, without emphasizing the irony, that Clinton and his supporters have supposed that the Clinton administration lacks a real legacy because there was no foreign-policy crisis, a necessary condition for a president to be remembered as a great leader. But the truth is, Clinton *did* face a foreign-policy crisis. Osama bin Laden declared and waged war on the United States during Clinton's two terms. Yet the president failed to adequately address this new challenge, "and it's far more our misfortune than his."[4]

The following glimpse into his actions should give an objective reader good reason to believe Clinton's mistakes were not simply an amazing series of coincidences, but the results of his own character and ideology. Unfortunately, these events also served to thwart antiterrorist efforts.

Who Leashed the Dogs?

Before Osama bin Ladin there was Imad Mugniyah.

Actually, there still is Imad Mugniyah, because we have yet to track him down. Like Osama bin Laden, he remains on the FBI's most-wanted list. Mugniyah is the star terrorist leader of Iran's Hezbollah, created to export terror to Israel and America.[5] Mugniyah has actually met with and helped Osama bin Laden.[6] As *60 Minutes II* reported, "Mugniyah was the mentor; Bin Laden was the disciple. The student has gone so much further than his teacher. Bin Laden has become modern history's most famous terrorist. His teacher remains a little-known and shadowy figure, a man whose photograph, captured only in black-and-white, appeared once in a French magazine."[7] Mugniyah is wanted in connection with the following cold-blooded acts of terror:[8]

- The bombing of the U.S. Embassy in Beirut in April 1983 that killed sixty-three.

- The bombing in October 1983 that killed three hundred U.S. Marines and French troops in Beirut.

- Numerous kidnappings, including the kidnapping, torture, and murder of CIA Beirut Station Chief William Buckley.

- The hijacking of TWA Flight 847 from Greece to Beirut in June 1985 (a crime that included the murder of Navy diver Robert Stethem).

- The bombing of the Israeli Embassy and a Jewish Cultural Center in Buenos Aires, Argentina, in March 1992 that killed a total of 115.

Yet on July 23, 1996, just a month after nineteen servicemen were killed in the Khobar Towers bombing, we had a chance to catch this murderer. U.S.

intelligence learned that Mugniyah was aboard the *Ibn Tufail*. Immediately, Navy and Marine forces in the area were scrambled on a secret mission. Four battleships began shadowing the vessel.[9]

Overnight, the armed forces planned a massive boarding, which involved parachuting onto the boat, climbing the side, and distracting the sailors so that there would be no resistance—all so they could locate and capture Mugniyah if he was, indeed, on board. As they stalked the boat, the soldiers reviewed their information and attack plans. "I'd never seen the kind of intelligence we had during this mission. I mean, in less than 48 hours," SEAL platoon commander Tom Short later said, "we had blueprints to the ship, the layout of the ship, pictures of the ship. Who was the crew, what they were carrying, what was their schedule. I mean it was just amazing to me the amount of intelligence that we had."[10]

At nightfall, July 24, sixty Navy SEALs, dozens of Marine commandos, and hundreds of other troops, including four groups of snipers arranged from bow to stern and on helicopters, were ready to move. Marine sniper Bill McSwain recalled, "We almost felt like we were dogs on a leash ready to go."[11]

But they never went. The White House reined them in.

We may never know what happened. President Clinton's deputy assistant to the president for national security affairs, Nancy Soderberg, insists that there was not even a slight possibility that Mugniyah was aboard the ship. Otherwise "President Clinton would have gone. No question about it."[12] Military sources familiar with the facts of the mission stated, "We didn't understand why we didn't go. Our intelligence was good and if we had boarded and he wasn't there, then 'no harm, no foul.'" All we can know for sure is that the military put together a plan based on reportedly good intelligence, and the White House pulled the plug.

We lost not only an opportunity to strike back at terrorism, but also what could have been an amazing source of intelligence on Al Qaeda.

Sending a Message to Terrorists

One way to lead a war against terrorism is with stiff punishments. Here, as elsewhere, Clinton showed that he didn't want to lead a war against terrorism; in fact, he was leading in the exact wrong direction.

For example, if Clinton took the escalating problem of terrorism seriously, why did his administration pressure the State Department to grant a visa to a known terror master?[13] Fernando Garcia Bielsa ranked high in the Cuban Communist party and supported terrorist operations on behalf of Fidel Castro's government. This was no secret. The State Department, then as now, had Cuba listed as a sponsor of international terrorism "on par with Iran and North Korea for engaging in terrorist activity themselves or by providing arms, training, safe haven, diplomatic facilities, financial backing, logistic and/or other support to terrorists," according to a report released the previous year.[14]

Bielsa was responsible for Cuba's covert operations as the chief of the America Department of the Cuban Communist Party Central Committee.[15] As scholar Michael Waller writes,

> The America Department, known by its Spanish initials DA, long has been Castro's main instrument for coordinating terrorism in the Western Hemisphere. A 1975 Senate investigation on Cuban support for terrorism found that the DA began directing terrorist operations in Puerto Rico and in the Midwestern and Eastern United States in 1974. Senate hearings in 1982 revealed that Cuban intelligence "organized" the Puerto Rican Armed Forces of National Liberation, known by its Spanish acronym, FALN.[16]

According to a 1981 State Department report, Cuba formed the DA to foster and support revolutionary groups in this hemisphere, "to centralize Cuban control over covert activities."[17]

As the head of DA, Bielsa was quite dangerous. The Cuban government wanted to move him to Washington, D.C., to work at the Cuban Interests Section on 16th Street in Washington. This would have put him only a few blocks from the White House and provided him with status and privileges as a diplomat.[18] According to a study done by Rex A. Hudson for the Cuban-American National Foundation, the Cuban Interests Section in Washington, D.C., had twenty-four staff members before Clinton took office in 1993. Almost all of them were spies. By 1999, after two terms of the Clinton administration, a Congressional source told Waller that the number of staff members had doubled.[19]

The kind of control Bielsa exerted over terrorist groups can be seen in the case of the secret terrorist organization the Machetero, which set off bombs in Puerto Rico. The Machetero want to see Puerto Rico become a Communist state, independent of U.S. control. In 1988, the Task Force on Combating Terrorism released a report calling the organization "a tightly controlled and extremely violent Puerto Rican terrorist group that has targeted primarily U.S. military personnel and Puerto Rican police." Further, the report noted, "The stated position of the group is that they have 'declared war' on the United States."[20]

After a 1998 bombing attack provoked by plans to privatize the telephone company, Bielsa convinced the Machetero leadership to stop, apparently because he and others in Cuba felt it was counterproductive. "He appears to have directly intervened to stop recent violent actions committed by the Macheteros in Puerto Rico," said a source in the U.S. government. "After that meeting, the violence abruptly ceased."[21]

Despite this background information, the Clinton White House undercut the FBI and pressured the State Department to issue Bielsa a visa. Technically, the Justice Department had to approve the application in the case of potential spies, but Reno caved under the weight of State Department pressure, and the visa application was approved. Cuba's director for terrorism in the Western Hemisphere was permitted to set up shop in our capital city.

Clemency for Terrorists

What is especially ominous about this move by the administration is that Clinton had already, inexplicably, granted amnesty to fourteen convicted Puerto Rican FALN terrorists—terrorists belonging to a group under the supervision of Fernando Garcia Bielsa. They were responsible for a hundred and thirty bombing attacks between 1974 and 1983 that left six dead, over eighty wounded, and caused millions of dollars in damage.[22] Some of those wounded would never recover. In the 1982 bombing of New York Police headquarters, Officer Salvatore Pastorella was permanently blinded, and the fingers on his right hand were blown off. Officer Anthony Senft lost one eye, and Officer Rocco Pascarella lost his right leg.[23]

The terrorists committed other violent acts in their own country. "In

Puerto Rico itself, they wrought even more bloody mayhem, beginning with the murder of a police officer in 1978," writes *Boston Globe* columnist Jeff Jacoby. "In December 1979, they ambushed a Navy vehicle in Sabana Seca, killing two of the 17 passengers and badly wounding nine. In January 1981, they bombed the Air National Guard base in Carolina and destroyed nine fighter jets."[24]

Not only did Bill Clinton grant them clemency, he did so knowing that they remained unrepentant of the murders and violence. Initially, the administration spokesman indicated the terrorists would be released from prison if they signed statements renouncing violence and pledging not to associate with other criminals.[25] When they refused to sign it, liberal activists continued to press for their release. Jesse Jackson, for example, claimed the proposed stipulations were "humiliating."[26]

Why would such luminaries as Bishop Desmond Tutu, Corretta Scott King, Cardinal John O'Conner, and several members of Congress advocate amnesty for such people? Allegedly, the punishment was too severe for the crimes. Congressman Louis Gutierrez, an Illinois Democrat, claimed, "They've done hard time. They are serving what is in effect a life sentence . . . and a life sentence is unreasonable."[27]

In the end, the felons were released because Bill Clinton wanted them released. None of the fourteen even applied for clemency, according to the *New York Times*, "as is usually required."[28] Instead of prisoners pressing for clemency, the White House and the Justice Department kept the issue alive.

When the issue was first broached, Margaret Love, assistant attorney general in charge of pardon applications, and the pardon attorney in 1997, wrote a letter to White House counsel Charles F. C. Ruff, recommending denial of clemency. But after Roger Adams replaced Love, the application was again considered. On November 5, 1997, Adams met with Deputy Attorney General Eric Holder and three Democratic representatives: Gutierrez and New York's Jose Serrano and Nydia Velasquez. According to Adams's notes of the meeting, Holder explained that the lack of any statement of remorse was a problem. Such a statement would help their chances for clemency from the president.

Six months later, Adams's notes say that he took it upon himself to telephone an aide on Gutierrez's staff to inform him that no statement of remorse had yet been received. According to Neil Lewis, writing for the *Times*, "Adams counseled the staff aide as to how the statement should be worded for maximum effect and he added that the department's new report would await the statement."[29] When the statement finally came, it was "a long ambiguous statement," that lacked any "explicit statement of regret." The prisoners admitted that "some people had been hurt," but added that "innocent victims were on all sides." In response, Adams filed a second report that contained no explicit recommendation for the president, as such reports usually do, but instead offered Clinton "a range of options."[30]

Eventually, fourteen of the terrorists signed a promise not to use violence in the future, and Clinton promptly commuted their sentences. At a time when terrorism was on the rise as never before, the leader of the United States publicly displayed our willingness to deal with terrorists by giving them a get-out-of-jail-free card.

Truth and Consequences

The pardons were met with strong bipartisan rebuke on Capitol Hill. According to the *Puerto Rico Herald*, both House and Senate passed resolutions that condemned the pardons. The House resolution declared that the Clinton administration's grant of clemency transgressed "longstanding tenets of United States counterterrorism policy." It was "an affront to the rule of law, the victims and their families, and every American who believes that violent acts must be punished to the fullest extent of the law." Passing by an overwhelming majority—311 to 41—the resolution also declared, "making concessions to terrorists is deplorable," and "President Clinton should not have offered or granted clemency to the FALN terrorists." While all Republicans voted for the resolution (218 to 0), a majority of Democrats did as well (93 to 41).[31]

The Senate's resolution condemning the pardons, which passed 95 to 2, also pointed out how gratuitous Clinton's actions were, since "no petitions for clemency were made by these terrorists, but other persons sought such clemency for them."[32]

Clearly, Clinton's actions were reprehensible to both political parties. The paper points out that, though several had advocated the release of the prisoners, no one spoke up to defend the president's action. In fact, many of the president's usual defenders condemned what he did. Diane Feinstein, the Democratic senator from California, said, "Some have described these prisoners as political prisoners. They were not. They were terrorists."[33]

Of course, no amount of condemnation from Congress could undo the results. The Constitution vests the president the power to pardon. He was not required to consult with the Department of Justice, and other presidents have issued pardons without consultation. But the question naturally arises: Why would he do such a thing? Getting any kind of verifiable answer from the White House proved impossible. While the president was happy to verbalize his own version of things, documents from the White House were suppressed. Neil Lewis reported that the exact order of events that led to clemency have "remained murky" because the administration, both the White House and the Justice Department, claimed executive privilege and refused to turn over requested information. The White House attorneys claimed that all the president's discussions with his subordinates regarding clemency did not have to be released to anyone because the Constitution gives the chief executive sole authority to grant pardons.[34]

Having evaded Congressional inquiry, on January 18, 2000, Clinton told two reporters that a president should "rarely commute sentences and should have good reasons for doing so if he does."[35] Then, apparently oblivious to the contradiction, claimed that Charles Ruff, his White House counsel, "handled it entirely, and only he handled it."[36] The president could not possibly "have good reasons" for commuting the sentence if he left the matter entirely in the hands of his attorney. In any case, the Constitution does not grant the president's attorney the authority to commute sentences. The buck stops with the president.

One month after clemency was offered, Attorney General Janet Reno wrote that FALN and the Machetero were an "ongoing threat."[37] In the Justice Department's Five Year Interagency Counterterrorism and Technology Crime Plan, Reno added, "Factors which increase the present threat from these groups include . . . the impending release from prisons of members of these groups jailed for prior violence."[38]

That Clinton would issue these clemencies to Puerto Rican terrorists working for Cuban-backed Marxist terrorist groups—knowing that the release of these criminals heightened the threat of future violence against Americans—and in the same year pressure the Justice Department to allow the head of Cuba's terrorist network to set up shop in Washington, D.C., makes the decisions look even worse in the eyes of many. Wrote Michael Waller for *Insight*,

> The White House isn't helping to clear the air. Rather than allay concerns about espionage and Cuban influence operations, it has quashed congressional inquiries about the decision-making process behind the president's unusual clemency offer.
>
> Many political observers following the clemency issue, particularly Republicans, have assumed that the decision was designed to help first lady Hillary Rodham Clinton curry favor with ethnic Puerto Rican voters in New York City for her anticipated Senate campaign. Evidently, there was more to it than that.[39]

Waller may be right or not. The stonewalling guaranteed that nothing can be proven. But what these decisions did indicate is that the president's alleged commitment to the war on terrorism had no credibility.

In their book *The Age of Sacred Terror: Radical Islam's War Against America*, Daniel Benjamin and Steven Simon, the former director and senior director for counterterrorism at the National Security Council during the Clinton administration, try to make the president and the president's defenders look good, while blaming as much as possible on those in the administration who were suspicious of Clinton. Missing from the book, however, is any reference to the clemency to Puerto Rican terrorists. In itself, there is nothing wrong with this omission. The subtitle states that the book is concerned with Islamic terrorism, not the Cuban/Marxist variety. It is easier to make Clinton look good if one excludes the evidence that runs counter to their preordained mindset.

Clinton's heavy-handed pursuit of unrequested clemency for these killers needs to be factored into any calculation about his administration's response to terrorism. Actions speak louder than words, and these spoke volumes. Whatever his rhetoric, his actions released terrorists and ignored the pleas of the victims and the safety of American citizens.

Investigating Charities, 1996

The October 6, 2003, *Newsweek* reported that Captain James Yee had been arrested when classified material about Guantanamo Bay was discovered in his possession.[40] Yee had just completed a tour of duty at that facility. The implications of his arrest go far beyond one man. Yee received his certification as an imam from the Graduate School of Islamic and Social Sciences. That organization is one of several under investigation for allegedly raising funds for terrorist groups. Furthermore, Chaplain Yee was endorsed by the American Muslim Council's Armed Forces and Veterans Affairs Office. The cofounder of that group, Abdurahman al-Amoudi, is also under investigation for the same problem: ties to fund-raising for terrorist organizations.

Federal prosecutors claim that al-Amoudi took $340,000 in cash through Damascus in order to distribute it to terrorists in Syria. He was detained in London, where that money was found in his possession.[41] Evidence showed that al-Amoudi's American Muslim Foundation had written checks to two Portland, Oregon, residents suspected of supporting Al Qaeda. At the same time, al-Amoudi has been quite involved in promoting Islamic chaplains for the U. S. Military. The *Washington Times* reports, "Over the past 10 years, Alamoudi has met dozens of times with senior government officials and helped establish the Pentagon's Muslim chaplain program."

Besides the American Muslim Council, there is one other organization that certifies Muslim chaplains for the military, the Islamic Society of North America. According to the *Washington Times,*

> One of its board members, Siraj Wahhaj, was named in 1995 by U.S. Attorney Mary Jo White as one of more than 100 "unindicted persons who may be alleged as co-conspirators" in the attempt to blow up New York monuments. Mr. Wahhaj also served as a character witness for Sheik Omar Abel Rahman, who was convicted in the 1993 World Trade Center bombing. Mr. Wahhaj was never convicted of a crime.[42]

While these arrests and impending trials are recent, it is important to keep in mind that the investigation resulting in these arrests is tied to an inquiry of Islamic charities and other groups. According to Douglas Farah and John

Mintz of the *Washington Post*, "Authorities described the arrest as an important step in the wide-ranging investigation of funding for terrorism in this country, *a probe that centers on a cluster of foundations and businesses based in Herndon, VA*" (emphasis added).[43]

In March 2002, federal agents kicked off Operation Green Quest, an investigation into the funding of suspected terrorist organizations by charities. Directed by the Treasury Department's counterterrorism task force, agents from the FBI, IRS, U.S. Customs, and Immigration and Naturalization Service seized more than twenty computers, financial papers, and other documents.[44]

At the time of this writing, this information is still being reviewed. Some people may be exonerated, others yet unknown may be accused, and some convicted. But it is a well-established fact that terrorism is supported through charities that solicit funds from American residents. And the investigation has barely begun. According to a recent book by Loretta Napoleoni, *Modern Jihad: Tracing the Dollars Behind the Terror Networks*, terrorist activities represent 5 percent of the world's gross domestic product, or $1.5 trillion—a figure that includes "charity donations."[45] Plainly, Islamic charities that transfer money overseas need investigation. The American dollar is the preferred terrorist currency.[46]

Now compare the present to the past. Obviously, it would have been good to look into the possibility that terrorists were getting funds from America through charities long *before* 9/11. But the fact is, such an investigation did begin back in the nineties, only to be brought to a halt before anything could be done. When we think of political correctness, most envision irrational rules being enforced on college campuses. The Clinton administration, however, allowed politically correct thinking to torpedo an investigation into domestic fundraising for terrorist groups.

According to a *Washington Times* story, in 1995 federal investigators were looking at tax-exempt Islamic charities suspected of supporting international terrorism, especially through Saudi Arabia. Saudi Arabia (or a substantial contingent within that country) has long been suspected of international money laundering for various terrorist organizations such as Islamic Jihad and Hamas. Nevertheless, despite the escalating threat of terrorism, including the 1993 attack on the World Trade Center, the Clinton

State Department pressured investigators to abandon their examination. "Former federal prosecutor John J. Loftus said four interrelated Islamic foundations, institutes and charities in Virginia with more than a billion dollars in assets donated by or through the Saudi Arabian government were allowed to continue under 'a veil of secrecy.'"[47]

While the criminal activity suspected in this case involved primarily Palestinian terrorism, Al Qaeda also benefits:

> One former and three current federal law enforcement officials said the new probe began after U.S. officials learned that intelligence agents in India had wiretapped the telephone of a Pakistani charity funded by the Saudi government and discovered the transfer of $100,000 to Mohamed Atta, one of the 19 al Qaeda hijackers in the September 11 attacks. That information helped U.S. officials identify the 19 hijackers, 15 of whom were from Saudi Arabia, the officials said.[48]

White House spokeswoman Julie Payne did not respond to questions about the State Department's rationale. Bill Clinton's politically correct view of the world would not allow for the perception. He could be accused of racial profiling. The same kind of political correctness was at work when the FBI considered investigating a similar situation in 1998.

> Federal law-enforcement sources tell *Newsweek* that FBI agents in Chicago first became alarmed five years ago that terrorist suspects with ties to one of the northern Virginia groups were compiling lists of Muslims in the U.S. military for possible recruitment. (The concern was fueled by the case of Ali Mohammed, a former U.S. Army sergeant who became a devotee of Osama bin Laden's and later pleaded guilty to charges related to the 1998 bombings of two U.S. embassies in Africa.) But a proposal to investigate the issue then was rejected by FBI headquarters—apparently because of concerns that, without hard evidence, a full-fledged probe might rile religious sensitivities.[49]

With three thousand deaths at the World Trade Center, the PC rationale of the 1990s has been rejected. After all, it is unusual to have hard evidence *before* starting an investigation. Usually one launches an investigation on the basis of probable cause and, if one finds evidence, charges are brought and the case moves to trial. Pursuing such leads may have saved lives on September 11.

"In cases like this one, it is very difficult to argue that Clinton lacked sufficient information to act against the terror masters," says Michael Ledeen, pointing to Clinton's culpability. "The American government had abundant information, and would have acquired much more if federal prosecutors had been permitted to shut down the Islamic organizations. Clinton prevented the Justice Department from acting on the information it had, and blocked its efforts to strike a meaningful blow against the terror network."[50]

A POINT OF COMPARISON

The American people were aware of possible abuses of the IRS by the Clintons during his two terms in office. *NewsMax* reported shortly after 9/11 that IRS priorities during the Clinton administration seemed somewhat odd, if one tried to believe national security was a concern to the president. Notable people who were audited included Gennifer Flowers and Paula Jones, but suspect Islamic charities were not. In September 2001, the legal watchdog group Judicial Watch filed a complaint with Charles Rossotti, the Clinton-appointed IRS commissioner, regarding sixteen known nonprofit entities based in the United States that were connected to Islamic terrorist networks such as Hamas and Al Qaeda. These charities had been permitted to operate without being audited or even being threatened with an audit to show where their money was going. As *NewsMax* pointed out, "The Judicial Watch complaint is hardly a state secret. On the contrary, the complaint is based largely on reports published over the last three years in venues like the *New York Times*."[51]

The point here is that the Clinton administration's aversion to investigating Islamic charities for possible connection to terrorist groups *cannot* be ascribed to an aversion to use the IRS to do audits. In fact, under the Clinton administration plenty of individuals and nonprofit organizations were investigated. The list includes:

- Gennifer Flowers, who testified she had an adulterous affair with Bill Clinton.

- Liz Ward Gracen, another woman who claimed to have had a sexual relationship with the president.

- Dolly Kyle Browning, another woman alleging an affair.

- Paula Jones, who accused Clinton of sexual assault (her tax returns were mysteriously put in the hands of *New York Daily News* reporter Lars Erik Nelson).[52]

- Juanita Broaddrick, who also accused Clinton of sexual assault.

- Katherine Prudhomme, who had the gall to confront Al Gore about Juanita Broaddrick's allegations.[53]

- Billy Dale, the White House travel office director, whom the Clintons wanted fired.

- Bill O'Reilly, *Fox News* critic of the Clinton administration, was audited three years in a row by the IRS.[54]

In addition to these people, the IRS audited the National Rifle Association, Citizens Against Government Waste, National Center for Public Policy Research, American Policy Center, The American Cause, The Heritage Foundation, *American Spectator*, Oliver North's Freedom Alliance, Judicial Watch, Citizens for Honest Government, the Progress and Freedom Foundation, Concerned Women for America, the San Diego Chapter of Christian Coalition, *National Review*, and the Western Journalism Center, founded by Joseph Farah.

The case of Judicial Watch is especially enlightening. Not only was the nonprofit advocacy group audited when it opposed Clinton, but the IRS admitted the audit's political motivation. Senior IRS official Paul Breslan said, in the presence of six witnesses, "What do you expect when you sue the president?"[55]

The chairman of Judicial Watch, Larry Klayman, told *NewsMax* that the audits were quite blatantly political: "The IRS asked for our political affiliations in the first notice of audit," claiming that they were "relevant" to their investigation.[56]

Worse still, each time Judicial Watch seemed to make legal headway against the White House, the IRS ratcheted up the pressure. "When we would accomplish something big, like the criminal finding by Judge Royce Lamberth against Clinton in the Kathleen Willey Privacy Act case, our lawyers would get a call saying, 'We just want you to know that Judicial Watch is still on the IRS's radar screen,'" Klayman said. "The same thing happened when we revealed the White House e-mail scandal," he added.[57]

While the abuse of the powers of the IRS by the executive office deserves its own book, the point of briefly mentioning some of the things that happened is to indicate that Clinton was not at all averse to using his power to investigate people. He simply was not interested in using that power to deal with issues of national security. His personal security was his only interest.

Whatever Happened to "Terror 2000"?

While the media was quite willing to ask what warning George W. Bush or his administration received before the attack, it is important to realize that plenty of warnings were given long before he ever took office. As the Manchester *Guardian* reported on 12 September 2001,

> Almost prophetically, the Pentagon has conducted a secret study, called Terror 2000, designed to consider and study the likely future of terrorism and help the intelligence world meet the threat. One of the main conclusions from the team of investigators, which included experts from the CIA and Israeli Mossad, and former KGB agents, is that the world is witnessing the dawn of a new age of "superterrorism," when men with no moral restrictions on mass killing will use weapons of mass destruction. "You're talking about taking large numbers of people out because that becomes theatre, because it attracts attention," said Marvin Cetron, one of the authors.[58]

The "Terror 2000" report, written in 1994, was indeed prophetic. It warned of the possibility that hijackers would use an airliner as a missile against the Pentagon. It also predicted the possibility of the World Trade Center being targeted.

Targets such as the World Trade Center not only provide the requisite casualties but because of their symbolic nature provide more bang for the buck. In order to maximize their odds for success, terrorist groups will likely consider mounting multiple, simultaneous operations with the aim of overtaxing a government's ability to respond, as well as to demonstrate their professionalism and reach.[59]

But "Terror 2000" did not have to be "a secret study." A few days after the *Guardian* story, UPI reporter Pam Hess showed that it contained specific warnings about airliners, the Pentagon, and the Twin Towers, and that it was also hushed up. Report coauthor Marvin Cetron told UPI, "I think they took the ostrich approach."[60]

According to Cetron, the Clinton State Department was responsible for withholding the report from the public. Furthermore, while it was distributed to government agencies and some members of Congress, certain details were left out—such as the use of planes as weapons. "They said: 'You can't handle a crisis before it becomes a crisis. It scares the hell out of people, and they can't do anything. It's like a person with cancer; some people don't want to know. Others want to know everything so they can fight it.'"[61]

Of course, whether or not a crisis could have been prevented by the free flow of information is now a question that can never be answered definitively, but it seems perfectly plausible that a warning like this, in the wake of the 1993 bombing of the World Trade Center, might have caused needed change to occur. If airlines had been made aware of the threat, things could have been different.

As we will see when we consider Clinton's response (or lack thereof) to the 1993 bombing of the World Trade Center, the president did not want to be distracted from his domestic agenda by foreign affairs. The refusal to release "Terror 2000" did prevent distractions, but it also made us more vulnerable to attack.

Palestinian Terrorists

Yasser Arafat is a terrorist.

When Clinton entered into talks with him, he undercut America's longstanding policy of refusing to negotiate with terrorists. In the hope of reaching peace and gaining a legacy, Clinton sent out a message to Islamic terrorists everywhere that terrorism pays.

In 1993, secret meetings sponsored by the Clinton administration in Oslo, Norway, culminated in the signing of the Oslo Accords. As Clinton's former Director of Central Intelligence James Woolsey said to me, "Clinton was convinced after Oslo and the Rose garden meetings that mid-east peace was achievable." In signing this document, Arafat promised to apprehend and punish terrorists, as well as disavow terrorism. Of course, this never happened. Pressured by the Clinton administration, Israel gave ground on issues, but Arafat refused to live up to his end of the agreement. "He repeatedly has pocketed concrete Israeli concessions, such as troop withdrawals from most of Gaza and about thirty percent of the West Bank, in return for promises which too often have gone unfulfilled."[62]

According to a report from the Heritage Foundation,

In direct contravention of the Oslo accords, Arafat's Palestinian Authority (PA) has permitted known terrorists to roam freely inside PA-controlled territory and has taken no action against 200 suspected terrorists identified to it by the Israeli government. It has failed to extradite 27 terrorists wanted by the Israeli government for crimes against Israelis, including at least six who continue to serve in the Palestinian security services. In addition, Arafat has expanded his police force far beyond the 30,000 permitted by the Oslo accords. The PA police, together with various internal security forces, now form an armed militia of up to 50,000 men. The PA already has violated the painstakingly negotiated Hebron agreement, signed January 15, which set the terms of Israeli military withdrawal from 80 percent of Hebron, the last major Palestinian city that had been under Israeli control. The New York Times reported that significantly more than the 400 PA policemen allowed under the agreement were deployed inside Hebron, armed with more than the allotted 200 pistols and 100 rifles.

Arafat also has raised the ire of Israelis through bellicose rhetoric that raises strong doubts about his peaceful intentions. He repeatedly has called for a jihad (holy war) to liberate Jerusalem and has described slain Palestinian terrorists as martyrs.[63]

Arafat also promised to get rid of references to Israel's destruction from the Palestinian Covenant. But that never happened either. The call for the destruction of Israel remains in the document.[64]

"I think Yasser Arafat is like Robert Mugabi, but that's unfair to Mugabi. Arafat is a terrorist killer who wants to destroy Israel," Woolsey said. "Some think Arafat is Nelson Mandela, but there's not an ounce of Mandela in him. Arafat got a very generous offer from [Ehud] Barak. Too generous. But he turned it down and you know he doesn't want peace. He wants a one-state solution to this problem with the destruction of the state of Israel."

Barak's offer was to grant the Palestinians a state made up of 95 percent of the West Bank, the Gaza Strip, and portions of Jerusalem, including the Temple Mount.[65] Not only did Arafat turn this down, he didn't even bother to make a counteroffer. Instead, he instigated low-intensity warfare, hoping the violence would win him even more concessions. Said Woolsey, "Once Arafat began the killing in September 2000, the second intifada, I knew there was no difference between Yasser Arafat and Osama Bin Laden."

Clinton's cozying up to Arafat was consistent with the rest of his record on terrorism. He failed to bring about any lasting peace, showing instead by public example that terrorism could impact U.S. foreign policy in their favor. Additionally, at a time when the CIA was needed to track down terrorists and prevent other attacks, President Clinton had CIA director George Tenet in Palestine dealing with the Israelis and Palestinians. According to Madeleine Albright, in October 1998, Tenet was working in the negotiations "to fine-tune the assurances on security."[66]

I asked Woolsey why the CIA would be used for political negotiations. "Presidents have always used the DCI to put people together," he said. "The difference was this time it was out in the open. Usually it's behind the scenes."

But Tenet's work was more than putting people together. As Woolsey told *Insight* magazine, from press accounts it appears that the CIA equipped and trained Arafat's security forces. "I'm sure that if any material or training was used to kill Israelis this brought about a great deal of soul-searching at the CIA. The CIA has a close relationship with Israeli intelligence dating back to the inception of the state of Israel."[67]

Clinton and the Taliban

Clinton's release of terrorists and negotiations with terrorists raises serious questions, one of them being, Why didn't the Clinton administration actively oppose the Taliban?

Congressman Dana Rohrabacher would certainly like an answer to that question. Rohrabacher was a special aid to President Reagan during the eighties. In that capacity, he made several trips to Afghanistan during the time that the Mujahedin were fighting the Soviets and afterward.

According to a *WorldNetDaily* report, Rohrabacher claims "he was belittled, stonewalled and ridiculed for three years for asserting the Congressional oversight role in the formulation of foreign policy toward Afghanistan during the last term of the Clinton administration."[68] The Clinton administration not only failed to show an interest in his efforts to help the Northern Alliance, they actively obstructed his work.[69] As he testified before Congress:

> In several personal instances I was involved with helping obtain medical and humanitarian support for people in the areas of Afghanistan that was not yet under Taliban control. I was thwarted by our own government. I was thwarted by our own State Department. NGOs [Non-Government Organizations] with aid for Afghans who were in areas that were controlled by the Taliban, on the other hand, had no trouble with our government. They had some other troubles that, of course, the Taliban gave them themselves, but our government was perfectly happy to have NGOs operating in Taliban-controlled areas but stopping people like myself who were trying to help those people in areas that were opposed to the Taliban.[70]

Far worse was done, however, after the Northern Alliance managed to win victories despite the Clinton administration's refusal to side with them. At that point, the State Department intervened to ensure that the Taliban remained in power and that victory was kept away from the Northern Alliance. On this point, Congressman Rohrabacher's testimony is quite valuable:

In mid 1988, however, even with this tacit support from the Clinton administration, the Taliban were incredibly vulnerable. They had overextended themselves in an invasion of the northern part of Afghanistan, and many of their best, if not most of their best, fighters were captured, along with huge amounts of war supplies. The road to Kabul was open. And who interceded to prevent the collapse of the Taliban at this pivotal moment? Who pulled their chestnuts out of the fire? President Clinton, personally.

At this moment of maximum Taliban vulnerability, the White House dispatched Assistant Secretary of State Rick Inderfurth and Bill Richardson, then our United Nations ambassador. They flew to northern Afghanistan and convinced the anti-Taliban forces not to attack and not to retake Kabul, but, instead, to accept a cease-fire and an arms embargo.

This is at the moment, and I cannot stress this more forcefully, it was at a pivotal moment. The Taliban could easily have been defeated. The Northern Alliance was willing to accept a return of King Zahir Shah to lead a transition government. Instead, under the direction of the Clinton White House, these two top U.S. Government officials, Assistant Secretary of State Rick Inderfurth and UN Ambassador Bill Richardson, arrived on the scene to convince the anti-Taliban forces to stand back. And we thus saved this fanatical, anti-western regime from being destroyed and being defeated.

This later led to a dramatic defeat of the anti-Taliban forces. The cease-fire lasted only long enough for the Saudis and the Pakistanis to fully rearm the Taliban. And the arms embargo that Bill Richardson and Rick Inderfurth talked about was only effective against the anti-Taliban forces, which are the people called the Northern Alliance. Think about that. We talked them into a cease-fire, which lasted only long enough for the Taliban to rearm. We talked them into an arms embargo, which was only an arms embargo against them.[71]

Here again, the Clinton administration failed to deal aggressively with terrorists or terrorist supporters. This cannot be ascribed simply to a run of bad luck or honest mistakes. Over and over again, the administration proved it had no concern whatsoever for terrorism or national security. Letting terrorists go free, suppressing reports on our vulnerability to terrorist attacks, and refusing to investigate terrorist financing operations while using investigations to harass conservative opponents, is the backdrop to Clinton's missed opportunities with Osama bin Laden. One could easily argue that Clinton's policies not only showed a lack of concern for terrorism, they actually *helped* terrorist organizations thrive.

And this barely scratches the surface. Further evidence exists showing how little concern Bill Clinton had for national security, as he allowed weapons and technology to flow from China and Russia to rogue states like Iran and North Korea.

CLINTON'S SILK TRAIL

China and National Insecurity

DURING THE 1992 PRESIDENTIAL CAMPAIGN AGAINST GEORGE H. W. Bush, Bill Clinton strongly criticized China for its human rights record and accused President Bush of "coddling" the regime in Beijing by continuing to allow it Most Favored-Nation status even after the brutal crackdown in Tiananmen Square.

Senator and vice presidential nominee Al Gore adopted the same position. In 1992, while serving in the Senate, Gore joined sixteen of his colleagues to write Secretary of State James Baker expressing concern that China might "gain foreign aerospace technology that would otherwise be unavailable to it" because Bush had signed a waiver allowing China to launch an American satellite. Gore went so far as to say in October 1992, "President Bush is really an incurable patsy for those dictators he sets out to coddle." Candidate Clinton agreed: "I believe our nation has a higher purpose than to coddle dictators and stand aside from the global movement toward democracy."

Once in office, however, the Clinton/Gore administration continued China's Most Favored-Nation status. Clinton also reversed Reagan- and Bush-era restrictions on the export of advanced technologies to China by removing satellite technologies from the State Department's munitions-control list and placing them, instead, on the less-restrictive Commerce Department dual-use technology list. This was in keeping with the incoming administration's emphasis on global economic security as the new primary national security concern.

Clinton's policies toward China are directly relevant to the war on terror and September 11. Weapons and weapons-related technologies that find their way to China frequently end up in North Korea and Pakistan.[1] North Korea is a problem in its own right, and Pakistan, while currently an ally in the war on terror, has a long history of support for Islamic extremists including Al Qaeda and the ousted Taliban regime in Afghanistan.

Quid Pro Quo

Understanding Clinton's changes in long-standing policies toward China requires a review of the donations to the Democratic party and the subsequent decisions made by Clinton.

In May 1993, the donation patterns of Bernard Schwartz, CEO of Loral Space and Communications, dramatically changed. Loral lobbied Secretary of State Warren Christopher to reclassify satellite technology to make it easier for U.S. companies to launch satellites on Chinese rockets. The interim report by the House Committee on Government Reform and Oversight, which investigated the matter, states:

> In the previous six years, according to Federal Election Commission data, Loral chairman and CEO Bernard Schwartz had made less than $100,000 in cumulative political donations, mostly to Senate Democrats. All of his donations from 1987 through 1992 were so-called "hard-money" contributions, regulated and limited by federal law. Mr. Schwartz made his first unregulated "soft-money" contribution to the Democrat National Committee (DNC) in May 1993.[2]

In January 1994, Clinton classified three communication satellites as "civilian" in order to get around the existing restrictions, thereby allowing the satellites to be launched from China. The General Accounting Office reported in April of that year, "The U.S. Embassy conducted no post-shipment verifications related to missile technology," because such efforts were always "hampered by the Chinese government's reluctance to cooperate."[3] Allegedly, one of the conditions of shipment to China was their agreement to inspections. After China received the materials, however, they refused to permit some of the inspections and "the State Department did not press the issue."[4]

In June of 1994, Schwartz sent the DNC a soft-money donation of one hundred thousand dollars, "eight times the size of his first soft-money donation in 1993."[5]

According to the Congressional report by Chairman Chris Cox, for the next two months,

> Mr. Schwartz goes to China, having received a highly coveted slot on Commerce Secretary and former DNC chairman Ron Brown's trade mission.[6] With Mr. Brown's help, Mr. Schwartz uses his Chinese contacts to obtain satellite-transmission rights for a mobile telephone network in China, a deal worth billions. In a Sept. 20 memo to the president, White House Deputy Chief of Staff Harold Ickes, who was directing the Democrat Party's fund-raising from his West Wing office, suggests a presidential follow-up to Mr. Schwartz's lucrative China trip: "In order to raise an additional $3,000,000 to permit the [DNC] to produce and air generic TV/radio spots as soon as Congress adjourns," Mr. Ickes advises the president to call Mr. Schwartz and invite him and others to a White House breakfast "to impress them with the need to raise $3,000,000 within the next two weeks."[7]

In early October of 1994, Clinton lifted the sanctions against China that had been put in place after China improperly sold missiles to Pakistan. Harold Ickes wrote President Clinton a memo stating that Schwartz "is prepared to do anything he can for the administration."[8]

Also in late 1994, Johnny Chung began raising soft money for the DNC, handing over $100,000 between August and December.[9]

Things heated up the next year. Schwartz wrote to the president and promoted the idea that responsibility for satellite exports should be shifted from the State Department to the Commerce Department. Secretary of State Warren Christopher established an interagency task force made up of representatives from the Commerce Department, the Defense Department, the CIA, and the National Security Agency (NSA). While this group studied and debated the issue, Schwartz stepped up soft-money contributions. According to a Congressional investigation into illegal campaign donations, Schwartz gave over $140,000 to the Democratic National Committee and related party committees from April 24 to September 30, 1995. Professional fund-raiser Johnny Chung came up with $175,000.[10]

In October 1995, Secretary of State Warren Christopher decided to keep the current satellite export restrictions in place. To his credit, Christopher resisted heavy lobbying from various aerospace firms, including Loral and Hughes Electronics Corporation. The *New York Times* reported that Christopher feared the proposed policy change would jeopardize "significant military and intelligence interests" by allowing China to get hold of new satellite technology.[11] Christopher's decision meant that satellites would continue to be listed as munitions under State Department technology export rules, rather than as dual-use technology under more liberal Commerce Department rules.

A few weeks later, on November 29, 1995, Schwartz gave another $100,000 to the DNC. That same day, a Chinese government agency wrote Loral. Beijing wanted the company's assistance in upgrading its dual-use imaging technology. Exporting such technology was prohibited under U.S. sanctions.[12]

On February 6, 1996, Clinton gave approval to launch four communications satellites on Chinese rockets, waiving the restrictions. He also had coffee with Wang Jun of CITIC.[13] CITIC owns interest in Chinese satellite companies and, as numerous Defense Department sources have stated, is tied directly to the Chinese military. Afterward, Chinese arms dealer Wang Jun had dinner with Ron Brown, the Secretary of Commerce. Two days later, the Commerce Department and the White House resumed talks on the issue of exporting satellites.

Wang is the son of one of China's "most reactionary leaders," the late Wang Zen,[14] who is described as the chief advocate of the Tiananmen Square massacre.[15] Jun had been the subject of a serious U.S. Customs Service investigation for the fifteen months prior to his White House visit, because his company had allegedly supplied two thousand AK-47s to arms dealers looking to smuggle the weapons into in the United States. His company was suspected of selling cruise missiles to Iran.[16]

One week later, on February 15, 1996, Schwartz donated another fifteen thousand dollars to the Democrats. That same day, the White House gave the State Department an urgent request to finalize the transfer of satellite licensing authority to the Commerce Department. At the end of February, Schwartz gave an additional $50,000 to the Democrats. Though it did not seem significant to U.S. national security at the time, on February 14 a Chinese rocket carrying a Loral satellite blew up and destroyed a local village.[17]

On March 14, 1996, Clinton overruled Secretary of State Christopher's decision to keep the satellite restrictions in place. The decision to put the Commerce Department in charge of licensing was kept secret for several months. During that time, Democratic fund-raiser Johnny Chung donated almost $100,000 to Democratic party causes. Chung later told federal investigators that he received the money to donate from Liu Chao-ying, an executive of the state-owned Chinese company China Aerospace.

In April and May of 1996, a commission for Loral investigated the cause of the February 14 rocket explosion. The commission determined that the crash was caused by a flaw in the rocket's flight-control system. The commission shared its two-hundred page report with the Chinese, without first having the report vetted, as required by the U.S. government. The vetting process ensures there is no unauthorized transfer of technology regarding missile guidance and control systems. In this particular case, such a review was vital. The same Chinese company that produces the space-launch missiles also develops China's strategic nuclear missiles. Schwartz gave another $50,000 to the Democrats on April 24, 1996, in the midst of the ongoing investigation.

During the summer of 1996, soft-money contributions to the Democratic party increased. Lieutenant Colonel Liu Chao-ying of the People's Liberation Army illegally passed Johnny Chung $290,000.[18] Chung told investigators later that the money was to be given to the Democratic party. In July, Chung donated $45,000 to the DNC to attend two fund-raisers in Hollywood, California.[19] Colonel Liu attended the July 22 event as well and managed to get a photograph with President Clinton.[20] Chung then gave an additional $35,000 to the DNC in September 1996. His contributions to the Democratic National Committee totaled $366,000.[21]

Colonel Liu had other connections to Chinese weaponry and technology as well. She worked as an aerospace executive for firms that had been sanctioned by the U.S. government in 1991 and 1993 for sharing missile technology with Pakistan. Her father was then the highest-ranking general in China's armed forces and was responsible for modernizing the Chinese military with Western technology.[22]

Meanwhile, Schwartz continued his donations to the Democratic party, giving an additional $235,000 between June and October 1996.[23]

On November 5, Bill Clinton was reelected to a second term. That same day his administration published the new guidelines on licensing satellites.[24] Those guidelines had been due in April but their release was withheld until after the election.[25]

In May 1997, the Pentagon released a report analyzing the impact to national security by the unauthorized transmission of the Loral Commission's report on the 1996 Chinese rocket crash. The classified report concluded that the national security of the United States had been permanently damaged because China had been given information that allowed it to improve its missile technology. In response to the report, the Justice Department and the U.S. Customs Service began a criminal investigation.[26]

The DNC was forced to acknowledge that it could not account for the source of the funds donated by Johnny Chung. Eventually, the DNC was pressured by Congressional investigators and the media to return $306,000 in illegal contributions.[27]

Then it was discovered that in July 1994, John Huang, friend of Bill Clinton and former employee of foreign bank the Lippo Group, accompanied Secretary of Commerce Ron Brown to China, where they offered Chinese companies $5.5 billion in militarily useful production technology.

Later, on February 12, 1998, National Security Adviser Sandy Berger sent Clinton a memo telling him that the Justice Department "has cautioned that a national interest waiver in this case could have a significant adverse impact on any prosecution [of Loral] that might take place based on a pending investigation of export violation." But he also wrote, "the advantages of this project outweigh the risk," and that "it is inappropriate to penalize [Loral] before they have even been charged with any crime."[28] Less than a week later, on February 18, President Clinton signed a waiver allowing a Loral satellite to be put into orbit by a Chinese rocket.[29] The launch allowed the Chinese access to essentially the same technology Loral had released to China in 1996.[30] Schwartz continued his giving during this time.

He contributed over $50,000 to the Democrats from January to March 1998.[31]

Wait, There's More

On May 22, 1997, in a letter to Attorney General Janet Reno, House Judiciary Committee Chairman Henry Hyde and Congresswoman Tillie Fowler of the House Committee on National Security asked the Justice Department to investigate alleged illegal foreign campaign contributions to the Clinton campaign and the DNC from Chinese donors.

In their letter, Representatives Hyde and Fowler pointedly questioned whether donations were tied to "the Clinton administration's loosening of export controls on sensitive dual-use equipment and technology, which has specifically benefited the military and intelligence services of the People's Republic of China."

The liberalization of policy restrictions seemed to parallel numerous Asian donors' visits to the White House, particularly members of the Riady family, owners of the Hong Kong Chinese Bank and the Lippo Group. Hong-Kong-based China Resources Holding Company had given a $26 million bailout to the bank after it realized the Riady family's close ties to Clinton. Defense Department sources stated the China Resources Holding Company was also known to have links to Chinese intelligence.

When the Lippo Group demonstrated its direct access to Bill Clinton and, thereby, its ability to influence American foreign policy, China Resources increased its shareholding in the bank to 50 percent. A key figure in the investigation was John Huang. He had moved to Little Rock in the mid-1980s to establish Lippo's operations in Arkansas, and he subsequently got to know the Clintons very well.

In January 1994, he left the Lippo Group, having received a $750,000+ severance package, and went to work at the Commerce Department.[32] Commerce Secretary Ron Brown gave personal instructions for Taiwan-born Huang to receive a top-secret security clearance, circumventing the background checks of the FBI and State Department's Office of Security, a strict requirement for somebody born in a foreign country. The *London*

Sunday Times stated that Huang, while at the Commerce Department, had access to intelligence from the CIA that related to economic and trade secrets.

This information speaks volumes about Clinton's lack of commitment to national security and, as such, the war on terrorism. President Clinton claimed in May 1998, "All the foreign-policy decisions we made were based on what we believed—I and the rest of my administration—were in the best interests of the American people."[33] Nevertheless, the numbers speak for themselves. Prior to Clinton's March 1996 decision to switch the licensing of satellite technology from the State Department to the Department of Commerce, Schwartz donated over a $150,000 to the Democratic party. After the decision was made, he donated another $300,000. Indeed, he was the party's largest soft-money donor during the 1996 election cycle.[34] It was also during this period that Johnny Chung laundered $300,000 in Chinese contributions to the Democratic party.

The New Policy of Globalism

One Defense Department official offered a *possible* rationale for Clinton's policy changes, aside from a purely mercenary willingness to sell out the American public for campaign cash. During the Cold War, the intelligence community had one major target—the Soviet Union and its Warsaw Pact allies. For at least a half-century the central focus was on developing and cultivating all forms of intelligence gathering against that target.

When the Cold War ended, however, there was a rapid effort to disassemble the Soviet monitoring apparatus. In so doing, the intelligence community under the Clinton administration failed to shift its resources in timely fashion to the new threat posed by weapons proliferators and sponsors of state terrorism. Indeed, the Clinton administration did not regard these as a significant national security threat.

The dismantling of America's intelligence and military apparatus made militarily useful technologies available to such emerging rogue countries as Iran, Iraq, Libya, Syria, and North Korea. It also made the technology available to India and Pakistan, who were in their own race to develop nuclear weapons. In addition, the policy shift allowed China to gain access to technologies for its nuclear weapons program, including the development of intercontinental ballistic missiles.

Clinton did not perceive national security as primarily a military and intelligence issue. Instead, weapons proliferation was regarded as a foreign policy issue, not a national security threat. Therefore, military concerns were often downplayed. The area of dual-use technology was but one example. The focus of the Clinton administration was economic security through globalization.

Globalization is a concept involving the free movement of money, people, information, technologies, ideas, goods, and services around the world at high speeds with few restrictions. Under the Clinton administration, it seems national security was viewed more in terms of economic strength than in military capability.

As a consequence, economic crimes and corruption were seen as the major national security concerns. For example, according to a Defense Department official, there were some twenty-three countries engaged in economic espionage against U.S. targets, thereby presenting unfair competition to U.S. companies. To counter the threat, the Clinton administration placed more emphasis on economic intelligence capabilities. It adopted a more aggressive strategy in acquiring clandestine economic intelligence to assist in areas such as contentious trade negotiations and the identification of emerging markets as a means to reduce U.S. trade deficits.

In the rush to exploit the China market, the Clinton administration allowed tens of billions of dollars in technology to be exported to China at serious expense to U.S. military superiority in critical special mission areas—nuclear weapons and intercontinental ballistic missile development, antisubmarine warfare, air superiority, power projection, and intelligence gathering. Defense Department sources said the Clinton administration granted no less than thirty-three waivers in export restrictions, allowing the transfer of technologies that assisted China in developing its ballistic missile program.

While leaving key restrictions in the federal regulations, Defense Department sources also claim the Clinton administration's actual practice over time reverted to allow exports, with the presumption of approval, to locations anywhere in China that the intelligence community said were not involved in production for the Chinese military. This allowed wholesale exportation from the United States of an array of technologies, including stealth and so-called hot-section technologies that would extend the life and range of jet engines, giving China power projection in the region.

Though information had been obtained proving that China was exporting to Pakistan missiles that exceeded multilateral levels under the Missile Technology Control Regime, then-Defense Secretary William Perry wanted "no less than pictures of the missiles in the covered facilities in Pakistan," Defense Department sources recalled. This kind of intelligence didn't exist.

The Rationalization of Globalism

Many U.S. companies that were major supporters of the Clinton administration benefited from the prioritization of exports over national security. The net effect of the transfers was to help China with militarily critical technologies. The U.S. may not realize the full impact on national security of those exports for another three to five years.

A knowledgeable Defense Department official stated that Clinton's foreign policy of globalism was formed in 1992 when he gained the support of some companies that demanded a new vision for an economic form of national security. The tone of that vision was laid out plainly in a September 15, 1993, letter from President Bill Clinton to Edward McCracken, then CEO of Silicon Graphics.

At that time, export-control policy remained a serious national security priority, particularly in the aftermath of the Cold War. The Clinton administration had made clear the direction it would take to assist U.S. companies, particularly those that had endorsed Clinton for president over incumbent President Bush. More than three hundred high-tech companies made such endorsements and provided substantial financial contributions to Clinton's 1992 election campaign, including businesses engaged in telecommunications, computers, and micro-electronics. McCracken's Silicon Graphics was one of those companies.

In his letter to McCracken, President Clinton outlined four areas for export control "reform" in the post-Cold War environment. They were:

113

- Liberalize computer and telecommunications controls

- Reduce processing times to obtain export-control licenses

- Expand the use of distribution licenses so that exporters would not have to come back repeatedly for licenses of controlled items

- Eliminate unnecessary unilateral controls of technologies that only the U.S. controlled. To the administration, such controls put U.S. exporters at a disadvantage in competition with companies from other countries.

"I expect that these reforms will help liberalize controls on tens of billions of dollars worth of U.S. exports," Clinton wrote. "It can help unleash our companies to compete successfully in the global market."

This sea change in policy would have a significant impact on national security.

Sharing Secrets with the Enemy

By the end of 1998, the House Select Committee on National Security completed its investigation of the effect on U.S. national security of technology transfers to China.[35] The report remains partially classified, but concluded, according to Committee Chairman Christopher Cox, that "United States transfer of technology to the People's Republic of China has been the target of serious PRC efforts over the last two decades."[36]

The report was a bipartisan effort to review policies of Democratic and Republican administrations. Democratic Congressman Norman Dicks hoped the report would be taken seriously by President Clinton, saying of the White House, "They recognize this is a bipartisan effort that has yielded a consensus product."[37] The Cox report specifically named Hughes Electronics Corporation and Loral Space and Communications as culprits. Hughes had lobbied for the same changes Loral had pushed for.[38]

When even more portions of the report were declassified, the extent of the damage caused by the technology transfer became apparent. The committee reported that China gave "ballistic missile technology to Iran, Pakistan, North Korea, Saudi Arabia, Libya and other countries."[39] The

report also said, "China supplies assistance to the nuclear weapons programs of Iran and Pakistan." This finding contradicted President Clinton's
certification to Congress that China was not supplying nuclear weapons-
related goods to rogue states.[40]

According to a senior Defense Department source, the Clinton administration put pressure on those within the DOD to say that China was in
compliance with the nuclear nonproliferation treaty and the Missile
Technology Control Regime. A few brave souls within the Department
dissented in that request and were summarily penalized by their managers.
The Clinton administration wanted to give the appearance that China was
conforming to international norms, when intelligence reports said just the
opposite.

Michael Maloof, a Defense Department official who made press as a
"hardliner" in 1998 because he got in the way of Clinton's ambitions, stated
in an interview, "Hughes Electronics Corporation had lobbied the Clinton
administration to proceed with a new telecommunications satellite deal with
China despite concern in Congress over such technology transfers that could
help the Chinese military."

According to Maloof, the satellite deal cost over $600 million. Failure to
gain approval for the transaction could have cost Hughes upward of $1.3 bil-
lion, as well as possibly billions of dollars in future high-tech deals with the
Chinese market. His concern was that six Chinese companies, including
some tied to the Chinese military, would oversee the spacecraft's operations
in handling mobile telephone calls for China and twenty-one other Asian
countries. While the satellite was intended for civilian use in Asia, the
Chinese military would also employ it, enabling them to address weaknesses
in their ability to communicate with widely dispersed military units, some of
which were engaged in routing out political dissidents in far-to-reach places
in western China.

Though Hughes stated that the Chinese would not learn technical
details of the satellite, called the Asia-Pacific Mobile Telecommunications
(APMT), the fact is that in 1995, Hughes hired Shen Jun, the son of
Lieutenant General Shen Rongjun, who helped run Beijing's space program.
He was hired as a linguist, as stated in its State Department munitions
license application; however, the reality is that Shen Jun worked for Hughes

as senior project manager, training Chinese officials to operate the APMT satellite.

According to Maloof, Hughes knowingly provided only partial information in seeking employment approval for Shen Jun in 1996, even though he had been at the Hughes facility since 1994. In seeking approval for the APMT, Hughes provided only the Singapore address of the APMT joint venture between China and Singapore. This had the deceptive effect of dis-associating the APMT project from the Chinese military and making it look benign, even though the Chinese sought configurations on the APMT satellite that would allow for eavesdropping. In April 1998, it was Feng Ruming, a major general at COSTIND in Hong Kong, who publicly announced the APMT project.

"Once these facts were revealed, the State Department suspended Hughes's munitions license," Maloof said. "My concern was that the father's assistants in the military were helping to run the Chinese venture that was to buy the APMT satellite from Hughes and would control it in space. Because of my concerns about Hughes and its close relationship to the Clinton White House I did an analysis that revealed the cumulative exports of selected sophisticated U.S. technology to China since 1994 had provided the Chinese military with a nationwide integrated command, control, communications, computers and intelligence encrypted network that will serve it well into the twenty-first century."

A special Justice Department group investigating Chinese contributions to the Clinton campaign asked Maloof for assistance in researching links to Chinese involved in its probe, but the DOD general counsel "nixed the request."

Terrorism's Friend

Aside from the current problems presented by China's assistance to the missile and nuclear programs in North Korea, the aid given to Pakistan may be directly relevant to the ongoing threat of Osama bin Laden. "The security of Pakistan's nuclear weapons components and nuclear design skills is . . . open to question," according to Daniel Benjamin and Steven Simon's *The Age of Sacred Terror*.[41] The authors relate one known instance in which a Pakistani nuclear scientist is believed to have made contact with Bin Laden. While this effort may have been "ineffectual," Benjamin and Simon explain that the greater issue is whether or not this incident was unique. It is hard to know whether or not it is representative of other Islamic radicals deeply involved in Pakistan's nuclear weapons program. To simply assume that those who are technologically sophisticated are also unlikely to be religious extremists is, according to the authors, quite unwarranted. "The apocalyptic mentality of the terrorists and their fantasies of omnipotence are driving them toward the use of weapons of mass destruction. Pakistan is probably their best potential source of the materials, or of the weapons themselves."[42]

With Islamic terrorism becoming an increasing threat throughout Clinton's first term, the importance of China's willingness to share information with Islamic countries should not have escaped his attention.

Computer Technology Sharing

Clinton's policies also made available technologies that potential enemies could acquire without U.S. knowledge. Questions of where such technologies would end up and the significant threats posed by such acquisitions would have significant implications on U.S. national security.

This impact could be seen in U.S. technology exports to China. Of the one thousand export license applications reviewed by the Defense Department during 1994, the Defense Intelligence Agency only saw six hundred of them. Of the four hundred it didn't review, most of these license applications were essential for Chinese rocket and satellite improvements, according to Defense Department sources. In effect, the Clinton administration had purposely done an end run around the very procedures set up to prevent militarily critical technologies from aiding the strategic capability of countries like China.

Clinton's policy decision in September 1993 to decontrol military technologies affected more than twenty-one areas of concern critical to the Defense Department. The more significant of those areas included:

- Semiconductor materials and microcircuits
- Software engineering

117

- High performance computers
- Machine intelligence and robotics
- Simulation and modeling
- Photonics
- Sensitive radars
- Passive sensors
- Signal and image processing
- Weapons systems enhancement
- Data fusion
- Computational fluid dynamics
- Air-breathing propulsion
- Hypervelocity projectiles and propulsion
- High energy density materials
- Composite materials
- Superconductivity
- Biotechnology
- Flexible manufacturing

Upon review of these technologies, it is apparent that export controls that would have an impact on U.S. strategic capabilities include antisubmarine warfare; stealth technologies for missiles and aircraft; command, control, communications, computers and intelligence; tactical weather forecasting; computer-aided design and manufacturing; and laser-blinding weapons. In addition, the elimination of such controls also freed up access for foreign nations to chemical, biological, and nuclear technologies, and the missiles to deliver them.

Concerns were raised in 1997 over a "shopping spree" that China began as a result of a major computer liberalization effort in 1995. China bought forty-six U.S.-made supercomputers that matched those used for U.S. national security purposes. Under the 1995 policy change, most supercomputers sold for civilian purposes did not need to be licensed for export by the federal government. Being dual-use, however, such computers had serious military capability.

As discussed earlier, China was known to be a major exporter of weapons technology to such countries as Iran, Iraq, Syria, and North Korea. These computers gave the Chinese or their trading partners the capability to design more efficient or lighter nuclear warheads that could be used on missiles capable of reaching the United States. The computers also allowed the Chinese to conduct tests with underground explosions so small that they would be undetectable by outsiders, thereby allowing them to skirt an international ban on underground weapons tests.

At the time, Gary Samore, senior director for nonproliferation and export controls at the Clinton National Security Council said, "We don't have any information that these computers are being used by the Chinese for military purposes, including nuclear weapons."[43]

The reason for this lack of information is that the United States did not have the human or technical intelligence to have obtained it, thanks to CIA mismanagement under Clinton. It was U.S. policy, at the direction of the Clinton Commerce Department, not to enforce rules that required so-called end-user statements or visits to locations.

Hardware Transfer

By 1997, members of the Republican-controlled House of Representatives were becoming more concerned over the national security implications of the Clinton administration's policies. In Hyde and Fowler's 1997 letter to Attorney General Reno, they listed exports that China had acquired that raised "questionable decisions" as to intentions.

For example, one of the deals that Ron Brown and John Huang took to China in their $5.5 billion sales package of militarily related technologies created a dangerous situation. A U.S. company, McDonnell-Douglas, was allowed to ship an almost completely intact missile and strategic bomber factory to the PRC, despite strong opposition from specialists at the Defense Department. They pointed to substantial evidence that equipment was going to be diverted to military production facilities. "News stories and a Government Accounting Office report requested by the House National

Security Committee all show that before the equipment was shipped, U.S. officials were aware that the conditions placed upon issuance of the export licenses were unenforceable, and that the Chinese possibly intended to divert the equipment they had purchased for civilian use to a military production facility."

Prior to approval of the licenses, Hyde and Fowler said, officials from the China National Aero-Technology Import-Export Corporation were allowed to visit the plant during operating hours. The plant produced significant B-1 bomber and C-17 cargo aircraft components. In going through the plant, the Chinese videotaped classified production lines in operation. This was a violation of current export laws which "was brought to the attention of (Clinton) administration officials and ignored."

"Once it was determined that the diversion had occurred," they added, "political appointees at the Departments of Commerce and Defense approved new licenses with different end-use conditions and destinations, rather than expressing displeasure with the Chinese or exercising their legal obligation to sanction the PRC."

In another case, Hyde and Fowler pointed to a 1994 export of sophisticated telecommunications technology to a U.S.-Chinese joint venture called Hua Mei, in which the Chinese partner is an entity controlled by the Chinese military. The U.S. partner was a business associate of then-Secretary of Defense William Perry. The transfer included fiber-optic communications equipment used for high-speed, secure communications over long distances. The export package also included advanced encryption software.

"The (Clinton) Administration's actions in these and other cases have resulted in a significant increase in indigenous Chinese military production capabilities," they wrote. "Given China's willingness to sell weapons and technology to the highest bidder—including rogue nations such as Iran, Iraq, and Libya—these transfers could represent a profound threat to U.S. military personnel.

"Moreover," they added, "the increased capabilities that China has gained portend a regional arms race and increase the possibility of conflict in a region in which the United States has major interests."

No such investigation ever took place.

Throughout all of this, Chinese technology acquisition efforts were not limited just to exports. Defense equipment was being auctioned off at pennies on the dollar. The Chinese purchased valuable U.S. military production equipment for prices low enough to avoid the so-called *deminimus* provision that would have otherwise embargoed the equipment from being shipped to China.

Is Clinton Defendable?

While underplaying the significance of President Clinton's actions and the likelihood that he compromised national security for political gain, Benjamin and Simon do show another way in which this scandal hurt us in the war on terror. By this and many other scandals, Clinton distracted the nation from real concerns. They don't explain it that way, of course. Instead of holding Clinton accountable, they justify everything in terms of the public's appetite for scandal:

> Why America became so enthralled by these scandals is something that will keep historians busy for years to come . . .
>
> However the factors are finally parsed, Americans' fixation on scandal left little space for the perception of new threats. This was a dangerous addiction, especially for the world's sole superpower and therefore the world's primary target of discontent.[44]

There you have it. A scandalous president who takes contributions for companies and then does them unprecedented favors is in the grip of "a dangerous addiction." That's not exactly what they say, but those are the facts that explain what they say. Blaming the American public for the addiction is not worth refuting. Several other presidents have served their country without committing such deeds. Clinton did it to himself, and he did it to the nation in the process. He "left little space for the perception of new threats," say Benjamin and Simon. True. That's another reason why September 11 is Clinton's legacy.

A former member of the House leadership explained it to me this way: "The transfer of dual-use technology to China was a treasonous act. It should never have happened, and no one was held accountable for it."

NEGLECTING THE BEAR

The Enemy of My Enemy . . .

IN JANUARY 1993, BILL CLINTON INHERITED A TERRIFIC relationship with China. He harshly criticized the Bush administration over this fact. Most experts also considered the United States relationship with Russia after the Soviet Union dissolved in 1991 to be excellent. From a U.S. foreign policy view, our relationship with both countries, as well as their relationships to each other, was optimal for the U.S. to capitalize on—that is, the U.S. was on excellent terms with both of these superpowers, but they were not all that friendly with one another.

This was an excellent situation for U.S. national security. The U.S. had no designs on China's or Russia's territory or sovereignty, but our interests were served by ensuring that they did not move closer together.

After eight short years of Clinton, however, the relationships reversed. The United States was the odd man out, and China and Russia were firm friends. This opened the door to them helping each other's weapons programs. Failed U.S. policy in both countries created economic conditions that forced them to sell weapons and weapons technologies to numerous other countries for much-needed cash. While the White House alienated Russia, it also turned a blind eye to intelligence showing that Russia was selling massive amounts of forbidden weapons and weapons technologies to enemies of the United States.

These transgressions are detailed in a Congressional report produced by the Speaker's Advisory Group on Russia. As Russia was about to hold presidential elections in March 2000, the speaker of the House tasked six Congressional committee leaders "to assess the results of U.S. policy toward Russia during the Yeltsin years." The report contains a stunning rebuke of

Clinton's policies. Due to Russian and Chinese technology transfers, a very dangerous situation now exists in Pakistan, North Korea, and Iran, where these governments either have or are developing weapons of mass destruction.

More Intelligence Failures

The disintegration of America's relationship with China exemplifies the consequences of Clinton's flawed military intelligence policies. As detailed in Chapter Four, the Central Intelligence Agency in the '90s became consumed with political correctness and neglected adequate intelligence-gathering capability. Time and again the CIA was surprised or shocked by what was happening in the Mideast, Russia, and China. Iran and its unknown dealings with Russia provide a perfect example of this.

In 1997, the U.S. government's original Initial Operational Capability (IOC) estimate for Iran predicted that the country was ten years away from testing its Shahab-3 missile. The very next year, due to information about Russian assistance, the IOC dramatically revised the estimate to say that Iran was only eighteen months away from a working missile system. But that, too, was wrong. In July 1998, Iran surprised the world by successfully testing the Shahab-3. "By mid-1998, the Iranian ballistic missile program was one of the most advanced in the world, due to Russian assistance."[1]

Ironically, only one month earlier, President Clinton had vetoed the Iran Missile Proliferation Sanctions Act, which would have required him to impose sanctions on governments that assisted Iran in the development of nuclear weapons—as Russia was doing.[2]

In 1999, George Tenet testified that it would take "many years" for Iran to develop a missile that could reach the United States. However, in February 2000, Tenet had to revise his estimate and tell the Senate Intelligence Committee that they would "probably" soon be able to reach North America with a ballistic missile.[3] The CIA had not sufficiently factored Russia's assistance into the initial estimate of Iran's missile capabilities.

Even in Russian-Chinese geopolitics, something that the CIA should be practiced in after the Cold War, the agency fell behind during the nineties. In 1999, George Tenet reportedly had to order a "crash effort" to evaluate ties between the two countries.[4]

We should temper our criticism and judgment of the CIA somewhat. After all, the agency was not always wrong. When it did deliver solid intelligence to the Clinton White House regarding China and Russia, it was frequently ignored or rejected. In one incident, the agency received its brief back with the word "BULLS—" scrawled over it.[5]

In 1995, the CIA delivered a report to Vice President Al Gore detailing the corrupt practices of then-Russian Prime Minister Viktor Stepanovich Chernomyrdin.[6] President Clinton had assigned Gore the responsibility for working with Russia, which meant working with Chernomyrdin. The Gore-Chernomyrdin Commission developed rules against weapons proliferation, but Russia ignored those rules. Clinton, in turn, chose to ignore intelligence reports of how Russia was breaking the rules. "Throughout the 1990s, despite repeated pledges by the Yeltsin government given during summits, Gore-Chernomyrdin Commission meetings, and ministerial-level meetings, Russian private and government entities continued to provide critical technological assistance to Iran's ballistic missile programs."[7]

As a result of Gore's repudiation of the CIA's work, the *New York Times* reported, "CIA analysts say they are now censoring themselves. When, for instance, the agency found that it cost a German business executive one million dollars just to get a meeting with Mr. Chernomyrdin to discuss deals in Russia, it decided not to circulate the report outside the CIA," officials said.[8]

In 1997, intelligence was collected indicating that three Russian companies had signed contracts to assist Iran's missile program.[9] Israeli military intelligence later confirmed this.[10] In March 1997, the CIA presented a secret report of a statement by then-President Ali Akbar Hashemi Rafsanjani of Iran, expressing hope that their growing relationship with Russia would allow them to obtain more military technology—a goal for which Iran had $10 billion to spend.[11] George Tenet also gave a report to Congress, in which he stated,

[In 1997] Russian firms supplied a variety of ballistic missile-related goods and technical know-how to foreign countries during the reporting period. For example, Iran's success in gaining technology and materials from Russian companies, combined with recent indigenous advances, means that Iran could have a medium-range ballistic missile much sooner than otherwise expected.

During 1997, Russia was an important source of dual-use technology for civilian nuclear programs in Iran and India. By its very nature, this technology may be of use in the nuclear weapons programs of these countries.[12]

The administration refused to confront Russia; instead, it told the Israelis that we had the situation "under control," while blindly accepting false assurances from Yeltsin that weapons proliferation would stop.[13] These actions clearly contributed to the decline of morale within the CIA.

The Hungry Bear

The fact was that Russia desperately needed money—specifically, hard currency. The Russian economy contracted by a whopping 25 percent from 1992 to 1999.[14] In 2000, unemployment was at 11.5 percent; it had been at 4.8 percent in 1992.[15]

The failure to produce a working free-market economy produced two mutually reinforcing results. First, it left the massively overexpanded military industry in Russia as the only way the country could produce cash, providing strong incentive to sell weapons to anyone who would buy. Second, with the drop in the economy came a drop in the popularity of the United States. This provided the rationale for spreading weapons abroad to encourage "multipolarity."[16]

Russia's huge military industry was a "paradox."[17] It had drastically reduced spending from the days of the old Soviet empire. In 1992, procurement was cut by 80 percent.[18] The Russian armed services acquired only two new fighter aircraft in 1995, as opposed to 581 in 1991.[19] "According to Russia's Defense Minister Marshal Igor Sergeyev, fifty-four percent of Russia's aircraft and forty percent of its anti-aircraft systems, helicopters, armored equipment, and artillery need repairs. Seventy percent of the navy's ships need major repairs."[20]

When an electric company threatened to stop service to a Siberian missile base in order to make the military pay them the $180,000 they owed in past-due bills, commandos from the base prevented the power cut-off by forcibly taking over four of the company's substations.[21] Worse, sailors starved to death, and soldiers were instructed to pick berries or mushrooms to supplement their meager rations. According to estimates, as many as a thousand draftees committed suicide every year.[22]

Under these circumstances, crime became rampant. Soldiers stole food in order to eat.[23] But other forms of crime were also common. The military lost communication with some of its operational nuclear weapons units because thieves cut wires in order to plunder the copper and sell it as scrap.[24] More seriously, "More than one hundred generals and admirals, a deputy minister of defense, and two other top officials of the Ministry of Defense were under investigation for corruption and embezzlement as of 1997."[25] In the war with Chechnya, soldiers were accused of profiting themselves at the expense of the military—from civilian leaders such as First Deputy Prime Minister Oleg Soskovets on down to officers and even enlisted men, who sold weapons and other items to the Chechens they were fighting.[26]

Yet in the midst of poverty and declining services, technology and morale were, paradoxically, "islands of excellence," as the Congressional report calls them.[27] "The anomalous Russian pattern is that while the bulk of its military assets are depreciating, it is still successfully targeting certain areas for investment in twenty-first century weapons technologies."[28] It isn't hard to understand why such technologies would pose a threat to the security of the United States. Demoralized, defunded, and sometimes literally starving, these weapons and weapons materials were able bring hard currency into the country from nations that wished to buy them—nations such as Iran, Iraq, North Korea, Libya, and China.

Temptation existed both on official and unofficial levels. Individual corruption and the rapid spread of Russian organized crime, as well as state policy, made selling weapons on the black market an attractive option. Russia possessed almost twelve hundred metric tons of enriched uranium and two hundred tons of plutonium.[29] Russia also had about twenty-five hundred scientists from the Soviet nuclear industry who were either unemployed or underemployed, as well as tens of thousands of support workers with experience in nuclear technology.[30] The Soviet biological weapons program had at one time employed sixty-five thousand people.[31] Economic decline meant that many of these were laid off and that security procedures were degraded.

"The decline in Russian military spending and the general failure of Russia's economy under the Clinton administration's tutelage gave this immense military-industrial complex the urgent incentive to sell as much as possible as quickly as possible—often irrespective of the long-term implications for Russia's own security."[32] Selling such contraband either officially in defiance of agreements with the U.S. or privately was attractive on several levels. Officially, it provided much-needed cash, "utilized existing Russian assets," and put to work "possibly hundreds of thousands of unemployed Russians,"[33] providing a source of investment into the development of new weapons and weapon systems.[34] Privately, it would "increase personal wealth" for those who demanded bribes.[35]

Finally, all this could be justified in the name of promoting "multipolarity," to the detriment of the United States. "Some Russian commentators even articulated a policy of Russian arms sales to anti-American forces as a means both of providing Russia with hard currency and of assuring that U.S. resources will be consumed in countering the weapons Russia has sold abroad."[36]

Breaking Up Is Hard To Do

From 1992 to 1999, Russian and Chinese feelings for America changed dramatically. In 1992, when Yeltsin addressed a joint session of Congress, the excitement was electrifying. He was interrupted nine times during his speech with standing applause and chants of "Boris, Boris."[37] Visits on the part of U.S. officials had allowed them to observe thousands of Russians parading through Moscow bearing American flags. In Beijing, tens of thousands came to Tiananmen Square to pay homage to the goddess of democracy statue erected there.[38]

But in 1999, when Clinton addressed the Russian Duma, he was received with indifference and even hostility. Only about a third of the representatives bothered to show up, and the president was "jeered and insulted" both "inside and outside the chamber." In both Moscow and Beijing, thousands participated in violent anti-American demonstrations.[3]

A comparison of the 1993 *Foreign Policy Concept of the Russian Federation* with later versions illustrates Russia's principles and objectives in international relations. In 1993 it said,

> For Russia, the time has become objectively ripe for close cooperation with the United States in the Asia-Pacific region, with whom we are today brought together by adherence to singular democratic values and an unconditional interest in stability in the region. It would be expedient for us to share responsibility with the United States for the provision of security in the Asia-Pacific region, to become strategic partners here. For these purposes, we should reorient our military potential in the direction of ensuring regional stability and creating reliable guarantees of common security together with the United States.[40]

Of China's relationship with Russia, the document said, "A realistic transformation of the nature of relations with China must consider the differences in ideology and the socio-political systems of the two countries."[41]

In the June 2000 version of the document, however, China has virtually replaced the U.S. as Russia's friend: "The concurrence of the fundamental approaches of Russia and the PRC to the key issues of world politics is one of the basic mainstays of regional and global stability. Russia seeks to develop mutually advantageous cooperation with China in all areas." It also refers back to the 1993 document saying that "certain plans relating to establishing new, equitable, and mutually advantageous partnership relations of Russia with the rest of the world have not been justified."[42]

In July of 2000 there was a summit in Beijing, "a who's who of the Russian military-industrial complex."[43] The "Beijing Declaration by the People's Republic of China and the Russian Federation" was one result, in which code words for the U.S., such as "hegemonism" and "power politics," made it clear that the point of the summit was to defy America. "China and Russia . . . defy hegemonism, power politics and group politics, and oppose attempts to amend the basic principles of international law, to threaten others by force or to interfere in other countries' internal affairs."[44]

By their own public statement, Russia's and China's leaders considered weapons trade and weapons technology "the glue" cementing the relationship between the two countries.[45] From 1991 to 1996, China spent about a billion dollars a year on weapons and weapons technology from Russia. In 1997, the amount doubled. In 1999, the two countries revealed a plan to do $20 billion in trade by 2004.[46]

Due to its acquisition of superior weapons systems, China has become a significantly more potent threat to the United States. For example, China has acquired Tu-22M Backfire bombers. "The Backfire's potential use as an intercontinental bomber made it the subject of rancorous arms-control negotiations between the U.S. and the U.S.S.R. Its capabilities against U.S. carrier battle groups would arguably be of still greater interest to the PRC."[47] In 1996, China ordered two *Sovremenny*-class destroyers. These destroyers came with Moskit SS-N-22 surface-to-surface missiles particularly "designed to destroy U.S. aircraft carriers and their AEGIS escort vessels."[48]

China's weapons trade, aside from threatening America's national security, adds to the threat of terrorism. In addition to selling technology and weapons to countries like Iran, Russia's trade with China creates secondary issues. China exports its newly acquired technology to rogue states and terror organizations once it learns to produce them itself. "Because of the PRC's track record as a significant weapons proliferator, these Russian exports can be expected to have a cascading effect in other regions of vital importance to the United States."[49] All of this is attractive in the short term to China because it is a way of weakening our perceived "hegemonism," even though China itself could suffer in the long term from these same weapons.

A Blind Eye

The Clinton administration's response was to pretend that there was nothing wrong with what was happening. The undersecretary of defense for policy, Walter B. Slocombe, claimed that "far from seeing a threat to U.S. interests . . . we welcome it, as a step toward Russia being a constructive partner in the region."[50]

When Secretary of State Albright was asked in February 2000 if the U.S. had told Moscow that we opposed their arms sales, she evaded the question.[51] Despite casual dismissals from the Clinton White House, their nonpolicies had opened up questions about their security planning, which was based on the idea that "the United States will face no peer competitor in the military field during the next two decades."[52]

Russia had also exported many weapons and weapons systems—some of which were designed specifically to counteract U.S. systems—to both North and South Korea and India.[53] Yet, as in the case of Russia's help with China, the Clinton administration displayed "willful blindness" regarding Iran. For example, President Clinton only signed an executive order on July 28, 1998, "utilizing existing law to ban trade, aid, and procurement from foreign entities assisting programs for the production of weapons of mass destruction in Iran or elsewhere" because the Iran Missile Proliferation Act, despite his veto, was about to become law.[54] In keeping with this order, President Clinton sanctioned seven Russian entities that were assisting Iran's missile program.

Yet there were questions about what Clinton had done allegedly to obstruct missile proliferation. Why were not similar corporations who had done similar things not also sanctioned? Furthermore, how could these sanctions actually sanction the companies they targeted? By executive order, Clinton gave himself the power to decrease or even cease United States aid for research and manufacturing. This might have been effective if the targeted entities received any such aid, but they didn't. Another question: What is the point of sanctions prohibiting entities from exporting goods to the United States when, in fact, there was no market in the U.S. for their wares? Also: Why address equipment when what was being traded was information and technology? "Moreover, the executive order did nothing to address Russia's export-control system, which even National Security Adviser Sandy Berger said was necessary when he announced the sanctions."[55]

Plainly, Clinton cared little about compliance or enforcing international sanctions or arms-proliferation agreements. Many examples of this are available. U.S. patrol ships stopped a Russian oil tanker on February 2, 2000, and discovered it was smuggling oil from Iraq. The Clinton administration never sanctioned Russia or even threatened to reduce U.S. financial support. "Instead, the Iraqi naval official on board the tanker was freed; the oil was diverted to Oman and auctioned off; and the tanker was returned to Russia."[56]

In 1995, Yeltsin fired a general when it was revealed that he tried to sell five tons of VX nerve gas to Syrian agents.[57] The VX gas had been stolen from Russian military facilities. The same general had allegedly sold over seventeen hundred pounds of chemicals to a Mideast buyer whose identity was never discovered.[58]

In both these situations, it is hard to know if those involved were simply acting on their own or following unstated government policy. When Jordan seized Russian parts for guided missiles destined for Iraq, in violation of UN sanctions, it was impossible to determine whether it was state sanctioned, part of organized crime, or a sporadic act of government corruption. Because "the Clinton administration never adequately pressed the Russian government for an explanation or adequately investigated the case," we will never know.[59]

This is just a sampling of massive exports of both conventional and unconventional weapons that Russia sold during the Clinton administration. One of the most serious developments was the Russian media's report that Vladimir Putin changed the law and allowed for the sales of nuclear technology and material to countries whose programs were not fully monitored by the International Atomic Energy Agency—such as Iran and North Korea.[60] The Clinton administration continually took assurances from officials in the Russian government as reliable and disregarded all intelligence reports to the contrary, even from our intelligence community.[61] They simply refused to deal with the problem effectively.

When President George W. Bush took office, he quickly worked to reverse the Clinton trend, stating in July 2001:

> I've spoken very clearly to . . . President [Putin] that it's time for new leadership to develop a new strategic framework for peace. . . . There are new threats, new forms of terror: cyberterrorism, fundamentalist extremists, extremism that certainly threatens us, threatens Israel, who is our strong ally and friend, threatens Russia. We've got to deal with it. The threat in Europe at sometime, perhaps. We must deal with that issue. And one way to do that is coordinate security arrangements, is to talk about how to . . . deal with the new threats, but also is to be able to have the capacity to rid the world of blackmail, terrorist blackmail.[62]

We live in a very different world from the one that existed when Bill Clinton came to office on January 20, 1993. George W. Bush and presidents who follow him will be dealing with the serious national security threats Clinton left behind for decades. We are now living Bill Clinton's legacy.

WORLD TRADE CENTER ONE

While Clinton Fiddles . . .

ON FEBRUARY 26, 1993, A BOMB DETONATED IN A RENTED ONE-TON Ford F-350 Econoline van parked on the second level of the World Trade Center parking basement. The explosion radiated outward from the south wall of Trade Tower Number One, displacing an estimated 6,800 tons of material. Despite having occurred in an area of the building made of steel-reinforced concrete, twelve to fourteen inches thick, the blast left a crater 150 feet in diameter and five floors deep.[1] Six people were killed.

According to U.S. District Court Judge Kevin Duffy, who presided over the trial of the terrorists responsible, the explosion caused "more hospital casualties than any other event in domestic American history other than the Civil War."[2] In addition to the six dead, 1,042 were injured.[3] It took 750 fire-fighters an entire month to get the damage under control.[4] Fifty thousand people had to be evacuated.[5]

The terrorist bomb was made of at least twelve hundred pounds of urea nitrate, a homemade fertilizer-based explosive. The bombers used two twenty-minute lengths of a nonelectric burning fuse to detonate the device, ending in lead azide as the initiator. The terrorists also placed three large metal cylinders of compressed hydrogen gas under the main explosive charge.[6]

The property damage went beyond the initial blast damage to the tower. During the ensuing investigation, inspectors realized that both the Trade Center buildings and the nearby Vista Hotel were in danger. The hotel might have collapsed within days had steel supports not been carefully placed to reinforce the structure. The structure of the tower was undergirded with steel supports as well.

The train system was also damaged—a part of a network that went from New York to New Jersey. Authorities evacuated the complex and ran a train through the station while collecting seismographic data. They found they were able to make temporary repairs that allowed the train to be used safely.[7]

Pollution was another concern. The blast exposed raw sewage and also threatened the area with asbestos, carcinogenic mineral wool, gasoline from damaged automobiles, and small fires caused by shorting circuits. Immediately after the blast, the Occupational Safety and Health Administration advised people working at the crime scene of the need to wear equipment to protect their breathing.

Thirty-six days into his presidency when the bombing occurred, it is important to remember Clinton's reaction. The president of the United States never went to the site to see the damage firsthand. He never witnessed the crime scene of what the *International Criminal Police Review* called "the most significant international terrorist act ever committed on U.S. soil."[8] The president may have received firsthand accounts and he may have watched the television coverage, but he never visited the site.

The Investigation

Immediately after the explosion, the race was on to find out who was responsible. A foreign terrorist attack on American shores was something Americans had never experienced. Remember that 1993 was a different world. Some early reports in the media suggested that a generator might have blown up.

The first investigators on the scene were bomb-technician agents sent by the New York office of the FBI. They quickly concluded an explosive device had detonated in the parking garage. The next day two experts arrived from the FBI Laboratory Explosives Unit. As Dave Williams recounts for the *International Criminal Police Review*:

> The initial inspection on 27th February was described as "a scene of massive devastation, almost surreal." It was like walking into a cave, with no lights other than flashlights flickering across the crater. There were small pockets of fire, electrical arcing from damaged wiring, and automobile alarms whistling, howling and honking. The explosion ruptured two of the

main sewage lines from both Trade towers and the Vista Hotel and several water mains from the air conditioning system. In all, more than 2 million gallons of water and sewage were pumped out of the crime scene.[9]

The two special agent examiners confirmed that the massive explosion was the result of an intentionally built bomb, not a freak accident. Not a week had passed before hundreds of investigators had combed through the debris— more than twenty-five hundred cubic yards.[10]

By assessing the damage done to the concrete, structural steel, and automobiles, the investigators were able to determine that the bomb exploded at a velocity of between 14 and 15.5 thousand feet per second. Correlating this with the kind of damage done by the bomb and other factors, agents were able to deduce that the bomb had been made up of between twelve and fifteen hundred pounds of explosive. The delivery vehicle was either a pickup or a van, since nothing larger would have been able to enter the parking garage.[11]

The investigation was difficult and complicated, but the agents also got some lucky breaks. In this case, a sizeable piece of the van used to bomb the World Trade Center survived the explosion. Contaminated by sewage, the heavy fragment yielded no useable residue for explosive analyses, but upon closer examination, investigators discovered a dot-matrix number imprinted on the piece. "The number was identified as the vehicle identification number of a van reported stolen the day before the bombing," writes Williams. "The vehicle was a 1990 Ford, F-350 Econoline van owned by the Ryder Rental Agency, rented in New Jersey and reported stolen in New Jersey. The frame fragment displayed explosive damage consistent with damage from a device exploding inside the vehicle."[12]

This gave the FBI an early lead. For the next several days investigators from several agencies stayed busy. On Monday morning, the work to secure the crime scene was done so that investigators would not be in danger of getting caught in a collapse. By Tuesday morning, law-enforcement personnel from eight distinct agencies assembled to begin collecting evidence. Even for an estimated two hundred officers, it was a huge undertaking.[13]

Arrests came shortly after the discovery of the van fragment. As Williams reports, while the FBI conducted an interview at the Ryder agency from which the van was rented, a man named Mohammad Salameh called to get his $400 security-deposit refunded. The FBI waited for Salameh to show and arrested him as he was leaving. An investigation following his arrest led to an Allied Signal Corporation chemist working in New Jersey named Nidel Ayyad, whom authorities linked to Salameh through phone records and joint bank accounts. Investigators seized Ayyad's work computer. They were also able to link Ayyad to a house in Jersey City where traces of nitroglycerine and urea nitrate were discovered. Phone records linked both Salameh and Ayyad to a nearby self-storage center.[14]

The manager of the storage facility told officers that Salameh and four other men, who appeared to be Arab, had been using a Ryder truck a few days before the attack. He also said that they had stored three tanks of compressed hydrogen from a welding company before he told them to remove them. A search of their storage space revealed chemicals used in the explosion, lengths of fuse, and lab equipment. Agents also found two bottles of nitroglycerine, a very dangerous and unstable explosive substance.[15]

As evidence continued to mount tying the tenants of the storage facility to the explosion, investigators got more clues when a letter was delivered to the *New York Times* claiming that the bomb was detonated in the name of Allah. From this letter, the FBI got DNA that matched Ayyad, showing he had licked the envelope to seal it. Also, the text of the letter was found in a file on his computer.[16]

Other suspects were quickly identified. Ahmad M. Ajaj arrived at New York City's Kennedy airport from Pakistan and was arrested on a passport violation. He was using a "poorly forged Swiss passport."[17] As a result, arrest officers were given a great deal of evidence. In a search of Ajaj's luggage, officials found manuals and videotaped instructions on how to make deadly explosives, including the explosive used in the bomb used to attack the tower.

Based on interviews and fingerprint evidence, authorities were able to tie Ajaj into a wider conspiracy, involving Salameh, a man known only as Yassin, who was likely involved in packing and delivering the bomb the morning of the blast, and Ramzi Yousef, who entered the U.S. on Ajaj's flight and whose fingerprints were discovered on the how-to materials in Ajaj's baggage.[18]

Yousef, carrying a suspicious Iraqi passport, requested and received political asylum.[19] In fact, he never even had to go through the interview process. The waiting room was so overcrowded with others requesting asylum that authorities merely photographed and fingerprinted him and gave him a court date. Yousef went on his way and never bothered to appear in court.[20]

The FBI and others had to work fast to find all the critical forensic evidence. Investigators also identified a fifth member of the conspiracy, Mahmud Abuhalima, through witnesses in the neighborhood that placed him with the other suspects. He fled to Egypt after the bombing but was eventually extradited back to the U.S.[21]

After a six-month trial involving over two hundred witnesses, four men were convicted on March 4, 1994, on a thirty-eight-count indictment. Mohammad Salameh, Nidal Ayyad, Mahmud Abouhalima, and Ahmad Mohammad Ajaj were each sentenced to 240 years of imprisonment without the possibility of parole.[22] But that left the person who appears to have masterminded the entire attack still at large. Ramzi Yousef was missing. He was a dangerous man to be roaming free:

> Yousef's terrorist crusade appears to have been driven by a confluence of anti-American and anti-Israeli rage and a significant dose of ego rather than religious ideology. He had more in common with the famous Latin American terrorist Carlos the Jackal than he did with the religiously inspired suicide-bombers of Hamas. Although he drew on the diaspora of militant Islamic fundamentalists, his attempt to inflict mass casualties in New York City did not stem from religious conviction. Instead, his twisted belief about how to respond to the plight of the Palestinian people seemed driven by the thrill of being an explosives expert, killing innocent people, and moving on to practice his brand of terrorism another day. His exploits as a transnational terrorist affirmed the high opinion he held of himself. A terrorist who thinks that he is a genius will set the highest goals for practicing his craft. In Yousef's case, that meant attempting to kill as many innocent people as possible.[23]

Yousef fled to the Philippines, where he began to plot even greater terror attacks. He studied explosives in order to improve his abilities.[24] He even experimented with a small transportable and undetectable explosive device to see if it would work, placing the charge under his seat on a flight from Manila to Tokyo. He disembarked at a stopover. A Japanese businessman was killed simply for having the misfortune of being next to sit in Yousef's seat.[25]

Yousef was also planning, among other horrors, to assassinate both the Pope and President Clinton and conduct a massive airline attack. He planned to blow up as many as twelve U.S. 747s simultaneously, in what was called the Bojinka plot. Simon Reeve and Giles Foden, reporting in the Manchester *Guardian*, refer to Bojinka as "an audacious plan to simultaneously destroy 12 airliners over the Pacific Ocean and have a suicide bomber fly a plane into the side of the CIA headquarters in Langley, Virginia."[26]

As covered in detail earlier in the book, the only reason he was stopped is that he accidentally set his kitchen on fire at three in the morning on January 7, 1995, and had to flee the scene.[27] He left his computer behind, which revealed what he intended to do with the explosives he was cooking up. He was arrested a month later.[28] In the days following the discovery of what he had been plotting, officers had no way of knowing whether he had already hidden bombs on planes. They did everything they could over the next few days to increase airline security in the Pacific Rim.[29] Yousef was obviously driven to kill. In fact, it is doubtful that he was really a religious fanatic in an ordinary sense of that term.

> [S]ources suggest that Yousef was motivated by an inchoate mixture of visceral hatred and personal affirmation, wrapped in a variety of geopolitical rationales. . . . Yousef's declared motivation was not religious but rather an anti-occupation crusade aimed against Israel and its main supporter, the United States. In contrast, Ayyad, Abouhalima, and Ajaj all expressed religious sentiments during their statements at sentencing but never admitted any connection to the WTC bombing. . . . Given that several of the conspirators were followers of Sheikh Omar [Abdul Rahman], Yousef's lack of religious justification is conspicuous by its absence. He appears to have been a secular terrorist who mobilized others by playing on their religious zeal. At the root of the WTC bombers' intent to inflict mass casualties was a strong desire to punish, to seek revenge, and to underscore the dignity of Muslims.[30]

Yousef was arrested only because one of his recent recruits had second thoughts about blowing up a plane. Instead of following through, he went home, poured the explosive liquid down the drain, and called the authorities to tell them what he knew.[31] On February 7, 1995, a team in Islamabad "rendered" Yousef to the United States—that is, they took him into custody, put him on a plane, and took him to the U.S. to stand trial.[32]

In the ensuing investigation, Yousef told agents that he intended to kill a quarter-million people in the bombing of the World Trade Center. His plan was to cause one tower to fall over into the other.[33] When the head of the FBI in New York later pointed out that the Twin Towers were still standing, Yousef replied in defiance, "They wouldn't be if I had had enough money and explosives."[34]

One of Yousef's accomplices, Eyad Ismoil, was also caught. He had helped Yousef drive the bomb-laden van to the parking garage. Like the others, they were each sentenced to 240 years in prison.

THE LIMITATIONS OF A CRIMINAL INVESTIGATION

The arrests and convictions were good news, especially the capture of Yousef before he carried out the Bojinka plot. However, as we will see in more detail later in this book, criminal investigations have limits.

What happened on February 26, 1993, was not simply a crime. It was an act of war. While criminal prosecution can assist with national security, it is also true that strictly favoring criminal prosecutions can compromise national security. A major reason is that "the Justice Department typically denies information to the national security bureaucracies, taking the position that passing on information might 'taint the evidence' and affect prospects for obtaining convictions," as Laurie Mylroie wrote in 1995. At the time, Ms. Mylroie was working with the Foreign Policy Research Institute of Philadelphia, having taught previously at Harvard University and the U.S. Naval War College. She writes:

> In effect, the Justice Department puts the prosecution of individual per-
> petrators—with all the rights to a fair trial guaranteed by the U.S. judicial
> system—above America's national security interest in determining who
> may be behind terrorist attacks. Questions of state sponsorship that are of

pressing interest to national security agencies are typically relegated to a distant second place, or never properly addressed at all, because the national security agencies are denied critical information. In particular, whenever early arrests are made regarding a terrorist incident on American soil, the U.S. government cannot properly address both the national security question of state sponsorship and the criminal question of the guilt or innocence of individual perpetrators at the same time.[35]

What this means is that a criminal case can be inherently obstructive to intelligence gathering by national security agencies such as the CIA. In this case, the investigation did catch some of the perpetrators. It also uncovered and prevented another attack when an informant "led [CIA intelligence to] a handful of local Muslims in a new bombing conspiracy, aimed at the United Nations and other New York landmarks. For this conspiracy Sheikh Omar Abdul Rahman and nine others were found guilty in early October 1995."[36]

But it didn't uncover the terror network behind these plots. When Mylroie met with federal prosecutors in New York, in January 1995, and questioned them about the issue of state sponsorship, they said, "'We don't do state sponsorship. We prosecute individuals.' Asked who does 'do' state sponsorship, they answered, 'Washington.' 'Who in Washington?' No one seemed to know."[37]

Yet in a matter of five weeks, the FBI declared there had been no involvement by any foreign government. Mylroie explains the problem with this hasty verdict:

[B]y April it was impossible to have conducted a sufficiently thorough investigation. Such an investigation required, at a minimum, a meticulous examination of all records associated with the defendants to insure that they had had no contact with foreign intelligence agencies—or at least that none could be found. That process simply could not have been accomplished in five weeks. And it must be kept in mind that, at the time, the mastermind of the bomb was a fugitive about whom almost nothing was known. How could anyone therefore declare confidently that he was not a foreign agent, especially in light of the fact that he had entered the United

States on an Iraqi passport and had been known among the New York fundamentalists as "Rashid, the Iraqi"?[38]

The fact is, the evidence needed to be meticulously reviewed by the Central Intelligence Agency. Mylroie points out that human intelligence and other forms of information gathered by the CIA are often important, but alone are never enough. They also need access to physical evidence. In 1993 no access was given to the CIA.

The Nonresponse

The 1993 bombing could have been much worse than it was. The actual plan was to destroy one or both towers, killing thousands. Instead, Yousef killed only six. Those six deaths and the over one thousand wounded should have served as a warning to the inexperienced Clinton administration to wage a war against terrorism. Instead of a forewarning, however, the victims became a foreshadowing of the carnage the future held.

After the World Trade Center bomb, it was vital to relentlessly track down and hold responsible *all* the terrorists and terrorist organizations responsible. While there was a full-scale manhunt conducted for Yousef, it was only by dumb luck that he was caught. If he had not set his kitchen on fire or if a recruit had not betrayed him, he might have killed hundreds more by this time. Terrorists see inaction as weakness, so Clinton's inaction sent a message that terrorists could attack the U.S. on its soil without fear of retribution.

Clinton's top political adviser, Dick Morris, has been quite candid about how little Clinton cared about terrorism or national security: "Nothing so illustrates the low priority of terrorism in Clinton's first term than the short shrift he gave the 1993 bombing of the World Trade Center, the first terrorist attack on U.S. soil."[39] Clinton aide George Stephanopoulos tried to cover for his boss, saying in the *New York Times,* Yousef's attack "wasn't a successful bombing. . . . It wasn't the kind of thing where you walked into a staff meeting and people asked, what are we doing today in the war against terrorism?" But Morris isn't buying. "Stephanopoulos was just the hired help. Clinton was the president and commander-in-chief. For all of his willingness to act courageously and decisively—against the advice of his liberal staff—on issues like deficit reduction and welfare reform, he was passive and almost inert on terrorism in his first term."[40]

The fact is, Clinton actively tried to downplay the national importance of the bombing. He may have been incapable of dealing with terrorism, so he tried to keep Americans from focusing on terrorism. "After the February 1993 bombing of the World Trade Center, President Clinton never visited the site and only alluded to it once in his regular Saturday radio address right after the bombing. Visiting New Jersey shortly after the attack, he urged Americans not to 'overreact.'"[41]

The evidence that Clinton was in no danger of "overreacting" to the murder of six Americans and the attempted murder of thousands more by an unknown power is revealed in the White House paper "The First 100 Days, Administration of President Bill Clinton, January 20–April 30, 1993."[42] The day after this bombing, Clinton was on the radio when he must have "alluded" to the attack, according to Dick Morris. From the White House's own summary of Clinton's first hundred days, even the allusion is missing:

DAY 39: FEBRUARY 27, 1993
　　Saturday radio address on the economic plan.

One looks in vain at the report of the first hundred days for any mention of, let alone concern for, foreign or domestic terrorism. The only time the word "security" is used is in the context of Clinton's health care ambitions; the words "national security" are nowhere to be found. The only mention of the bombing treats it as equivalent to a natural disaster.

DAY 73: APRIL 2, 1993
　　Holds Forest Conference, Portland, Oregon; conference convenes interests at odds over management of the Nation's forests in the Pacific Northwest.
　　Declares major disaster in the State of New York due to effects of the bombing of the World Trade Center and in the State of Nebraska as a result of severe March flooding and ice jams, authorizing emergency relief assistance.[43]

President Clinton clearly did not risk "overreacting" to the World Trade Center bombing. Columnist Andrew Sullivan summarized the nonresponse of the president:

> Did the Clinton administration overhaul its intelligence and defense priorities in response to the 1993 warning? No. No effort was made to co-ordinate the mess of agencies designed to counter terrorism—the FBI, the CIA, the Pentagon, the State Department, the airlines, local law enforcement, the Coast Guard. No effort was made to recruit more spies who could speak Arabic or go undercover to pre-empt such attacks.[44]

Morris concurs: "Everything was more important than fighting terrorism. Political correctness, civil liberties concerns, fear of offending the administration's supporters, Janet Reno's objections, considerations of cost, worries about racial profiling and, in the second term, surviving impeachment, all came before fighting terrorism."[45]

The Learning Curve

The United States could not afford Clinton's nonreaction. As the former director and former senior director for counterterrorism at the National Security Council explain in their *pro*-Clinton book, "Beginning slowly—too slowly—after the first World Trade Center bombing, officials in the White House, the CIA, and isolated offices in a scattering of other agencies began to scale the steep learning curve."[46] But the "isolated offices" in their "scattering of other agencies" required an engaged president as a unifying force—someone who would set the agenda, make sure they stayed focused on the mission, and wouldn't allow turf battles to outweigh the greater good.

Former CIA Director James Woolsey agreed in an interview for this book that there needed to be a change in perspective. Director Woolsey said, "Until November 9, 1989, the Soviet Union was front and center. After their fall, we never adapted to a new world view." In that era, terrorism was done differently. "In the 1970s and 80s, terrorist attacks were driven by Iran and the Hezbollah. State sponsorship is really not accurate; it's more like a limited partnership."

With the first World Trade Center bombing things should have begun to change. "At the time, Al Qaeda was still in its embryonic stage," Woolsey said. "The summer and fall of 1995 time period was crucial because we were just able to see the trail of documents from the first World Trade Center bombing and the Riyadh, Saudi Arabia, bombing that had taken place. By the end of 1995, John Deutch should have been burrowing in on this and his people should have seen a problem, a pattern developing." Of course, as we saw in Chapter Four, Deutch had other things on his plate.

A disengaged president who didn't travel to New York to see "the most significant international terrorist act ever committed on U.S. soil" is not going to try to scale a learning curve. As James Woolsey pointed out to me, "Clinton went along with the first World Trade Center bombing as a law-enforcement matter." This was the habit of the administration in the 1990s. "The White House focused on terror cases as law-enforcement matters. You're bound to catch somebody, so try and claim victory when you do."

Like Mylroie, Woolsey thought this method left unanswered questions for the World Trade Center bombing. "Were the Iraqis involved in World Trade Center One, that was the question. We should have scrutinized Iran closer in the 1980s and we should have scrutinized Iraq closer in the nineties."

Shockingly, Woolsey stated that "the president did not ask me ask to do anything in response to the bombing of the World Trade Center, nor [did he ask] me to be part of any committee or commission that would deal with the disaster." He went on to say, "President Clinton did not speak to me directly after the bombing. He did not direct me to do anything related to the attack." The president regarded the issue, said Woolsey, as simply "a law enforcement matter." On his own initiative as CIA director, Woolsey did direct his people to pursue "all avenues to gather information."

Woolsey's hands were tied to some extent by the lack of a presidential mandate, and he also had to be careful not to get in the way of the FBI, since they were assigned the case. "The FBI worked on it fulltime with a massive taskforce, but they could not share anything with us because it was an ongoing criminal investigation. And they could not share 6e material gathered in the grand jury. The system was set up that way on purpose so that the FBI and the CIA would have different missions and protect the American public from an out-of-control government. The Patriot Act has solved some of those problems and created new ones."

I should point out an oddity here. Even though Woolsey's relationship with FBI director Freeh had degenerated into a "cool" one, he did not express any frustration with the bureau for their refusal to share information, as if it was a personal problem on the part of Freeh in particular or the FBI in general. Yet in their book, *The Age of Sacred Terror: Radical Islam's War Against America*, Daniel Benjamin and Steven Simon portray the FBI's adherence to "Rule 6e of the Federal Rules of Criminal Procedure, which forbids disclosure of grand jury material," as purely an excuse devised to protect the FBI's turf.[47]

That interpretation is, to say the least, debatable. It took a new law—the Patriot Act—to allow the sharing of 6e information between counterintelligence agencies. In an interview with Oliver "Buck" Revell, former executive assistant director of the FBI, he said the same thing. Though Revell is an FBI man, he truly dislikes Louis Freeh. He told me, "Recommending Louis Freeh for director of the FBI was the sorriest mistake I ever made." Freeh was, in his view, a poor manager. But the need to share information was not something that Freeh could do much about. "FISA threshold problems and Grand Jury 6e material were the two biggest barriers to gathering and sharing information that there was. The FBI and CIA could not talk to each other and share intelligence because of the rules that came from Washington."

After the bombing, the president needed to show leadership to America and the world. Clinton should have gotten his agencies equipped so that they could do the job of counterterrorism. As Mylroie wrote in the midnineties, "But there was no intelligence investigation of the World Trade Center bombing. The CIA is, after all, prohibited from operating in America. Of course, a crack interagency team could have been established to examine the question of state sponsorship. But Clinton administration officials set up no such team."[48]

12

THE SOMALIA MASSACRE

U.S. Soldiers Left To Die

IN 1998, WHEN PRESIDENT CLINTON AND HIS ADMINISTRATION were justifying his missile attacks against Afghanistan and Sudan, their charges against Osama bin Laden included "attacks on U.S. and UN peacekeepers in Somalia."[1]

Many years later, in 2002, long after the destruction of the twin towers, President Clinton again mentioned Somalia, but his remarks about the country had absolutely nothing to do with the situation he was addressing. The former president was making remarks about scandals involving corporate greed. Some claimed that the corporate malfeasance being uncovered had begun under his own watch as president. In response, he threw out this little gem about the Bush administration, apparently off the cuff: "These people ran on responsibility, but as soon as you scratch them they go straight to blame. Now, you know, I didn't blame his father for Somalia when we had that awful day memorialized in *Black Hawk Down*. I didn't do that."[2] Of course, he had just done exactly what he said he didn't do. He blamed his predecessor, George H. W. Bush, for what happened in Somalia.

Why were our armed forces even in Somalia on "that awful day memorialized in *Black Hawk Down*"?

Congressman Bob Livingston characterized the situation as "mission creep"—the original peacekeeping mission had turned into something allegedly more glorious, but unquestionably much more dangerous.

> Our policy in Somalia has suffered from a . . . lack of clear objectives. As originally envisioned by President Bush, our role in Somalia was to ensure safe passage for relief supplies, end the horrible mass starvation, and then

let the UN take over to keep the supply lines open. That's pretty much what happened—except that by moving UN troops to the forefront, our mission changed, and instead of neutrality, U.S. soldiers have now been forced to lead in fighting the forces of warlord Mohammed Farah Aideed. It was a peacekeeping operation, but now it's a "containment" effort aimed at something called "nation-building."[3]

Livingston quoted columnist Jim Hoagland in a speech on September 1, 1993, saying "modest, worthwhile U.S. achievements" pursued by George Bush "are now at risk as U.S. troops are being drawn deeper into Somalia's war of the warlords."[4] But Somalia, said Livingston, is of marginal interest to the national security of United States. The administration was unwise in claiming that it was a good "test case" for our military power. "But I think we should beware, lest a test case turn our policy there into a basket case. Military force and U.S. personnel aren't toys to be tested. Real war is serious business."[5]

Livingston had no idea how prescient his comments were. Only twenty-three days later, Les Aspin made a fateful decision about a request for more equipment for rangers in Somalia. Ten days later, America got an object lesson. But did Bill Clinton learn from it? Al Qaeda had declared a real war on the United States, but Bill Clinton and his national security team did not recognize it.

Real war is serious business.

What Happened

On October 3, 1993, U.S. forces were informed that two high-ranking advisers to General Mohammed Farrah Aideed, a warlord who had proven hostile to the United States and the United Nations, were at the Olympic Hotel in the capital of Mogadishu.[6] Quickly, ninety-nine soldiers, mostly members of Task Force Ranger who had been sent there to capture the aides and break Aideed's power, were mobilized to conduct a helicopter attack. Good intelligence, a good plan, and effective execution allowed the rangers to succeed in their mission, capturing the two advisers and twenty-two other Aideed supporters. It looked as though it would be a perfectly successful mission.

But then everything changed. The soldiers became targets of a well-organized ambush. As the troops prepared the prisoners for transport, two of their helicopters were shot down. Another was damaged so badly that it had to crash land at the Mogadishu Airport. The rangers were attacked by a force of over one thousand Somalis. This dramatic firefight continued over eleven hours, until they were finally rescued by United Nations troops. The daring rescue required soldiers with tanks and armored vehicles. The American Army Rangers had requested this same support, but the request had been denied. In the end, Pakistani and Malaysian troops came to rescue our soldiers because they had the armored vehicles necessary to survive the fierce gun battle. But it took them ten hours to arrive.[7]

Army Rangers' lives were lost because they were ill equipped for the mission. As one ranger's father explained, "Rangers are highly mobile because they travel lightly. This means they are lightly armed. Light infantry should never be committed with no means of reinforcement."[8]

The next day, Aideed's men threw a gruesome celebration for their victory, dragging corpses of American soldiers down the streets. Reportedly, over seven hundred of Aideed's gang had been killed. Eighteen U.S. soldiers died, and seventy-eight were wounded.

The Importance of Somalia

The fact that Clinton can't leave this incident alone is significant. The truth is that what happened in Mogadishu was quite important both as a window into Clinton's competence with the military and his legacy in regard to Al Qaeda. The incident to which Clinton referred as "that awful day memorialized in *Black Hawk Down*" cost the lives of American men in uniform.

President Clinton initially attempted to portray "toughness," as he would try to do again later. When word that Americans had been taken prisoner reached him, he declared that any mistreatment would invite reprisals. "The United States will view this matter very gravely and take appropriate action." Clinton emphasized he was speaking of unilateral U.S. action, not what the United Nations might do.[9] Eventually, the captured soldiers were returned unharmed.

However, the president took no action in response to the loss of life. On

October 19, President Clinton ordered the withdrawal of the Rangers from Somalia.[10] Those who opposed the United States watched as seven hundred and fifty American troops left the region after suffering one major defeat. "Right now we are engaging in a political process to see how we can resolve our mission in Somalia," the president said, "so right now we're in a stand-down position."[11] I doubt this sounded convincing to people who supported the president, and it certainly didn't fool our enemies. Clinton sent additional troops in order to facilitate a general withdrawal from the area. Seven months later, American forces pulled out of Somalia entirely, and no action was ever taken regarding the killing of American soldiers.[12]

When the attack first occurred, President Clinton had insisted that "U.S. achievements in Somalia 'must not be lost' because of reaction to Aideed's challenges to UN authority."[13] But Somalia was eventually abandoned by Clinton no better than before troops were sent to the region. This withdrawal sent a clear message to Osama bin Laden, giving him "great encouragement" that Al Qaeda could succeed against America.

Bin Laden's Role in Somalia

The impact of our defeat and withdrawal from Somalia is all the more important since, as the Clinton administration itself claimed, Osama bin Laden was aiding and abetting the warlords who killed our soldiers.

Terrorism expert Yosef Bodansky, in *Bin Laden: the Man Who Declared War on America*, writes, "Osama bin Laden has said that he considers his experience in Somalia a milestone in his evolution."[14] It was in Somalia that he was first exposed to some of the major complexities of leadership and decision-making at that level in a terrorist operation.[15] It also led him to the firm conviction, according to Bodansky, that "it would be possible to ultimately evict the United States from Saudi Arabia and the Persian Gulf States as well."[16] Further acts of terrorism became potentially profitable.

Most Americans are unaware that, to some Islamic fundamentalists, Somalia was a prize to be defended from an American presence. National Security Council authors Daniel Benjamin and Steven Simon write, "The Americans' appearance in the horn of Africa was a catalytic event for Al Qaeda, which interpreted the deployment as another unmistakable step in the campaign against Islam."[17] Bodansky writes of the surprise that awaited us when our troops first landed in December of 1992:

> The initial impression of relative tranquility was deceiving. For more than a year Iran and Sudan had been engaged in a fierce campaign to consolidate their control over the Red Sea and the Horn of Africa. Somalia, a Muslim country stretching along the all-important littoral of the Horn of Africa, attracted the attention of Khartoum (Sudan) and Tehran. The chaos in Somalia, fractured along tribal lines and immersed in a fierce struggle for self-determination and power, made segments of the population and their power-hungry leaders amenable to close cooperation with and susceptible to manipulation and exploitation by [the religious leader of Sudan] Turabi's people in Khartoum. Islamism was spreading in the ranks of the various tribal militias in Somalia, and by fall 1992 the armed Islamist movements in Somalia were growing fast.[18]

In this unstable situation, Bin Laden was able to exert influence. Years before Americans arrived, Sudan and Iran were funneling money into Somalia, and Bin Laden was responsible for getting the money through a network to its destination.[19] Additionally, Bin Laden, working on very short notice, helped pull together a protest to the U.S. presence in Somalia by organizing attacks in Yemen.

On December 29, Bin Laden's men detonated bombs at two Aden hotels. Three died and five were wounded, but it could have been much worse. Ready to attack U.S. Air Force transport planes, a strike team of Islamic terrorists was discovered at the Aden airport with RPG-7 rocket launchers. They were caught just before they could fire on a parked C-5 Galaxy.[20]

According to Bodansky, this operation was pulled together in such haste that Bin Laden took extra risks. This earned him credit with his allies, who took note of how well he handled the situation as well as his use of his own personal assets to get the job done. As a result, "he would play an even greater role in the forthcoming confrontation."[21]

When resistance escalated in the fall of 1993, Osama bin Laden was instrumental in secretly and quickly getting ammunition to where it was needed. "The entire Islamist operational plan was based on the sustained availability of large quantities of ammunition and supplies, which was Bin Laden's responsibility," writes Bodansky. "To ensure surprise and avoid pre-emptive strikes by UN forces these supplies had to be pushed forward from the storage sites in Somaliland to Mogadishu at the last minute. Bin Laden tackled this challenge successfully, presaging future Islamist operational successes."[22]

One of Aideed's major field commanders, Ali al-Rashidi, was a personal friend of Bin Laden's. They had met after al-Rashidi escaped an Egyptian prison and fled to Afghanistan in 1986. Egyptian sources indicated "al-Rashidi was Osama bin Laden's right arm." His job for Bin Laden was to supervise base camps designed to train the incoming Arab mujahideen, men who had volunteered from other Muslim nations to fight the Russian invaders.[23] Al-Rashidi was influential on linking Bin Laden with Egyptian allies and also traveled to several places to organize terrorists. By fall of 1993, he was put in charge of a unit in Mogadishu, Somalia. Writes Bodansky:

> For the main infiltration of experts and sophisticated equipment, Abdallah Jaweed and Osama bin Laden recruited several ex-DRA Afghan military pilots, all veterans of the massive resupply efforts into besieged DRA garrisons, to fly small transport planes into isolated airfields in Somalia at night. Heavier equipment was smuggled into Somaliland by Bin Laden's flotilla of small fishing boats operating out of neighboring countries, mainly Yemen and Kenya. From these points of entry the weapons and people were smuggled by small nomadic caravans into safe houses in the Mogadishu sites. A major outcome of this resupply surge was the establishment of a well-organized clandestine headquarters in Mogadishu from which a few Somalian, Afghan, and Algerian experts in urban guerilla warfare would run the imminent escalation.[24]

The victory over American troops, under these circumstances, was perceived by Osama bin Laden and his terrorist sympathizers as a victory. No one in the Clinton administration realized it, but Al Qaeda had just been handed a public relations triumph in the Middle East and Africa.

Shifting Blame

Instead of worrying about the message being sent by allowing our troops to be killed with impunity, then pulling out of that region of the world (close to the Middle East), Clinton immediately began shifting blame. As the *New York Times* reported, eleven days after the massacre, "Mr. Clinton said the aggressive effort against the faction leader Mohammed Farah Aideed 'never should have been allowed to supplant the political process that was ongoing when we were in effective control, up through last May.'" Clinton even claimed that he didn't know that the military was trying to capture the renegade general.[25]

One of the many tragedies of this story is that the Congressional hearings in its aftermath claimed that no one was really to blame. Senator Sam Nunn held hearings in the Senate Armed Services Committee. After the hearing, President Clinton met privately with retired Col. Larry Joyce, a Vietnam veteran who attended the committee meeting. His son was one of the Rangers killed in Somalia. Col. David Hackworth reports that Joyce questioned Clinton during their Oval Office meeting. "Since you had decided on a diplomatic solution, why was the 3 October raid launched?" Joyce told Hackworth that Clinton said, "That's the key question," and claimed that it was what he asked his own staff when he first heard the report of the deaths. Hackworth's response is on target: "If the president didn't know the biggest ground combat operation since Desert Storm was going down, our warriors and U.S. national security are in deeper trouble than I feared."[26]

The fact that the president claimed not to know in advance about the military strike is ludicrous and means that someone in the chain of command should have been fired for not informing him. But Clinton never made any such claim. That would have involved the admission that he was not actively involved in national security affairs or engaged when our men and women went into harm's way. He simply pleaded ignorance, as if such ignorance was excusable. Part of the rationale for this was the claim that the United Nations was calling the shots in Somalia. But the military commanders testified unanimously that the administration, not the United Nations, was giving the orders.[27]

None of the former president's claims withstand scrutiny. The United

Nations objective to remove Aideed from power was agreed to by "top Administration officials" in the summer of 1993. The military began having second thoughts about the viability of such a plan, but it was not until September that the administration began to question it. However, they never changed the military's orders. As far as the Pentagon was concerned, they were still assigned the mission of finding and defeating Aideed.[28]

President Clinton seemed quite in favor of this plan during the summer. After troops bombed General Aideed's armories and headquarters, Clinton spoke approvingly of the operation as a complete success. "The purpose of the operation was to undermine the ability of Aideed to wreak military havoc in Somalia," he claimed. "The military back of Aideed has been broken. A warrant has been issued for his arrest."[29]

In order to capture Aideed, the military wanted Rangers sent in. While the administration resisted the idea at first, the mission was eventually approved. Of course, this contradicts what some in the administration tried to say about top-level people not paying attention to the decision-making process. Clinton may have tried to sound humble by saying that his administration was insufficiently attentive, but it may actually have been an attempt to shift blame.

Secretary of State Warren Christopher admitted to the *Washington Post* that cabinet-level officials "were not sufficiently attentive" because the operation was under the eye of the Deputies Committee. "But," according to the *New York Times*, "senior Administration officials said the decision to send the Rangers was approved by Mr. Clinton, Mr. Aspin, Gen. Colin L. Powell, who was then the Chairman of the Joint Chiefs of Staff, and Anthony Lake, the national security adviser."[30]

As the summer came to an end, the Clinton administration began to advocate a more ambitious approach to Somalia's problems. The very day after the Rangers arrived, reported the *Times*, "Mr. Aspin called in a speech for more work on the political and economic reconstruction of the country. He also said United States troops would stay in Somalia until violence was quelled, the clans gave up their heavy weapons and a national police was created."[31] This was a tall order. Tragically, the administration wanted to pursue such broad goals *without* increasing the military presence in the country.

Worse yet, they began looking at political or diplomatic solutions without changing their military policy. "[A]s the administration sought to move to a political strategy, policy became less clear. Washington was looking for some sort of political settlement but had not yet given up its military approach."[32] This indecisiveness led to disaster. Requests for critical armored troop backup days before the Ranger disaster were denied by Les Aspin on September 23, because he worried it would appear as if military operations were being emphasized while the higher-ups were busy trying to emphasize diplomacy and wrap up the mission. But despite the diplomatic push, the Clinton team still wanted to bag Aideed—a confusion of purpose that led directly to the October 3 debacle, in which eighteen Americans died and several more were wounded.[33]

While it was true that the United Nations favored more military involvement rather than reliance on new diplomatic efforts, the decision to keep the Rangers on their mission to capture Aideed was the responsibility of the administration, as was the decision to do so without providing them with the armored support that they needed—a request supported by Generals Joseph Hoar and Colin Powell.

Hoar's position arguably should have contained special weight. The general had earlier opposed increased military presence in the area, writing a memo stating, "If the only solution for Mogadishu is large-scale infusion of troops and if the only country available to make this commitment is the United States, then it is time to reassess."[34] His decision to throw his support behind the tanks and armored personnel carriers was obviously not the result of bias toward increasing firepower. His advice should have been heeded.

The spin from the Pentagon was that the decision to deny armored support wasn't instrumental in most of the deaths, claiming that backup wouldn't have lessened the casualties much because most of the casualties occurred early on. But military officials noted that armor could have helped in the rescue operation,[35] and after interviewing the rangers, David Hackworth called the official story "pure Pentagon propaganda."[36]

Indeed, Clinton wasn't the only one covering himself. According to Hackworth, military officers were also basically aiding and abetting the administration's incompetence. General Thomas Montgomery defended himself by pointing out that he had requested the extra tanks and armored transports, but Les Aspin turned him down. True, but the fact remains that the general proceeded to put troops in harm's way without adequate protection. It does look like the unquestioned assumption of such a defense is that it is perfectly all right to take unnecessary risks with soldiers' lives rather than resign or otherwise engage in potentially career-ending resistance to bad decisions by one's bosses.[37]

The same problem is evident in the case of General William Garrison, who had command of the rangers. Garrison claimed he requested Air Force AC-130 gunships for the raid instead of "thin-skinned Army choppers." Hoar and State Department officials denied his request. Nonetheless, without proper equipment, Garrison still sent the rangers in.[38]

So Who's To Blame?

All of this blame shifting is *still* going on in the case of Bill Clinton. He still blames former President Bush for his own bad decisions. But it was not Bush's decision to keep troops in Somalia after the mission was over. Larry Joyce's Op-Ed in *USA Today* provides insight into who might be held responsible:

> Last December, we sent 21,000 troops to Somalia to provide security for a humanitarian mission. Once that was completed, all but 4,700 came home. Of those 4,700, only about 300 were combat troops—including 145 Rangers who were sent there in late August. And, suddenly, with this bare-bones force and no American armor or mechanized equipment and troops, the mission changed to one of very direct combat. Who changed the mission? The United Nations? The multinational commander on the ground in Somalia? Who in the American chain of command concurred? The president? The secretary of State? The secretary of Defense?[39]

James Smith is another father who lost a son, a ranger, in Somalia. He is a disabled Vietnam veteran invited to the White House to meet with Clinton, probably because Clinton staffers knew he was planning to give testimony before the Senate, which they expected would not put the administration in a good light. His testimony is that Clinton attempted to point the finger at "everybody except himself," including Les Aspin, the Defense Department, the Joint Chiefs, and even the Rangers "for being too aggressive."[40] At the time, Smith simply refused to shake the president's hand, instead giving him a Third Ranger Battalion patch, saying, "Don't forget them."[41]

Smith was prompted to make public comments about that meeting in response to the president's public blaming of former President Bush for what happened in Somalia. He responded that Clinton "seems to forget that when Bush number one sent troops into Somalia he sent them in by the tens of thousands. And they had complete armor, mechanized infantry, artillery, air cover support." But things changed under Clinton's leadership for the worse.[42]

If Clinton really had a case to make against Bush, he could have done so when he was president. His claim that he wouldn't do such a thing is contradicted by the fact that he *did* make the accusation in the process of denying that he would ever level such a charge. Instead, he forced Secretary of Defense Les Aspin to resign, since it was he who had allegedly made the decision that denied the Rangers the armor support they needed.

According to syndicated columnist Paul Greenberg, "When the awful toll became clear, some of us wanted Secretary Aspin to resign then and there. Instead, he waited two months. To his credit, when he did quit, he acknowledged his responsibility for the terrible events of that day, and the terrible decision of his own that had led to it."[43] The military's own Web site doesn't portray this acknowledgment as all that genuine a confession. "In the face of severe congressional criticism, Aspin admitted that in view of what had happened he had made a mistake, but stated that the request for armored equipment had been made within the context of delivering humanitarian aid to Somalia rather than protecting troops."[44]

Nevertheless, Clinton has plainly admitted that the responsibility lay within his own administration. Aspin admitted he made a mistake and, when Clinton announced Aspin's resignation soon after the Somalia debacle, "Observers assumed that the president had asked him to step down."[45] Former President Bush had nothing to do with it.

The resignation of Les Aspin may have been an encouragement to many in the military. As Greenberg points out, he was "a Congressman chosen mainly on the basis of his criticisms of the previous administration."[46] In his editorial, "Did my son have to die?" Larry Joyce is even more negative about

Aspin's role. He asks the president "Why is Les Aspin our Secretary of Defense? Why is a man who made a career of criticizing and reviling the military put in charge of the military? This makes as much sense as appointing an atheist to be a cardinal."[47]

Not everyone thought that Les Aspin was the real decision maker, however. Retired Colonel James Smith, a Vietnam veteran, has no real reason to defend Aspin, but he pointed out that it was unbelievable that Aspin wasn't doing what the White House wanted.

> Although then-Defense Secretary Les Aspin was forced to resign over the deadly blunder, Smith said he had no doubt that the decision to under-equip his son's unit came directly from the White House. When he testified before the Senate Armed Services Committee on the episode, the former soldier said reporters privately agreed, telling him, "Les Aspin had nothing to do with this. This was a White House decision. They knew how the White House works. They knew there was no way Les Aspin made that decision on his own."[48]

Whoever made the decision, it was done at the administration level when Clinton was commander-in-chief of the armed forces. His indecisiveness and simple lack of concern for the military's mission cost American servicemen their lives. As Ed Offley summarized in *Defense Watch*:

> And, of course, with political controversy growing at home in Congress over the "new" Somalia mission, then-Secretary of Defense Les Aspin, Clinton's affable and incompetent Pentagon chief, refused (1) to allow an expansion in the number of combat troops as violence surged in the summer of 1993, (2) declined the ground force commander's request for M1A1 tanks, M2 Bradley Fighting Vehicles and AC-130 gunships, but (3) insisting that American commandos continue their attempts to seize Somali clan leader Mohammed Farah Aideed and his top lieutenants, while (4) the administration explored ways to negotiate with those same warlords.[49]

Those four decisions are obviously in conflict with one another. It should come as no surprise that it resulted in unnecessary deaths. What is a surprise is how little attention the Clinton administration received from the major media regarding an issue that would years later become a major motion picture, *Black Hawk Down*. While the story was printed, it was never treated like a major scandal. Veteran officer Rick Erickson thinks the story is simply an example of the president mistreating the military and, thus, is not a story the media wants to draw attention to. "The story was, after all, the first indication that the elected Democrat would allow his obvious rift with the military to become a deadly one," writes Erickson. "The story further demonstrated Clinton's audacity for putting helpless causes for peace ahead of firsthand reports from in-theater military commanders, who assured the president that our troops were at war."[50]

Whether or not Clinton should have ever allowed troops to stay in Somalia with a changed mission is a question open for debate. He certainly should have provided them with the needed protection. There are many conservatives who think that policy and humanitarian efforts are outside the scope of the military's mission. But it is important to note that Clinton expressed agreement with former President Bush when his decision to send troops was announced. In fact, when a large number of troops initially returned, Clinton did his best to associate himself with the mission. He gave a speech on the South lawn of the White House, saying, "If all of you who served had not gone, it is absolutely certain that tens of thousands would have died by now." In the words of the president, the "successful mission" had "proved yet again that American leadership can help to mobilize international action."[51]

But it was Clinton who kept troops there, and it was Clinton who changed the mission. It was also Clinton who gave up right at the time when he could least afford to do so. As the *Wall Street Journal* editorialized, the results of the debacle in Somalia went beyond the needless loss of life. Rather than allowing the military to stay and finish off Aideed, Clinton aborted the mission. "The U.S. released the criminals it had captured that same day at such great cost, and the UN, lacking U.S. support, was powerless to keep order." Somalia quickly returned to its usual chaos, and worse, "the terrorists of al Qaeda interpreted the U.S. retreat from Somalia as a sign of American weakness that may have convinced them we could be induced to retreat from the Middle East if they took their attacks to the U.S. homeland."[52]

Clinton's mission change resulted in two simultaneous calamities. After the loss of American lives, the troops were suddenly withdrawn without anything being done to address the deaths. This demoralized our Armed Forces while simultaneously encouraging our enemies to attack us.

Somalia's Influence on Bin Laden

On January 31, 2002, CNN aired excerpts from Bin Laden's only post-September 11 interview. During that interview, he referred explicitly to Somalia as a great encouragement to him. "Our brothers with Somali Mujahideen and God's power fought the Americans. God granted them victory. America exited dragging its tails in failure, defeat, and ruin," Bin Laden said.[53]

But this was not the first time Bin Laden cited Somalia in an appeal to Islamic extremism. In a 1998 interview with ABC reporter John Miller, the terror master referred the to the Somali disaster.

MILLER: Describe the situation when your men took down the American forces in Somalia.

BIN LADEN: After our victory in Afghanistan and the defeat of the oppressors who had killed millions of Muslims, the legend about the invincibility of the superpowers vanished. Our boys no longer viewed America as a superpower. So, when they left Afghanistan, they went to Somalia and prepared themselves carefully for a long war. They had thought that the Americans were like the Russians, so they trained and prepared. They were stunned when they discovered how low was the morale of the American soldier. America had entered with thirty thousand soldiers in addition to thousands of soldiers from different countries in the world. . . . As I said, our boys were shocked by the low morale of the American soldier and they realized that the American soldier was just a paper tiger. He was unable to endure the strikes that were dealt to his army, so he fled, and America had to stop all its bragging and all that noise it was making in the press after the Gulf War in which it destroyed the infrastructure and the milk and dairy industry that was vital for the infants and the children and the civilians and blew up dams which were necessary for the crops people grew to feed their families. Proud of this destruction, America assumed the titles of world leader and master of the new world order. After a few blows, it forgot all about those titles and rushed out of Somalia in shame and disgrace, dragging the bodies of its soldiers. America stopped calling itself world leader and master of the new world order, and its politicians realized that those titles were too big for them and that they were unworthy of them. I was in Sudan when this happened. I was very happy to learn of that great defeat that America suffered, so was every Muslim.[54]

Bin Laden also made similar comments in Mach 1997 during an interview with Robert Fisk of the *Independent*: "[O]ur battle against America is much simpler than the war against the Soviet Union, because some of our mujahideen who fought here in Afghanistan also participated in operations against the Americans in Somalia—and they were surprised at the collapse of American morale. This convinced us that the Americans are a paper tiger."[55]

Bill Clinton's legacy from Somalia is that the United States became less safe and Bin Laden became more dangerous.

KHOBAR TOWERS
Bill Clinton's Blind Justice

KHOBAR TOWERS WAS A HIGH-RISE APARTMENT BUILDING IN Dharan, Saudi Arabia. It was used to house American servicemen stationed in the Persian Gulf, including two thousand American military personnel assigned to the King Abdul Aziz Airbase. On June 25, 1996, a tanker trunk packed with five thousand pounds of plastic explosives parked outside the perimeter fence. Three rooftop sentries saw the truck park and the occupants flee the scene. Previously, "the area had been declared a likely target for a terrorist attack."[1]

For several months before the bombing, al-Khobar compound guards recorded incidents of professional surveillance being conducted from outside—slow, scoping drive-bys, men with binoculars. "At least one truck tried the strength of the fence by ramming it. Also, two weeks before the bombing a tanker truck, similar to the truck that carried the bomb, was seen trying to enter the compound and then driving around."[2]

The guards' reaction to the possible threat was quick, as they hurriedly began to knock on doors to rouse the sleeping residents. One of those guards, Sergeant Alfredo Guerrero, is one of the heroes of that day. He reacted from instinct after seeing the men flee from the truck. "I didn't feel scared. I just knew I had to do something," he said later.[3] What he and others did in the minutes they had left was a lifesaver for many. Before the explosion, two floors of the building had been emptied. "We went suite by suite, room by room, and tried to get everybody on the way down."[4]

The truck explosion resulted in a massive fireball that left a crater thirty-five feet deep[5] and tore one entire wall off the building.[6] The blast killed nineteen U.S. servicemen. Those Americans were not alone—

dozens of Saudi citizens were also killed,[7] and an estimated five hundred people were wounded, 372 of whom were Americans.[8] While those numbers seem small after September 11, at the time this was a catastrophic event. As CNN reported, "It is the deadliest bombing involving U.S. citizens in the Middle East since the 1983 Beirut attack that killed 241 Americans."[9]

Technically, however, from the terrorists' point of view, this was an unsuccessful attack. The drivers attempted to get the truck inside the compound but failed because of the late hour. So instead, they parked at the perimeter barrier eighty to a hundred feet from the building.[10] If they had successfully parked the truck right next to the building, many more lives would probably have been lost. Ironically, U.S. army officials had tried to get local Saudi authorities to move the perimeter farther out from the building, but their request was denied.[11]

While there is some debate over whether Osama bin Laden or Al Qaeda were involved in what happened at the Khobar Towers complex, it is virtually certain that they were. Desmond Ball is one of many who are quite sure of this. The special professor in the Strategic and Defense Studies Center at the Australian National University in Canberra writes, "[Bin Laden's] network was responsible for the bombing of the U.S. Air Force complex in the Khobar Towers in Dhahran, Saudi Arabia, on June 25, 1996, which killed 19 U.S. military personnel and disrupted U.S. Air Force operations over Iraq." Indeed, soon after the attack, Bin Laden capitalized on it. "In August 1996, he issued his first *fatwah*, a religious decree which declared war on the U.S. and condoned the killing of innocent civilians in carrying out that war."[12] As he said in an interview:

> We have roused the nation and the Muslim people, and we have communicated to them the fatwahs of our learned scholars who the Saudi government has thrown in jail in order to please the American government for which they are agents. . . . We have communicated their fatwahs and stirred the nation to drive out the enemy who has occupied our land and usurped our country and suppressed our people and to rid the land of the two Holy Mosques from their presence. Among the young men who responded to

our call are Khalid Al Said and Abdul Azeez Al . . . and Mahmud Al Hadi and Muslih Al Shamrani. We hope Allah receives them as holy martyrs. They have raised the nation's head high and washed away a great part of the shame that has enveloped us as a result of the weakness of the Saudi government and its complicity with the American government . . . . *Yes, we have instigated and they have responded.* We hope Allah grants their families solace.[13]

Andrew Sullivan notes that the failure of the Clinton administration to grab Bin Laden when they had a chance probably resulted in this tragedy. As mentioned in Chapter Three, Clinton repeatedly turned down offers by the Sudanese to hand over Bin Laden.[14] Finally, Sudan allowed Bin Laden to move to Afghanistan at the administration's request. "Within a month, al-Qaeda struck again in Saudi Arabia, killing 19 American soldiers with a 5,000-pound bomb. Even senior Clinton officials concede that allowing Bin Laden to go free was a massive mistake."[15]

Bill Clinton's response to this horrific attack is important to understanding what happened on September 11. If the United States had acted with speed and determination to deal with these murderers and had shown to the world our willingness to stand up and fight terrorism, things might have been different. Khobar Towers fits into a pattern of attacks starting in 1993 with the first bombing (and attempted destruction) of the Twin Towers, and culminating in the hijacked airline attacks on September 11, 2001. The question is: In the ongoing and escalating war on terror, did the Clinton administration take any appropriate steps to convince terrorists and their state sponsors that they would pay a heavy price and be held accountable for their actions?

What Happened?

In the summer of 2001, a federal grand jury in Alexandria, Virginia, handed down a forty-six-count indictment alleging that terrorists backed by Iran, along with leaders of the Saudi Arabian Hezbollah terrorist group, had been planning the attack for three years.[16] The indictment indicated a great deal of effort and patience was behind the attack. Despite widespread suspicion that Osama bin Laden played a major role, he was not named.[17]

The significance of what happened at Khobar Towers went beyond the attack itself. A few days later, Saudi rulers began receiving threats via fax. "The importance of the faxed letters lay not in their content but in the mere fact that they existed. The private fax numbers were for exclusive use by the uppermost members of the House of al-Saud—they were not even known to, let alone used by, senior officials and other functionaries."[18] This provided a chilling indication of how extensive the terrorist network was, even reaching within Saudi's royal family.

The fact that Iran was involved and that the terrorist network reached into Saudi Arabian society, and even into the ruling regime, put Saudi Arabia in a delicate position. This caused a real problem for the U.S. in its effort to find out what had happened and to strike back at those responsible. "We may never know the full story," writes scholar Michael Ledeen, "for when the Saudis found convincing witnesses, they promptly decapitated them before any American could interrogate them."[19]

The Saudi government did not want to risk further anger from domestic extremists who were sympathetic to Iran's desires. They feared retaliation or that Iran itself might respond. Thus, they were not as cooperative as had been expected. Additionally, the FBI's involvement in the case was sometimes resented as an intrusion, even though the bureau was obligated to try to find out what had happened. All of this obstructed the collection of evidence. Worse, instead of giving the Saudis greater reason to help by pressuring them, the law-enforcement and intelligence communities were told not to offend the Saudis. According to *U.S. News & World Report*, even before the attack, the CIA in Saudi Arabia was instructed not to collect information about Hezbollah for fear of offending Saudi terrorist sympathizers. A former CIA official is quoted as saying, "We willingly put on a blindfold and left ourselves wide open."[20]

Obviously, our policy of blindness cost many American lives. The situation needed to change. The only way we would make significant progress was to put real pressure on the Saudi government to cooperate with the investigation. Pressure needed to be applied directly from the White House, but it never came.

How Clinton Handled It

At the memorial service for the slain servicemen, President Clinton appropriately stated, "America stands with you in your sorrow and your outrage. Your loved ones were taken before their time, felled by the hands of hatred in an act whose savagery is matched only by its cowardice."[21] The president knew better than to give those families and America anything more than an I-feel-your-pain speech. However, the administration made empty promises, nonetheless. The day after the Khobar Towers bombing, Secretary of State Warren Christopher promised, "We will not rest until these terrorists are brought to justice. We will hunt them down."[22] The president was also quite aggressive in his words: "The cowards who committed this murderous act must not go unpunished," said Clinton. "Let me say again: We will pursue this. America takes care of our own. Those who did it must not go unpunished." The following day, en route to an economic summit in France, Clinton had more to say. "Let me be very clear . . . we will not rest in our efforts to find who is responsible for this outrage, to pursue them and to punish them."[23]

But besides talking tough, Clinton's closest advisers urged him to actually *be* tough. His political life depended on it. As Byron York reported, Clinton was running for reelection, and his team was relieved when they found the American people by and large did not blame Clinton for the loss of life. But when TWA Flight 800 blew up in flight over the Atlantic Ocean three weeks later, Americans feared it was another terrorist attack. Though officially it would later be ruled an accident, the public polls showed Clinton's approval rating slipping. The public's view of Clinton's ability to deal with the Khobar Towers bombing tumbled, and they began to question whether Clinton was doing everything possible. Dick Morris, Clinton's political strategist, was worried that Bob Dole would be able to use national security against him in the election campaign.

"We tested two alternative defenses to this attack: Peacemaker or Toughness," Morris wrote in a memo for the president. In the "Peacemaker" defense, Morris asked voters to respond to the statement, "Clinton is peacemaker. Brought together Arabs and Israelis. Ireland.

Bosnia cease-fire. Uses strength to bring about peace." The other defense, "Toughness," asked voters to respond to "Clinton tough. Stands up for American interests. Against foreign companies doing business in Cuba. Sanctions against Iran. Antiterrorist legislation held up by Republicans. Prosecuted World Trade Center bombers." Morris found that the public greatly preferred "Toughness."[24]

But would Clinton really project power? Or would he just use tough rhetoric while sticking with the same failed policies?

A couple of months after the attack, it was reported that there was almost certainly an international conspiracy behind the terrorist assault. On December 2, then–Secretary of Defense William Perry made open statements about retaliation. "The United States will take 'strong action' if there is compelling evidence that Iran or another country was involved in the blast near Dhahran that killed 19 U.S. airmen."[25] Ten days later CNN reported that Saudi Arabia alleged that Iran was involved.[26] Of course, nothing ever happened.

The president promised to accomplish international cooperation at the G7 summit meeting saying, "We expect the allies to walk with us hand in hand."[27] But the president never used his powers as commander-in-chief to penalize or even pressure a state that was involved in killing Americans. Instead, he relegated the issue to the criminal justice system and failed to press the investigation to uncover what had actually happened.

Toughness with Saudi Arabia was essential to get to the bottom of the Khobar Towers investigation. Initially, the Saudis promised to work with the FBI. However, by November 1996, the FBI began pulling many agents out of Saudi Arabia because of a lack of cooperation from Saudi authorities. The White House response was expected. CNN reported, "White House Press Secretary Mike McCurry flatly denied reports of uncooperative Saudi officials, telling reporters that he is working to find out the real reason behind the pullout."[28]

The Saudis had arrested many suspects, some with ties to Iran, including one who they suspected was the driver of the truck. But U.S. officials claimed that the investigation was inconclusive: "We have reached no conclusions about who was responsible for this."[29] Saudi government officials were declaring their own findings but not giving the FBI access to their evidence or the suspects they interrogated. They provided videotapes of some of their interrogations, but that was not sufficient for a U.S. criminal investigation. "FBI Director Louis Freeh has made three trips to Saudi Arabia . . . in an effort to gain better access to evidence for American investigators. The videotape falls short of what the FBI wanted."[30]

The fact is, the president had promised justice, and he needed to make sure his promise was kept. Clinton should have pressured the Saudis. "It's their country, after all," one official pointed out. "FBI jurisdiction overseas is limited by the invitation of the host country."[31] That makes perfect sense for the FBI. But the president could make it clear that they needed an invitation.

The results of this impasse were embarrassing to the FBI. The *Washington Post* was actually able to come up with details from the Saudi investigation that U.S. officials had not yet learned. The newspaper reported from "sources, who are familiar with the Saudi portion of the intensive probe," that the Saudi government had captured the suspected driver of the explosive-laden truck, and he was being held along with forty Saudi Arabians on suspicion of involvement in the plot—some of whom had confessed their guilt.[32]

Obviously, when newspapers report information about an ongoing FBI investigation that the FBI is unaware of, somewhere there is a failure to communicate. As a result, what started as the largest overseas investigation ever conducted by the FBI quickly dwindled. "Immediately after the bombing, more than 70 FBI agents, including bomb and forensic experts, were sent to help—the largest contingent ever sent abroad on one investigation. But by September, their number had dwindled to a handful."[33]

As the *Washington Post* stated, "The investigation was championed by top officials but was also constrained by diplomatic sensitivities as the United States sought to improve relations with Iran and to preserve its ties with Saudi Arabia."[34] This certainly fits the pattern of conflict within the Clinton administration, and Bill Clinton did not weigh in.

This conflict was especially evident in the relationship between President Clinton and his Louis Freeh. The FBI "was furious" at the White House because they had not pressured the Saudis to support the bureau in its necessary job of investigating the Khobar Towers killings. "You wonder why we didn't push the Saudis harder," the *New Yorker* quoted Leslie Gelb of the Council on Foreign Relations as saying. "You wonder why we didn't say to them, 'If you don't turn over the people we need to talk to, we're going to stop supplying you with military equipment.'"[35]

During Clinton's first term, Louis Freeh and the White House became rather alienated from one another. Clinton defenders claim it was opportunism on Freeh's part, because he realized his funding came from a Republican Congress.[36] However, the evidence doesn't point to such a far-fetched explanation. Elsa Walsh reported in the *New Yorker* what everyone knows, that the relationship between Louis Freeh and the Clinton administration went south rather early and never recovered. With the president's attempt in 1993 to involve the FBI in his firing of the travel office staff and Freeh's public opposition to the White House's proposal to cut the bureau's 1995 budget, there was plenty of reason for conflict. Then, Freeh was angered by the 1996 Filegate scandal, during which Republicans attacked the bureau for colluding with the Clinton administration in handing over confidential information on their political opponents to the White House. "The Filegate scandal struck at Freeh's most treasured principle: the independence of the bureau."[37]

Filegate, if you remember, elicited quite a reaction from Freeh, who had been chosen in large part because of his reputation for personal integrity, in hopes that he could rebuild the FBI's reputation. He went on record as accusing the White House of "egregious violations" in their quest for the secret background files of their political enemies and said that the administration had not acted in "good faith and honor." As a result "the FBI and I were victimized."[38]

White House staffers and Democrat operatives loyal to the president would have said virtually anything to destroy Louis Freeh's credibility. His investigation into the Khobar Towers bombing was an embarrassing testimony to the difference between the Clinton administration and the Bush administration before him. Freeh had to ask for the cooperation of George H. W. Bush to get the Saudis to allow his investigation to go forward.

Sandy Berger, Clinton's national security adviser, assured journalist Elsa Walsh that he tried to impress the Saudis with the importance of the FBI's investigation into the Khobar Towers bombing. One especially important meeting occurred when Crown Prince Abdullah came with an entourage to stay in Washington, D.C., for six days and met with both President Clinton and Vice President Gore.

According to Walsh, there are differing reports on both President Clinton's meeting and Vice-President Gore's meeting with the crown prince, though all seem to agree they were watershed moments in the FBI's investigation. Soon afterward, the Saudis began showing the FBI their evidence. One eyewitness, Sandy Berger, claimed that the president brought up the subject with the prince, pleading for families who needed closure. Berger remembered Clinton saying, "Even if they can't always get full justice, they can get the truth." Berger also told Walsh that Clinton "talked about how important it was to the U.S.-Saudi relationship, and that if Americans didn't believe the Saudis were helping the United States in the investigation then the American public would not support the U.S. defending Saudi Arabia." According to Berger, Clinton also reassured the prince that he would not retaliate militarily against Iran without consulting the Saudi government.[39]

But other witnesses tell a different story. According to two who were present, neither Clinton nor Gore showed much interest in the investigation. Clinton's appeal hardly sounded like it meant much to him. "It was along the line of 'Would you be kind enough to continue cooperation?'"[40] Additionally, the president spent more time dwelling on his various legal problems, getting Abdullah's friendly advice on how to deal with the Monica Lewinsky scandal.[41]

The prince had expected tough questions from the president and vice president but left the meeting under the impression that there was no real need for the Saudis to cooperate. "What's going on?" he reportedly asked an associate.[42] Gore never asked any questions about it and only touched on the issue as if it were an incidental matter. A terrorist suspect in the attack was appealing to the Saudis for political asylum. The prince asked Gore some questions about that issue. Otherwise, the investigation of the Khobar Towers bombing was not a major topic of discussion. Thus, the cumulative effect of these lackluster conversations "was to persuade the Crown Prince that the case was no longer of great importance to the United States."[43]

At that point, former President Bush was brought in to help in the war on terror. Freeh realized that the prince did not feel the urgency of the matter, so he went to the former president without asking permission or even informing Bill Clinton. Bush agreed and interceded with Prince Abdullah on Freeh's behalf. "The intercession worked; Bush has been regarded as something of a savior in Saudi Arabia since the Gulf War."[44] This resulted in a meeting between Freeh and the crown prince.

The results were successful for Freeh, bringing his two-and-a-half year struggle to a close. On November 9, 1998, the Saudi government agreed to give the bureau new access to their investigation. FBI officials were allowed to watch and listen through a one-way mirror as Saudi interrogators asked suspects questions the FBI had given them for that purpose. The eight suspects were each asked 212 questions. They confessed to their part in the attack and said that Iran was involved in the attack both by authorizing it and providing for it. "Khassab, the cell member who had been turned over by the Syrians, claimed that he had met directly with Ahmad Sherifi, the Iranian Revolutionary Guard official who had selected the Khobar barracks as a target, and that Sherifi always announced that he was acting at the behest of Ayatollah Khamenei."[45] In addition to the information from these interrogations, the FBI also received samples from all the physical evidence the Saudis had collected and transcripts from other interrogations.[46]

If it hadn't been for Freeh's initiative apart from President Clinton, and for the proactive work of former President Bush, the United States would not have received that level of access to the evidence and witness testimony. However, the roadblocks to getting something done about the Khobar Towers investigation did not end there. There are, predictably, contradictory accounts of who was responsible for the ongoing record of inaction. The Congressional inquiry into the September 11 attacks gives us one example of this:

> Regarding Saudi Arabia, former FBI Director Louis Freeh testified that, following the 1996 Khobar Towers bombing, the FBI "was able to forge an effective working relationship with the Saudi police and Interior Ministry." A considerable amount of personal effort by Director Freeh helped to secure what he described as "unprecedented and invaluable" assistance in the Khobar Towers bombing investigation from the Saudi

Ambassador to the United States and the Saudi Interior Minister. By contrast, the Committees heard testimony from U.S. Government personnel that Saudi officials had been uncooperative and often did not act on information implicating Saudi nationals.[47]

One major difference of opinion exists as to what happened after Freeh got his information from Saudi Arabia's interrogation of their prisoners. According to the *New Yorker*, Freeh went to see Sandy Berger with the reports to show him that there might be enough evidence to indict some of the perpetrators. Admittedly, he had a tough road ahead because the idea that the U.S. government could take testimony in another country and present it to a grand jury "was a novel legal concept."[48] Freeh stated he was researching that possibility. Another hurdle was the fact that the Saudi government had not agreed to this use of the evidence collected. As Freeh tried to relate all this, Berger demanded to know who else had this information. Freeh was caught by surprise by this line of questioning and assured the national security adviser that not many had access to the information.[49] Berger didn't seem to want to accept the possibility of any legally provable connection between Iran and Khobar Towers.

"That's just hearsay," Berger said.

"No, Sandy," Freeh replied. "It's testimony of a co-conspirator in furtherance of a conspiracy."[50]

In response to this skepticism, Freeh eventually decided that the administration was more interested with how things were perceived by the press rather than real national security issues. He came to the conclusion that the White House was not really interested in dealing with the terrorists behind the Khobar Towers bombing.[51]

Sandy Berger, as one would expect, tells a quite different story. He made it clear to Elsa Walsh that he held to an entirely different opinion about the meeting. His question about who else knew of Freeh's plan was not an attack but simply proper caution: "I didn't want to see this in the *Washington Post* before I had a chance to talk to the president about it. I thought it was a fair question."[52]

Berger also defended his inquiry into possible leaks. He believed it was his job to allow the president to make decisions with as little pressure as possible, pressure that would be felt if others knew about the FBI's evidence regarding Iran's involvement. He also defended his concern that the FBI could quite possibly leak information, pointing out that it had done so in the past. As an example he mentioned that someone in the bureau had accidentally sent out a mass mailing to hundreds of government employees that contained classified information on the Khobar Towers investigation, including interview transcripts.[53]

Berger also defended his concern that the suspects' statements were "hearsay," because the suspects spoke primarily of meetings in which they had not personally participated. He told Walsh, "I asked Louis whether what he had was hearsay. 'Can you use it in a courtroom?' . . . I wanted to know how we could use it" in court to indict terrorists.[54] He did not realize that Freeh was upset by their meeting.

But wherever the truth lies, plainly, they were increasingly at odds with each other. Two Saudis told Walsh that they "concluded that the relationship between the administration and Freeh had completely deteriorated. Whenever Freeh's name came up, they noticed that Berger's body language signaled discomfort."[55]

The fact remains: Of fourteen defendants eventually indicted, eleven are in Saudi Arabia and three are in hiding.[56] Despite Warren Christopher's promise, or that of President Clinton himself, the administration never got around to indicting anyone. The second Bush administration was saddled with the task of actually making the indictments, and they had to rush to beat the five-year statute of limitations attached to conspiracy charges. However, despite the fanfare of the indictment,[57] an official in the U.S. Attorney's Office for the Eastern District of Virginia said shortly before the September 11 attacks, "Nothing has happened," and it was doubtful anything would.[58] Indictments looked good on paper, but actually prosecuting and punishing terrorists requires finding them first.

What Did Law Enforcement Actually Accomplish?

We have to ask if these complex criminal investigations, including the hard work of former President Bush and the current Bush administration, really accomplish anything worthwhile—justice for the victims or security for the nation.

When Freeh finally got the indictment, Attorney General John Ashcroft hailed it "as an important milestone toward justice in a case that has long frustrated U.S. authorities and has served as a symbol of U.S. vulnerability to terrorism."[59] He proclaimed, "The indictment filed today means that next week's five-year anniversary of this tragedy will come with some assurance to victim family members and to the wounded that they are not and will not be forgotten."[60]

The basic question is one we have already raised: Why is our criminal justice system being used to deal with foreign attacks that are really acts of war? Remember, the indictment mentioned involvement of Iranian officials. It didn't actually include charges against any of them. This may have contributed to the belief inside Iran that they could get away with killing Americans.

Those in the criminal justice system who pushed for an indictment are to be praised for their dedication, but the basic policy question remains: Is this the right way to fight terrorism? Those prisoners in Saudi Arabia were never extradited. Despite whatever so-called Saudi cooperation Freeh may have secured, there remains no extradition treaty between our countries. Siobhan Roth in the *Legal Times* writes of the prisoners:

> Among them is Hani al-Sayegh, who was arrested in Canada in 1997 and then paroled into U.S. custody via Dulles International Airport. Al-Sayegh, the only one of the defendants who has come into U.S. custody, was thought to be the government's best chance. He is alleged to be a prominent member of Saudi Hezbollah, active in recruiting new members, and with close ties to the Iranian government. But negotiations for a plea agreement between al-Sayegh and U.S. prosecutors fell apart. The United States handed him over to Saudi authorities in October 1999.[61]

Allegedly, al-Sayegh drove a car that scouted ahead of the truck and then gave a signal for the driver to go ahead with his mission.[62] The charges brought against him were not for his involvement in the Khobar Towers bombing, but rather for a separate plot to kill Americans in Saudi Arabia. With U.S. charges dropped, al-Sayegh could be deported to Saudi Arabia, something he resisted because he claimed he would be tortured and executed. If he was indeed the lookout driver, then one irony of this tragedy is that the U.S. government intervened and got promises from Saudi Arabia before deporting him that he wouldn't be mistreated.[63]

Prior to bringing him to the U.S. from Canada, the FBI interrogated al-Sayegh for twenty-five hours and obtained his promise to assist them in the investigation. Once in the U.S., al-Sayegh reneged on his agreement. Since the FBI could get no evidence from Saudi Arabia to convict him, the government could not bring him to trial. He was simply sent back to Saudi Arabia. This is as close as we ever got to actually holding anyone accountable for the bombing of the Khobar Towers.

The fact is, locating a suspect in Saudi Arabia is relatively easy compared to other countries where terrorists hide out—places in which the criminal justice system has even less chance of finding then, let alone sending them to the United States to stand trial. As Siobhan Roth reports,

> Members of terrorist organizations "typically hang out in no-man's lands like the Western part of Lebanon or Afghanistan," says William Barr, attorney general under former President George Bush and now general counsel at Verizon. Others may find refuge among sympathizers in Yemen or the Sudan, countries that don't have what Montclair, NJ, defense attorney David Ruhnke terms a "let's go get 'em" approach to law enforcement.[64]

Another serious failure is the way political considerations delayed and perhaps warped the indictment itself. Louis Freeh and his FBI team had to do some hard work to get things done before the statute of limitations ran out. Unfortunately, he was up against a culture in the White House that wanted to treat Iran with deference. According to *U.S. News & World Report*, the press announcement of the indictment was quite revealing. "Elements of the Iranian government inspired, supported, and supervised the terrorists behind the act," Attorney General Ashcroft announced.[65] When asked why Iranians were not specifically indicted, Louis Freeh pointed out that Iran was mentioned thirty-five times in the indictment, and he emphasized that new defendants could be named as the investigation continued.[66] "If officials were being cautious, it was understandable; the case long has been a political minefield. Eager to engage Iranian moderates, Clinton administration officials were lukewarm in pursuing the case."[67]

The previous March, Freeh had moved the case to the U.S. attorney's office in eastern Virginia, because he felt that Washington, D.C., prosecutors were not really interested in producing indictments. Thus, prosecutors were rushed in order to beat the five-year statute of limitations. The indictments were announced the same week that time would have run out on "key murder and conspiracy charges."[68]

Freeh found a much more favorable attitude in the Bush administration. As the *Washington Post* reported when the indictment was made:

Behind the scenes, Freeh had feuded with Attorney General Janet Reno and other Clinton administration officials over prosecution strategy. Earlier this year, after Ashcroft was named attorney general, Freeh moved the case from the U.S. attorney's office in Washington to the federal prosecutor's office in Richmond. After praising the Bush administration and Ashcroft yesterday, Freeh declined to comment on the previous administration's handling of the case. "I'm leaving very satisfied and very pleased," he said.[69]

No doubt Freeh *was* pleased to finally get an indictment before leaving office. He had struggled for years to get this accomplished and had faced opposition in his quest to find justice for the victims and their families. But from a national security standpoint, how helpful was it to bring an unenforceable indictment five years after the fact? What terrorist organization is going to be deterred from striking at the United States again when they see how ineffectually President Clinton dealt with such an attack?

In reporting on the story, the *Washington Post* described the indictment: "For the moment, it is largely symbolic because the United States does not have custody of any of the defendants and even deported one of them to Saudi Arabia two years ago."[70] Now that we are on the other side of September 11, that certainly seems like a more realistic assessment than the naïve statements coming from the military:

The charges were hailed by officials in the military, which tightened security at all overseas bases in the wake of the attack. "The Air Force lost 19 dedicated airmen, in addition to hundreds who where wounded in this cowardly attack by terrorists," said Gen. Mike Ryan, Air Force chief of staff. "These indictments send the message to all terrorists that they will be hunted down and will pay for their crimes."[71]

Without the ability to actually hunt down and kill terrorists, the indictments could hardly be considered a matter of substance. David Horowitz summarized the issue succinctly: "The White House response was limp, and the case (in the words of FBI director Louis B. Freeh) 'remains unresolved.'"[72] Freeh's description is still true today, despite his success in getting an indictment. Because of Clinton's inaction, the late indictments became a symbol of the United States' impotence.

Clinton and his administration promised the relatives of victims and the U.S. public that they would deal with the terrorists behind the Khobar Towers bombing. But did the president ever intend to produce the "expansive, unmistakable, and unwavering" response to the terrorists "across all levels of the United States government"?

Instead, Clinton fought terrorism with rhetoric and, for the most part, took no action to bring about justice for the nineteen victims of the Khobar Towers attack. Andrew Sullivan sums up the administration's response rather well: "Clinton did little that was effective. The 1996 antiterrorism bill, while modestly helpful, was focused on domestic terrorism after Oklahoma City and was still reactive, not proactive."[73] The main provisions, such as a death penalty for terrorists and chemical tags for tracing explosives, were simply not sufficient for dealing with Al Qaeda. But Clinton did not face any pressure to make him take real action. "Clinton had such a commanding lead over Bob Dole that the difficulties of corralling Congress, browbeating the bureaucracy, or mounting a sustained military campaign against terrorism didn't seem worth the effort."[74] So even though he knew more drastic measures would have been politically popular, he simply didn't bother.

According to Sullivan, Clinton substituted real leadership in the war on terror with a transfer of responsibility to the vice president. He had Al Gore chair a commission on airline safety and security. When the commission came out in February of 1997 with proposals such as federalizing the airline gate security and implementing computer screening that would allow airlines to check for known potential terrorists, nothing was done about its recommendations. Sullivan points out that "simple computer checks could have exposed two of the terrorists who boarded American Airlines flights under their own names on September 11."[75]

The Clinton administration's treatment of the attack on Khobar Towers as a law-enforcement issue rather than an act of war is Bill Clinton's legacy of inaction and poor leadership. The overwhelming evidence shows that the administration did not push the FBI investigation to the center, claiming they lacked information. All the while, nothing was being done to pressure Saudi Arabia to cooperate with the FBI. Bill Clinton failed to lead in all aspects of the case. "Saudi investigators have given the United States evidence of alleged Iranian involvement in a deadly terrorist bombing of a U.S. military housing complex in Saudi Arabia," CNN reported six months after the attacks. "But U.S. officials have not yet concluded who was behind the incident, and the White House says President Clinton has made no decision about any possible U.S. retaliation."[76]

There is no record, of course, of Clinton deciding against retaliation. President Clinton never made a decision since that would have left him open to criticism. He simply ignored the issue until the public's memory faded and his promises were forgotten.

EMBASSY BOMBINGS

Clinton's Third Strike

ON AUGUST 7, 1998, TERRORISTS EXPLODED BOMBS OUTSIDE TWO U.S. embassies in Africa, approximately 450 miles apart.[1] The attacks occurred almost simultaneously in Nairobi, Kenya, and Dar-es-Salaam, Tanzania, at about 10:45 A.M. local time.[2]

Eleven U.S. citizens died in the two explosions.[3] The total death count reached 224, and over five thousand more were wounded.[4] Within days of the attacks, the Department of Defense sent or scheduled fourteen special flights to both countries with over a hundred security personnel, thirty-six medics, and sixty firefighters from Fairfax County, Virginia, as well as 360 units of blood and 150,000 pounds of medical equipment.[5]

Promises, Promises

President Clinton's secretary of state, Madeleine Albright, was in Rome for the wedding of her spokesman. In a press statement she declared, "Let me assure the American people . . . that if, as seems probable, these attacks are confirmed to have been terrorist in nature, the United States will spare no effort and use all means at our disposal to track down and punish the perpetrators of these outrageous acts."[6] President Clinton himself promised from the Rose Garden to do whatever was necessary to deliver justice to the perpetrators: "These acts of terrorist violence are abhorrent; they are inhuman. We will use all the means at our disposal to bring those responsible to justice, no matter what or how long it takes."[7] Vice President Al Gore echoed Clinton's statement, saying, "Let no one doubt that the United States will do whatever is necessary to pursue the perpetrators of this evil and cowardly act, and bring them to justice."[8]

Speaker of the House Newt Gingrich reacted similarly, though he also commented on our need to improve our intelligence-gathering capabilities. "We should do everything we can to track down the people who've done this and to make them pay to the fullest extent," he said. "This should be a reminder to all of us that it is a dangerous world as we enter the twenty-first century. We need much better human intelligence, much more sophisticated efforts to go after terrorists and others."[9]

Gingrich's statement was perceptive, since it mentioned holding those responsible accountable, and also focused on how the United States could actually find the terrorists and take steps to ensure our intelligence services provide protection from further attacks.

Clinton Strikes

President Clinton did make an attempt to strike back at the terrorists and show the world that the United States could not be attacked with impunity. On August 20, less than two weeks after the attacks on our embassies, the president announced from Martha's Vineyard, Massachusetts, "Today I ordered our Armed Forces to strike at terrorist-related facilities in Afghanistan and Sudan because of the threat they present to our national security."[10] He made it clear that the missile strikes were first and foremost reprisals for the attacks on the embassies.[11]

The strikes were initially perceived as a great improvement over his past reactions to terrorism. The president was not relying on the Justice Department to prosecute this as a matter of criminal law. Clinton was treating Al Qaeda as an enemy that had attacked our nation and using his powers as commander-in-chief to deal with them. Republicans were among the first to praise the response. Newt Gingrich spoke for many when he said Clinton "did exactly the right thing," and that he hoped the administration would do whatever else was necessary "to ensure that . . . our interests remain secure."[12]

Plenty of other Republicans spoke out as well. Senator Jesse Helms said,

"I, for one, am exceedingly proud of the U.S. military for their valor. . . . Sooner or later, terrorists around the world will realize that America's differences end at the water's edge, and that the United States' political leadership always has, and always will, stand united in the face of international terrorism."[13] Republican New York Senator Alfonse D'Amato called the action "bold and appropriate." The House majority leader, Texas Republican Dick Armey, also supported the missile strikes: "The United States has an absolute duty to attack terrorism where it lives and breeds, in order to prevent future attacks on American citizens around the world. The American people stand united in the face of terrorism. The men and women who undertook this mission deserve our praise and prayers."

Steven Forbes, who ran for the Republican presidential nomination in 1996, even compared Clinton to Reagan: "This is also a reminder of how important it is that we keep our intelligence and military capabilities strong and vigilant. President Reagan had it right: terrorists can run, but they cannot hide. Hopefully, this action marks the return to that sound approach."[14]

Clinton's Follow-Through

The embattled president could have followed the advice of Speaker Gingrich and others and taken further action to protect our interests since he had stated, "Terrorists must have no doubt that, in the face of their threats, America will protect its citizens and will continue to lead the world's fight for peace, freedom and security."[15] Additionally, a CNN/Gallup poll found that not only did 75 percent of the American people favor Clinton's decision to order missile strikes in Sudan and Afghanistan, but three-quarters of Americans approved of future attacks. Sixty-five percent even favored the future use of ground troops.[16] The time was right, given Clinton's own rhetoric, for a return to the "sound approach" to terrorism of Ronald Reagan.

Clinton understood that responding to terrorism and deterring future attacks required the use of force. Striking back and showing terrorists that they could not kill Americans and get away with it would be an essential part of any war against terrorism. Striking back aggressively and accurately would be essential. It was widely acknowledged that there was virtually no amount of additional security that would keep potential targets safe from terrorism.[17]

"You can't guarantee physical security anywhere on earth for anybody," former FBI agent Rosemary Dew was quoted as saying. "Guarantee is a very strong word. You can strengthen it, and we could do better, but . . ."[18] Our embassies were tempting targets, and Clinton knew that increased security was not enough.

Clinton Strikes Out

The president assured Americans that the initial targets had been carefully chosen so as to do the most damage to Al Qaeda. "Our forces targeted one of the most active terrorist bases in the world," Clinton said when he announced the simultaneous strikes in Sudan and Afghanistan. Referring to the "terrorist facilities and infrastructure" in Afghanistan, he promised, that we were attacking "one of the most active terrorist bases in the world" where "key elements of the Bin Laden network's infrastructure" were held and where thousands of terrorists had trained from all over the world. In Sudan, we attacked a factory "associated with the Bin Laden network" that was "involved in the production of materials for chemical weapons."[19]

Then the president spelled out the sort of attitudes and sacrifices that were necessary to win the war against terror.

> My fellow Americans, our battle against terrorism did not begin with the bombing of our embassies in Africa, nor will it end with today's strike. It will require strength, courage and endurance. We will not yield to this threat. We will meet it no matter how long it may take. This will be a long, ongoing struggle between freedom and fanaticism, between the rule of law and terrorism. We must be prepared to do all that we can for as long as we must. America is and will remain a target of terrorists precisely because we are leaders; because we act to advance peace, democracy and basic human values; because we're the most open society on earth; and because, as we have shown yet again, we take an uncompromising stand against terrorism.
>
> But of this I am also sure; the risks from inaction to America and the world would be far greater than action, for that would embolden our enemies, leaving their ability and their willingness to strike us intact.[20]

The missile strikes were not even remotely successful.

As later admitted by Defense Secretary William Cohen, Sudan should never have been targeted. The targeted factory was not a chemical weapons productions facility, as initially announced by the administration. Nor was it ever shown to have a connection with Bin Laden's terror network.

Besides the misidentified target, the strike on Sudan came close to driving a country *toward* terrorism rather than away from it. Prior to the missile strike, Sudan actively and repeatedly tried to reach out to the administration and offered unconditional help to the United States in tracking and capturing Osama bin Laden. When we asked the Sudanese government to expel Bin Laden from their country, they immediately complied. Sudan had previously extradited another well-known terrorist, Carlos the Jackal, to France. In other words, Sudan was an ally in the war against terror. If we had a problem with Sudan, we had other ways of dealing with them. Decorated ex-CIA officer Milt Bearden, who was station chief in Sudan, told journalist Christopher Hitchens:

Having spent 30 years in the CIA, being familiar with soil and environmental sampling across a number of countries, I cannot imagine a single sample, collected by third-country nationals and especially by third-country nationals whose country has a common border, serving as a pretext for an act of war against a sovereign state with which we have both diplomatic relations and functioning back channels.[21]

When you consider that the local informant who was later fired was almost certainly Egyptian, a country that has reason to portray Sudan in a bad light, the whole rationale for an attack without warning against the plant makes no sense.

The target in Afghanistan was also ill-planned. The missile strikes were supposedly aimed at a gathering of Osama bin Laden and many other important people in his organization. Somehow, the missiles managed to miss every single one of the suspects. Instead, they killed Pakistani intelligence officers who were equipping Kashmir guerrillas. Pakistani leaders were so outraged, they released two suspects they had arrested in connection with the bombing of the embassies.[22]

The administration claimed a victory in attacking Al Qaeda's "infra-structure." Milt Bearden responded to that story by asking, "What 'infra-structure'? They knocked over a lean-to? If the administration had any-thing—anything at all—the high-resolution satellite images would have been released by now."[23]

The bottom line is, the strike did little if anything to advance the war on terror. It proved to Bin Laden and his Al Qaeda leadership that they could kill at will.

Most significantly, the president never attempted to strike back at Osama bin Laden again. Instead, his one attempt at hurting Al Qaeda amounted to little more than an empty gesture, a lesson to terrorists that the United States was incompetent in dealing with them and they could strike without fear of any real retribution.

Wag the Dog?

Despite a great deal of public and Republican leadership support for the strikes, some questioned President Clinton's motives right from the start. Pennsylvania Republican Senator Arlen Specter and Indiana Republican Senator Dan Coats thought that the attacks might have been motivated by a need to distract attention from the Monica Lewinsky scandal. In addition to what they thought was suspicious timing, they were miffed that some members of Congress were not briefed on the strikes until after the missiles were launched. White House officials immediately denounced the accusa-tions. Defense Secretary William Cohen insisted that the "only motivation driving this action today was our absolute obligation to protect the American people from terrorist activities. That is the sole motivation."[24] These suspi-cions gained credibility with revelations that the attacks were ill-conceived.

Regardless of whether President Clinton timed the attacks for personal benefit, that was their effect. As the Media Research Center noted, the attacks kept the news media focused on international problems rather than his domestic scandals:

President Clinton's decision to launch a bombing strike at terrorists con-sumed the entirety of CNN's 8pm ET news show and nearly all of the

ABC, CBS, FNC and NBC newscasts Thursday night, thus nearly elim-
inating Monica Lewinsky news. CNN skipped Lewinsky's second
appearance before the grand jury while the other networks managed to
squeeze in a story near the end of their shows.[25]

Whatever the merits of the "wag the dog" accusation, one Clinton administration defender unquestionably used the strikes to defend the president's
behavior. The reason that the president refused to apologize for his behavior,
insisted George Stephanopoulos on ABC, was that "he was afraid of projecting weakness" to the terrorists.[26]

The Iraq Attack Factor

Suspicion that the August missile strikes were designed "to distract from
his own impeachment woes" was greatly enhanced by a new series of missile attacks in December. This time, Al Qaeda was not even mentioned.
They were forgotten. Instead, a surprise missile attack was launched on
Iraq.

Saddam Hussein continued to violate his agreement to allow UN
inspectors to confirm that he was not developing or storing weapons of
mass destruction, so technically the attack was justified. The timing, however, was clearly questionable. Hussein's defiance had been apparent for
many months, but Clinton showed no interest in doing anything about it.
Now, suddenly, missiles were launched on the heels of the House impeachment vote.

The story even goes further than that. Clinton's official reason for the
timing of the attack was a report handed in by UN weapons inspectors.
Curiously, the *Washington Post* reported a less than unbiased relationship
between the White House and weapons inspector Richard Butler. The *Post*
story claimed that two days before the bombing, "Clinton administration
officials played a direct role in shaping Butler's text during multiple conversations with him at secure facilities in the U.S. mission to the UN."[27] A few
days later, the *Washington Times* reported that former UN inspector Scott
Ritter claimed that the UN Special Commission team leader Richard Butler
intentionally provoked Iraqi defiance at the behest of the White House.[28] As

in the *Post* story, he also claimed that the Clinton administration had ensured that the language of the report would justify their missile strikes by working with Butler on the actual text of the report before it was submitted. "I'm telling you this was a preordained conclusion. This inspection was a total setup by the United States," Ritter said. "The U.S. was pressing [the UN] to carry out this test. The test was very provocative. They were designed to elicit Iraqi defiance."[29]

Naturally, Butler and the White House denied Ritter's accusations. The administration claimed the report was the factor that triggered Clinton's order. But the facts simply don't line up. When Cohen was asked if he had any advance warning about the content of the UN report before it was released, he said, "No. There was some speculation about what it might contain. And frankly, we had assumed that it might be mixed. We didn't know."[30] But on the Sunday before the attacks, two days before the inspection report was submitted, sources in the armed forces said that the White House notified the Pentagon that air strikes would begin that week. By coincidence, this was the same day that Mr. Butler ordered an end to UN inspections.

The administration attempted to rectify the discrepancy:

> Pentagon officials, rebutting an impeachment motive, said Thursday that Mr. Cohen and the Joint Chiefs of Staff had been looking for another opportunity to strike since mid-November, when Mr. Clinton called off a planned attack after Saddam pledged to cooperate with the UN inspectors. They said they wanted to take action before the month-long Islamic holiday Ramadan began this weekend and they grew tired of seeing badly needed budget dollars drained by on-and-off military buildups in the Gulf.[31]

The Ramadan excuse didn't work either. The bombing of Iraq continued until the nineteenth of December, the beginning of the Ramadan holiday.[32] In fact, it continued as long as Congress was holding impeachment hearings and, coincidentally, ended only a few hours after the last impeachment vote.

The timing and the accusations of massaging the report made the entire endeavor look suspicious. These factors also played into the hands of Saddam Hussein, whose overthrow was the stated U.S. policy since the first Gulf War. According to reporter Christopher Hitchens, "In February 1998, faced with a threatened bombing attack that never came, Iraqi state TV prophylactically played a pirated copy of *Wag the Dog* in prime time."[33]

Whether or not the president deliberately provoked a military conflict to draw attention away from his impeachment problems, Clinton's defenders in the House of Representatives did not hesitate to use the questionable military action in order to pressure his opponents. "We're concerned, obviously, because we don't believe we should be here today while our men and women are fighting abroad," Democrat minority whip David Bonior of Massachusetts lectured, "and we have expressed that in the first motion of the day with respect to adjournment. We don't believe this is a proper time to be debating removing the commander in chief while thousands of men and women are fighting abroad."[34]

Bonior's statement helps substantiate Hitchens's contention that "[d]uring the debate, the House Democratic leadership took the position, openly encouraged by the White House, that a president should not be embarrassed at home while American troops were 'in harm's way' abroad."[35]

There was still further reason the timing looked suspicious. Hitchens also points out that, from the standpoint of rational policy, the attacks on Iraq should have occurred the previous month:

> By November 14, 1998, Saddam Hussein had exhausted everybody's patience by his limitless arrogance over inspections of weapon sites, and by his capricious treatment of the United Nations Special Commission (UNSCOM) inspectorate. In a rare show of Security Council solidarity, Russia, China, and France withdrew criticism of a punitive strike. The Republican leadership in both houses of Congress, which had criticized the Clinton administration for inaction, was ready to rock 'n' roll with Iraq. The case had been made, and the warplanes were already in the air when the president called them back. No commander in chief has ever done this before. Various explanations were offered as to why Clinton, and his close political crony Sandy Berger, had made such a . . . decision. It was clearly understood that the swing vote had been the president's,

and that Madeleine Albright and William Cohen had argued the other way.[36]

Why did Clinton cancel the attacks? What was he thinking? "But now we understand what in November was a mystery," writes Hitchens. "A much less questionable air strike was canceled because, at that time, Clinton needed to keep an 'option' in his breast pocket."[37]

Another curious question about Operation Desert Fox is why the bombing ended when it did. The administration had already undercut its rationale for launching the attack by extending the campaign into Ramadan. Why not continue the attacks until Hussein was defeated, or at least cooperative? Said Cohen at a Department of Defense news briefing given the evening of the day the attacks ended,

> [W]e were pursuing clear military goals. And as President Clinton has announced, we've achieved those goals. We've degraded Saddam Hussein's ability to deliver chemical, biological and nuclear weapons. We've diminished his ability to wage war against his neighbors. Our forces attacked about 100 targets over four nights, following a plan that was developed and had been developed and refined over the past year. We concentrated on military targets and we worked very hard to keep civilian casualties as low as possible. Our goal was to weaken Iraq's military power, not to hurt Iraq's people.[38]

It is unclear from this statement if this was a four-day plan, or if the one hundred targets were part of that plan. The "clear military goals" represented here were to have "degraded Saddam Hussein's ability to deliver chemical, biological and nuclear weapons" and "diminished his ability to wage war against his neighbors." But those are hardly clear goals. Virtually any amount of damage, either from one day of attacks or ten, from hitting a hundred targets or a thousand, could be said to degrade Saddam's capabilities. As Hitchens put it, "We were incessantly told that Iraq's capacities were being 'degraded.' This is not much of a target to set oneself, and it also leads to facile claims of success, since every bomb that falls has by definition a 'degrading' effect on the system or the society."[39]

Hitchens and others may be wrong. Not all of Clinton's opponents share the view that Clinton timed the attacks on Iraq for his own political benefit. California Republican Congressman Tom Campbell articulated the feelings of many during the impeachment debate:

> I cannot trust him again. Today, we are engaged in war in the Persian Gulf. I was assured by Secretary Cohen and by the director of our Central Intelligence Agency that the timing was justified. Those are honorable men. And because of their testimony, I believe the timing was justified. But I do not believe it was justified because of what President Clinton has said, because I can no longer believe him.[40]

International Fallout

Regardless of Clinton's actual motives, timing the attack on Iraq to coincide with the House impeachment debate and vote undermined America's credibility in the international community. Following the strike, Russia, which supported the aborted strike scheduled for Iraq in November, withdrew its ambassador from Washington, D.C., in protest.[41] Russia's UN ambassador, Sergey Lavrov, called for chief weapons inspector Richard Butler to resign.

Reportedly, China's UN Ambassador Qin Huasen, was "visibly angry" when he came from the UN Security Council meeting, having learned for the first time that the U.S. claimed Chinese support for the December attack. "There is absolutely no excuse or pretext to use force against Iraq," he declared.[42] While France did not condemn the attacks, it is reported to have distanced itself from them.[43]

While there is question whether or not Saddam Hussein was cooperating with inspections before Operation Desert Fox, there is no question that he refused to do so immediately afterward. Saddam continued to cripple the weapons inspection system. Further, as the *Washington Post* reported, the UN Security Council tried to help Saddam:

> After bombarding Iraq for four nights in the name of United Nations arms inspectors, the Clinton administration began fighting a rear guard battle at

the world body yesterday to save the inspectors from diplomatic extinction. Three of five permanent members of the Security Council—Russia, France and China—have now called for swiftly lifting the eight-year oil embargo against Iraq, recasting or disbanding the UN Special Commission and firing its executive chairman, Richard Butler. At the commission, known as UNSCOM, a strong sense of the end of an era prevailed.[44]

Far from building an international coalition, Clinton's unilateral action fractured the international community and jeopardized the inspection system that he claimed he was fighting to protect.

Not many in the Middle East considered the missile strike against Iraq to be a justifiable action for their benefit. Israeli Prime Minister Benjamin Netanyahu refused to publicly endorse the strikes, saying only that "Israel is outside the dispute, and, in any case, will take care of defending itself if the need arises."[45]

According to the *Washington Post*, among our Islamic allies, public reaction "ranged from begrudging, indirect endorsements to outright condemnation of the attacks."[46] To many, the attacks were seen as strengthening rather than weakening Saddam Hussein. "Fearing that Operation Desert Fox could inflame opinion in the streets without ever toppling Iraqi President Saddam Hussein—their private wish—the conservative Gulf States were deeply conflicted about the aerial bombardment of Iraq."[47] In Kuwait there were also misgivings about what had happened. "The operation did not have a very clear goal," said the deputy speaker of the Kuwaiti parliament, Talal Ayyar. "If the aim was to topple Saddam, then there would have been complete support from the Gulf States. A limited operation only strengthens Saddam."[48] In general, the Arab media was certain that this attack was all about Monica Lewinsky.

The punitive strikes had no deterrent value on Saddam Hussein. One of the stated reasons for the mission against Iraq was "sending a message." As Clinton said in explaining his order to strike, "At the same time, we are delivering a powerful message to Saddam. If you act recklessly, you will pay a heavy price."[49] From the Iraqi viewpoint, the missiles were not about anything that Hussein did, but simply an extension of the president's Monica Lewinsky scandal.

Reinterpreting the Attack on Sudan and Afghanistan

With the Iraq missile strikes, observers began to openly ask the question murmured behind the scenes following similar strikes: Is this attack simply a way of diverting attention away from the domestic political situation? Bruce Sullivan, writing for the Conservative News Service, noted the shift in opinion. Before, only unofficial sources had questioned the president, but now "[e]ven Senate majority leader Trent Lott (R-Mississippi) publicly questioned the president's motives. 'Both the timing and the motive are subject to question,' he said."[50]

Others continued to question the president's motives as well. As the *Washington Times* editorialized the day after the attacks on Iraq commenced, "If yesterday's American airstrike on Iraq was not the act of a desperate man, it indisputably looked like one."[51] It was simply too much, they said, to believe that on the eve of the day on which the House would vote on his impeachment, the president just happened to call for an assault on Iraq. Even if the attack was justified, the fact that the president did not choose a different time and that he could not help but raise suspicions by ordering the attack, proved both "personal recklessness," and a loss of the ability to lead the country.[52]

For the editors of the *Washington Times,* the latest missile attacks put a new perspective on the various strikes launched against Sudan and Afghanistan. "What makes Mr. Clinton's action particularly appalling is that it fits a pattern we have come to recognize over the past year, known in popular short-hand as the 'wag the dog' scenario." This was the second time in the year that Clinton had ordered an assault on Iraq; the first had been ordered on the day that the Lewinsky scandal headlined the news, January 22, 1998. Then in August, the president launched his ineffectual attacks on Sudan and Afghanistan after an ill-received televised apology for the Lewinsky scandal on August 17. It was not perceived as very apologetic and soon thereafter, the missile attacks commenced. Then, "In November, as impeachment hearings geared up in the House of Representatives, the president began another build-up against Saddam, which culminated in the charade of November 11, when the president called back U.S. planes already in the air." Supposedly, this recall was due to a promise of compliance, but the

Clinton administration had warned Iraq to make the promises, only to find a later pretext to resume the attacks when the impeachment vote was about to actually take place.[53]

If this was the suspicion of many in America, imagine what our foreign enemies would believe! Looking back to the missiles launched against Sudan and Afghanistan the previous May, it is quite understandable that Osama bin Laden and Al Qaeda leadership and sympathizers would not have taken the U.S. seriously. The attacks were unsuccessful militarily and suspiciously timed to the Monica Lewinsky scandal. When the political heat was off, there were no further missile strikes. Bill Clinton caused Al Qaeda no harm and bolstered their belief that they were impervious to attack. They had every reason to pursue more opportunities to attack United States interests in the future. The only time Bin Laden needed to worry was when the president required a distraction from his domestic scandals. But even then, the terror masters knew the action would be badly aimed and quite short-lived.

Criminal Justice Takes on Terrorism

Having failed militarily, the Clinton administration continued to pursue the terrorists through the immensely slow, inefficient, and mostly unsuccessful route of the criminal justice system.

As in the case of the Khobar Towers, criminal charges were pursued against the perpetrators of the embassy bombings; only this time indictments were made quickly, while the case of Khobar Towers attacks languished. On November 7, 1998, not quite three months after the attacks, Osama bin Laden and several associates were indicted in Manhattan federal court. The 238-count indictment went beyond the bombing of the embassies, charging that Osama bin Laden, Muhammad Atef, Wadih el Hage, Fazul Abdullah Mohammed Sadeek Odeh, Mohamed Rashed Daoud al'Owhali, and other members of Al Qaeda conspired to murder Americans. Among the targets were members of the U.S. military stationed in Saudi Arabia following the Gulf War and in Somalia as part of UN Operation Restore Hope, as well as those employed at American embassies in Kenya and Tanzania. "They established front companies, provided false identity and travel documents, and provided false information to authorities in various countries."[54]

Mary Jo White, the U.S. attorney in New York City, and Lewis Schiliro, assistant director of the FBI office in New York, were at the press conference that announced the indictments. Once again promises were made. This time, since military options were off the table and the people involved were part of the FBI and the U.S. Attorney's Office, they were promises from the criminal justice system. One FBI official, for example, promised, "We will identify, locate, and prosecute all those responsible right up the line from those who constructed and delivered the bombs to those who paid for them and ordered it done."[55]

Ms. White declared, "It is up to the authorities of the world to respond vigorously and relentlessly to such terrorist attacks."[56] Yet, instead of Osama bin Laden being captured, extradited, and tried for his crimes, the future held the bombing of the U.S.S. *Cole*, followed a year later by the attacks of September 11. The simple fact is that Bill Clinton was the one authority in the world who had *not* responded "vigorously" or "relentlessly" to the terrorist attack. He had ordered notoriously unsuccessful missile strikes and after the embassy bombings, shifted the responsibility for Osama bin Laden to law enforcement. The safeguard between terrorism and the American people was now reduced to the work of a well-meaning but overworked U.S. Attorney's Office and the ill-equipped and underfunded FBI.

Even before the October 2000 attack on the *Cole*, it was obvious that indicting Bin Laden had done nothing to enhance national security. On June 24, 1999, nearly a year after the embassy bombings, the United States closed six of its embassies in Africa due to reports of suspicious surveillance. The reported reason was fear of Bin Laden and suspicion that he was planning an attack on American interests. Kenneth Katzman of the Congressional Research Service, a division of the Library of Congress, told CNN, "The focus now is on Africa and the Middle East, but I think we have to be very expansive," because Bin Laden "could try to strike in Latin America. He could strike in Mexico, the Far East—even in Washington, D.C."[57] CNN dutifully reported that Osama bin Laden was "on the FBI's ten-most-wanted list" and was one of ten fugitives out of fifteen who was "on trial" in New York City. Yet this fugitive had the power to force the United States to close its embassies. He was hardly on the run from the law. With Clinton depending on the criminal justice system to deal with Bin Laden, he and his network were free to, in Katzman's words, "come into a position where he threatens a broad range of U.S. policy interests."[58]

Harvey Kushner, chairman of the Criminal Justice Department at Long Island University's C. W. Post campus, criticized the embassy closings: "When you close six embassies in a region in the world, you send a message to the world that not only have the terrorists made us blink, but we have written off a large number of people in a part of the world."[59] While it is better to be safe than sorry when lives are at stake, Kushner's comment does show how terrorists across the globe must have laughed at the incompetence of the United States, confident that they had power to intimidate us. That knowledge reinforced their belief that they could act with impunity, which is why they attacked again and again.

As in the case of the missile strikes, the administration's pursuit of a criminal case against the bombing perpetrators accomplished very little. According to Siobhan Roth, as of September 2001,

> Perhaps the gravest issue is that the directors of a terrorist attack often remain outside the reach of U.S. law enforcement. For example, of the 21 men—including Osama bin Laden—indicted for the 1998 bombing of American embassies in Tanzania and Kenya, 13 remain fugitives. Only four have been tried and convicted. Others are awaiting trial in New York or are fighting extradition from Britain.[60]

Roth wrote her story before September 11. It makes chilling reading now in the post-9/11 environment.

THE U.S.S. *COLE*

Bill Clinton's Record—Cause and Effect

ON OCTOBER 17, 2000, SAILORS WERE STATIONED ON THE DECK OF the U.S.S. *Cole*, armed with machine guns to keep civilian vessels away—the ship was on a heightened state of alert called "condition bravo."[1]

Intelligence and law-enforcement communities had learned of an Al Qaeda plot to bomb a U.S. warship,[2] but that was not the reason for the armed sailors on the *Cole*. The state of alert was in response to the fact that they were refueling in the Aden Harbor in Yemen. It was a dangerous place for American servicemen to be. Both the U.S. and Yemen governments had issued warnings that Americans were unsafe there. Yemen is a country of seventeen million, where the men still wear swords and the women traditional garb. In 1999, it was one of the four countries listed as a place of increasing terror against Americans.[3] Considering this heightened state of alert, oddly enough, Naval ships docking in the Mideast took no real additional steps for ship security.

The only way sentries could stop a ship from being attacked was to observe an approaching vessel from a distance and fire on it immediately. It is not surprising then, that when a sailor saw a speedboat coming toward the *Cole*, he did not open fire. Clearly, without express orders to fire on the incoming vessel, seamen pulling guard duty were wary of starting an international incident and feared not being backed by superiors. The driver of the boat cut the engine so that it bumped softly against the side of the warship and then exploded. "Looking over the rail, the sentry saw one of the two men wave before the blast knocked him back."[4]

The explosion blasted a hole in the side of the ship forty feet in diameter.[5] Seventeen Navy seamen were killed, and thirty-nine were injured.[6]

Additionally the entire 505-foot-long ship was endangered. It began to list four degrees to port.[7]

No Response

Reading the "Joint Inquiry into Intelligence Community Activities" report combined with other reports shows a complete lack of response by the Clinton administration. With the U.S. election around the corner, the document tries to let Clinton off the hook: "Transitions between administrations always take considerable time. For some high-level positions, such as National Coordinator for Counterterrorism, it is difficult if not impossible to maintain continuity or an intense daily focus on an issue, if the status of the person holding the position is unclear." That may be true, but the election had not yet taken place, so it was his responsibility alone.

Clinton's further drive to pull together a last-minute peace agreement between Israel and the Palestinians undermined this contention. As late as January 6, 2001, he feverishly worked to arrange a settlement in the two weeks he had left in office.[8] If a Middle East peace agreement didn't have to wait until the transition, there was certainly no credible reason not to respond to the *Cole* bombing. While there may have been "slippage in counterterrorism policy . . . in late 2000 and early 2001," because of the "unresolved status of Mr. [Richard] Clarke as National Coordinator for Counterterrorism," the fact is that there was no reason for Clinton to pass the buck to the Bush administration. As with other important national security issues, the outgoing president could have done something about it himself. Indeed, it would be very difficult for President-elect Bush to have a policy in place regarding the Cole in his first days in office. By leaving this "legacy" for the Bush administration, President Clinton knowingly allowed the attack on the U.S. military and the killing of seventeen soldiers to go by without any real response.

In fact, President Clinton promised that his administration would do something about the attack, though in the next breath he also revealed what he actually cared about—the issue that would consume his time and energy right to the point of leaving office: "We will find out who was responsible and hold them accountable. If their intention was to deter us from our mission of promoting peace and security in the Middle East, they will fail utterly."[9]

What this meant, in Clintonspeak, was that the FBI would be dispatched but the military would not be used. Over the next few months, newspapers would not be filled with stories of missile strikes or the use of Army Special Forces or Marines, nor with some new hard-line policy toward the Taliban. Rather, newspapers would be filled with stories about President Clinton trying to broker a deal with terrorists and desperately attempting to cement a legacy for his administration by forging peace between Israel and the Palestinians. Further, "as late as December 2000, he was still weighing whether to go to Pyongyang to try to strike another arms control deal with the North Koreans."[10]

From the day of the attacks, it was evident that President Clinton's legacy aspirations for the Mideast were going to rule out any real action regarding the *Cole*. At the president's request, a "strongly worded" measure to be debated in Congress was pulled from consideration without explanation. The nonbinding resolution condemned "the Palestinian leadership for encouraging the violence and doing so little for so long to stop it, resulting in the senseless loss of life."[11] According to a CNN report, "Senior Capitol Hill staffers cited concerns that moving ahead with the resolution during this critical juncture could inflame tensions and make it appear that the U.S. government is issuing an ultimatum to the Palestinians."[12] As Byron York wrote for the *National Review*:

> Clinton's reaction to the Cole terrorism was more muted than his response to the previous attacks. . . . [H]e seemed more concerned that the attack might threaten the administration's work in the Middle East (the bombing came at the same time as a new spate of violence between Israelis and Palestinians). . . . The next day, the Washington Post's John Harris, who had good connections inside the administration, wrote, "While the apparent suicide bombing of the U.S.S. Cole may have been the more dramatic episode for the American public, the escalation between Israelis and Palestinians took the edge in preoccupying senior administration officials yesterday. This was regarded as the more fluid of the two problems, and it presented the broader threat to Clinton's foreign policy aims."[13]

The Clinton administration's excuse was that there was no proof of Al Qaeda's involvement until after the president left office. The "Joint Inquiry into Intelligence Community Activities," for example, gives us an account of the time-consuming investigation of the *Cole* attack. One would think, from this account, that the terrorists and these organizations were a complete mystery to U.S. intelligence, that it took at least a couple of months to put together who was responsible, and many more for the different agencies to actually share the information.

But the FBI was able to show a connection to Bin Laden within forty-eight hours of the explosion. An Egyptian informant recognized mugshots of two of the suspects as Al Qaeda terrorists.[14] Thus, on December 1, James Phillips was able to publish that "[b]y all accounts, the Oct. 12 bombing appears to be the work of the loose terrorist network headed by Osama bin Laden, an exiled Saudi now based in Afghanistan."[15] And according to *Time* magazine, Richard Clarke, whom Clinton made the nation's first national coordinator of counterterrorism, knew quite well that the *Cole* attack required a response against Al Qaeda. He came up with a strategy paper that he presented to the national security principals on December 20, 2000. But Sandy Berger, Clinton's national security adviser, and others in the Clinton administration shelved the plan.[16]

According to the *Washington Times*, soon after the attack Clarke argued for striking known Al Qaeda and Taliban targets. But all the other national security principals opposed taking action.[17]

The official line for Clinton's inaction with regard to Clarke's December 20 proposal was that the outgoing administration did not want to commit the next administration to anything. "We would be handing (the Bush administration) a war when they took office on Jan. 20," a former senior Clinton aide, told *Time*. "That wasn't going to happen."[18] But the administration's last-minute dealings with Korea or Israel and Palestine would have also handed the Bush administration new commitments as well. These events are common during periods of presidential transition. Once again, Clinton selectively acted where his interests lay and nowhere else. That inconsistency continues to be his legacy.

By default, the bombing of the U.S.S. *Cole* was treated like other terrorist attacks—as a law-enforcement matter. And as evidenced in the Khobar

Towers case, in law-enforcement matters, justice was abandoned in favor of international relationships in the Mideast.

Bodine v. O'Neill

The New York field office of the FBI was given responsibility for the *Cole* investigation, led by special agent John O'Neill.[19] Special Agent O'Neill had extensive experience in terrorism cases and was involved with the 1993 World Trade Center bombing case, the New York landmark plot, and security of New York City's millennium celebration. O'Neill was also instrumental in the "Borderbomb" case and brought Judge Bruguière from France to assist in a case in Los Angeles. Director Freeh also sent O'Neill to investigate the Khobar Towers and embassy bombings.

O'Neill ran into roadblocks right away. He attempted to conduct his investigation effectively and track down the terrorists responsible for the assault on our Navy, but Barbara Bodine, Bill Clinton's U.S. ambassador to Yemen, ordered O'Neill to keep the team small. O'Neill, from an FBI vantage point, brought in the appropriate manpower to conduct a proper crime-scene investigation, run forensics, take photographs, and do everything else necessary.[20] Ambassador Bodine, however, arbitrarily told him to keep the number down to around twenty-seven agents—a number she came up with that had absolutely no bearing on the needs of the investigation.[21] O'Neill's priority was the integrity of the crime scene and determining, if possible, who was responsible for this terrorist act. O'Neill did not play politics, and he showed up in Yeman with a hundred and fifty agents.[22]

While stationed in Yemen, O'Neill had concerns about the safety of the personnel under his command. Because of the danger posed to Americans on the streets, he wanted his agents to be equipped with automatic weapons for self-defense.[23] More concerned about the sensibilities of the Yemeni government than the safety of American FBI agents, Ambassador Bodine refused O'Neill's request. O'Neill and Bodine clashed again later when the Yemeni refused to allow the FBI to interrogate suspects. O'Neill requested that Ambassador Bodine exert pressure on the government,[24] but instead, Bodine barred O'Neill from Yemen by revoking his visa after he left the country for Thanksgiving.[25]

While personality conflicts may explain some of what happened, the fact remains that John O'Neill received little support from the Clinton administration in a very important investigation. Special Agent O'Neill not only had to deal with the Yemeni government refusing to cooperate and electronically eavesdropping on his daily briefings, he also needed to determine if a high-ranking general in the Yemeni armed forces, who happened to be the Yemeni president's half-brother and a known associate of Bin Laden, was involved in the attack.[26] O'Neill desperately needed, but did not get, support from the Clinton State Department. President Clinton should have put pressure on the Yemeni government. Instead, Agent O'Neill was consistently undercut by Bodine.

Unfortunately, Ambassador Bodine, who was part of the problem before September 11, is still at the State Department. She last made the news on May 12, 2003, when President Bush fired her after only three weeks as the U.S. Coordinator for Central Iraq.[27] Agent O'Neill eventually retired from the FBI in frustration. He was killed during the September 11 attacks on the World Trade Center where he had recently become head of security just two weeks before.[28]

In May of 2003, the *Washington Post* reported that a federal grand jury in New York City had handed down a fifty-count indictment against two men, Jamal Badawi and Fahd Quso.[29] However, they had both conveniently escaped from a Yemeni prison the previous month.[30] Once again, the criminal justice system was shown to be insufficient in dealing with international terrorism.

What is Clinton's legacy in regard to the attack on the U.S.S. *Cole*? Remember what Madeleine Albright said in defending the missile attacks in response to the earlier bombings of the U.S. embassies in East Africa: "While our actions are not perfect insurance [against future terrorism], inaction would be an invitation to further horror."[31]

Less than a year after the attack on the U.S.S. *Cole*, America and the world discovered new meaning in the term "further horror." As Albright herself admitted, Clinton's inaction remains his legacy.

TURNING ON A DIME

America at War

"IT'S EXTREMELY HARD TO TURN THE SHIP OF STATE ON A DIME."
That is what Oliver "Buck" Revell said regarding what the new administration had to do once George W. Bush's election was finally upheld. "To create a different focus from what it had been is very difficult."

Passing the Buck

Since Bill Clinton left office, he looks for every opportunity to regain the limelight and be considered relevant. The aftermath of 9/11 was no different. President Clinton tried to spin things in a way that would make him look good. He told a group of people gathered for a luncheon sponsored by the History Channel that he attempted to warn Bush about Osama bin Laden. According to Reuters, Clinton said, "In his campaign, Bush had said he thought the biggest security issue was Iraq and a national missile defense." But Clinton disagreed. "I told him that in my opinion, the biggest security problem was Osama bin Laden."[1]

Clinton's former national security adviser, Sandy Berger, has refuted that claim. In testimony to Congress, he said, "[T]here was no war plan [to fight terrorism and Al Qaida] that we turned over to the Bush administration during the transition. And the reports of that are just incorrect."[2]

Clinton's assertion is quite galling, not just because it is false, but because he presents misleading information to place blame on President Bush in order to vindicate himself. As the evidence clearly proves, President Clinton and his administration seriously and grievously weakened and hampered our intelligence-gathering and antiterrorism capabilities through negligence and bad decisions. Under Bill Clinton's watch, time and again he allowed Bin Laden to slip away.

This last point is the most important to understanding any warning that Bill Clinton claims to have given to President Bush. If he had really thought that Osama bin Laden posed the most serious threat to America's national security, he could have pointed this out in public speeches during his presidency and had his administration develop an offensive, proactive plan to deal with Bin Laden and his Al Qaeda network.

Even Reuters had to admit in its story that "Clinton's Vice President Al Gore, who ran against Bush in the 2000 Election, did not make the threat from Al Qaeda a major focus of the presidential campaign, which both candidates kept focused mainly on domestic topics." Clinton's claim to have warned President Bush about this threat, when Clinton's entire eight-year record demonstrates utter unwillingness to deal with it, seems rather disingenuous. According to Clinton, "I would have started with India and Pakistan, then North Korea, and then Iraq after that." And "I thought Iraq was a lower order problem than Al Qaeda." But at no time did Clinton ever show that these were his priorities. These concerns sound good today in a post-9/11 world, but where is the evidence that he cared about these things during his two terms in office? Whatever he may have said to "warn" President Bush, it certainly wasn't very convincing. The response of Sean McCormack, a White House spokesman, was quite on target: "The Clinton administration did not present an aggressive new plan to topple al-Qaeda during the transition."

There is, of course, no record of Clinton giving this warning to President Bush. The American people are just supposed to take his word for it. For his part, Clinton didn't consider it important enough to mention in public until after September 11, when reporters began to question the previous eight years.

Bill Clinton was the president from 1993 to 2001. During that time he set budgets and made critical decisions that affected the intelligence community and the military. He had numerous opportunities to confront Al Qaeda and bring down Osama bin Laden, yet he chose not to act. What are we to make of his decisions? There is only so much George W. Bush could do in eight months to correct Clinton's eight-year legacy.

And Bush did try. Deputy National Security Adviser, Steve Hadley, testified before the Joint Inquiry that "countering terrorist threats to the United States was a top intelligence priority from the first days of this Administration." He also told the committee that the Clinton administration's strategy against Al Qaeda, such as it was, remained in place in early 2001, but the Bush administration was considering a better strategy during that time. From January 2001 through September 2001, the Bush White House "conducted a comprehensive, senior-level review of policy for dealing with Al Qaeda," he said. "The goal was to move beyond the policy of containment, criminal prosecution, and limited retaliation for specific attacks, toward attempting to 'roll back' Al Qaeda."[3]

The outgoing administration, however, failed over Clinton's two terms to issue a clear message about the importance of fighting terrorism and Al Qaeda. You'll recall from an earlier chapter that in a meeting between Attorney General John Ashcroft and Janet Reno, Ashcroft's deputy chief of staff, David Israelite reported that, "Fighting terrorism was not on her list of priorities."

Attorney General Ashcroft had other things to occupy his attention. "At his swearing-in party," Israelite said, "FBI Director Freeh pulled Ashcroft aside and informed him about the Hanssen Case." Freeh was referring to the case of Robert Philip Hanssen, an FBI agent who sold our secrets to the Russians for fifteen years in exchange for money and diamonds.[4] Determined to find out what this meant for national security, within two months Ashcroft ordered two probes to find out what went wrong and how to fix it.[5]

The Justice Department "also had to deal with the Timothy McVeigh death-penalty case. The FBI field offices allegedly did not turn over all of the documents as the government prepared to execute McVeigh. This was the first case of a federal prisoner being sentenced to death."

With these pressing issues at hand and with the low priority placed on terrorism by the outgoing administration, it is difficult to see in a pre-9/11 world how Ashcroft could have been expected to make fighting terrorism a top priority. The Clinton administration never criticized the early months of the Bush administration for not dealing with terrorism. In Bush's two major speeches before September 11, he showed concern for national defense, but he never specified terrorism—and no Democrat criticized this as neglect. In his Joint Session of Congress address on February 27, 2001, President Bush spoke of rebuilding the military to deal with rogue nations and terrorists. Reversing the Clinton administration's practice, he declared, "I'm requesting $5.7 billion in increased military pay and benefits, and health care and housing. Our men and women in uniform give America their best and we owe them our support." This was consistent with the promises of his inaugural address:

> We will build our defenses beyond challenge, lest weakness invite challenge.
> We will confront weapons of mass destruction, so that a new century
> is spared new horrors.

Neither Clinton nor the Democrats changed. But Michael Elliot wrote for *Time* that Clinton's national security adviser Sandy Berger "was determined that when he left office, [National Security Adviser Condoleezza] Rice should have a full understanding of the terrorist threat. In a sense, this was an admission of failure. The Clinton years had been marked by a drumbeat of terror attacks against American targets, and they didn't seem to be stopping."[6] Even this sent a mixed signal. If terrorism was so important, why had this not been a focus of Clinton?

Bill Clinton served eight years in the White House. George W. Bush served eight months prior to 9/11. It is important, for perspective, to remember that Bush v. Gore ended a long and treacherous election season culminating with a Supreme Court decision. This ate into the time set aside for the new president to face the daunting task of assembling his cabinet and making appointments to the FBI, CIA, NSA, and other agencies geared to national security and federal law enforcement. All presidents must be brought up to speed on world events, present threats to America, economic matters, trade issues, national security matters, and a litany of other important issues. Appointments then undergo background checks and receive security clearances. All of this takes time, but it must be done as quickly as possible.

George W. Bush was delayed for six weeks from beginning this process because Vice President Gore contested the election. These delays clearly hurt our chances to stop 9/11.

The Road Before Them

The incoming administration knew that they had a lot of work to do to make up for eight years of Clinton and Gore. Recall Secretary of Defense nominee Donald Rumsfeld's response during his confirmation hearing when asked what "kept him up at night." He answered, "Intelligence."[7] At his swearing-in ceremony Bush promised to rebuild the military.[8]

Bush took immediate steps to prioritize intelligence. He resumed the presidential daily briefing as a face-to-face encounter between the president and a CIA briefer.[9] "Though CIA Director George Tenet has told others he had always had as much access to President Clinton as he needed, other officials privately argue that the Clinton administration did not always pay as much attention to what U.S. intelligence was gathering as it should," claimed a CNN report. "'We like it' said an official, that the new president wants to resume face to face briefings. 'It means we get more direct feedback and can tailor the product' better to the customer, the official said."[10]

The Bush administration also attempted to solve other problems started or aggravated by the eight years under Bill Clinton. In the Hanssen case, the White House dealt firmly with the intelligence failure by removing the diplomats who worked with him, while trying to stay on good terms with Russia by striking a conciliatory posture.[11] They moved to deter China by showing support for Taiwan[12] and held Arafat accountable for the violence he encouraged.[13] President Bush resumed the missile defense program that the Clinton administration had halted.[14]

There was a lot of lost time to make up for.

Clinton staffers attack the Bush administration for not immediately buying into and implementing counterterrorism plans developed in the last days of the Clinton administration. Daniel Benjamin and Steven Simon claim it was "hubris" for the Bush White House to implement reviews before acting, even though they admit in the same paragraph that Bush would not come into office on a blank slate.[15] Michael Elliot also displays impatience with the review process. But it is naïve to expect the Bush White House to embrace the foreign policy wisdom of the previous administration. If something had backfired, Clinton would certainly not have stood up to take the blame for it.

In February 2001, Bush ordered a terrorism policy review. But it was slowed by turf conflicts initiated during the prior administration.[16] Instead of allowing the feuds between agencies to fester, Bush took action. During a face-to-face briefing by CIA Director Tenet, the president was informed of the search for Abu Zubaydah, Al Qaeda's head of international operations, wanted in connection to the planning of the U.S.S. *Cole* bombing. Afterward, Bush told Condoleezza Rice that the prior administration's way of dealing with Al Qaeda was not working. They had been "swatting at flies."[17] He wanted a comprehensive plan for defeating terrorism. Rice delivered the message to the National Security Council, saying "The president wants a plan to eliminate Al Qaeda."[18]

In May 2001, President Bush announced a new philosophy relating to U.S. national security:

Many [countries] have chemical and biological weapons. . . . They seek weapons of mass destruction to intimidate their neighbors, and to keep the United States and other responsible nations from helping allies and friends in strategic parts of the world. . . . They hate our friends, they hate our values, they hate democracy and freedom and individual liberty. Many care little for the lives of their own people. In such a world, Cold War deterrence is no longer enough. To maintain peace, to protect our own citizens and our own allies and friends, we must seek security based on more than the grim premise that we can destroy those who seek to destroy us.[19]

By July 2001, the president reissued an executive order declaring a national emergency due to the threat posed by the Taliban. He stated,

The Taliban continues to allow territory under its control in Afghanistan to be used as a safe haven and base of operations for Usama bin Laden and the al-Qaida organization who have committed and threaten to continue to commit acts of violence against the United States and its nationals. For these reasons, I have determined that it is necessary to maintain in force these emergency authorities beyond July 4, 2001. . . . I am continuing the national emergency declared on July 4, 1999, with respect to the Taliban.[20]

Earlier, on April 30, 2001, Clarke presented a draft plan to the Deputies Committee. It took the Deputies Committee less than ninety days to agree upon and submit the plan to the Principal Committee. While Deputy Secretary of State Richard Armitage was "enthusiastic" about the proposal, the CIA, still under Clinton-appointed George Tenet, was averse to taking risks.[21] Nevertheless, the deputies kept meeting until a plan was agreed to on July 16.

The Principal Committee includes members of the government's national security agencies who meet to discuss and develop national security policy. Following a comprehensive review of the proposal, they approved the plan on September 4, 2001. The new proposal was delivered to Rice, who was set to hand it to President Bush on Monday, September 10.[22]

But by then, obviously, it was too late. According to Richard Clarke, the review process had been "as fast as could be expected."[23] The responsibility for September 11 is not to be found in the previous eight months, but the prior eight years.

It is Bill Clinton's legacy.

AFTERWORD

Bush vs. the 9/11 Commission

SECRETARY OF DEFENSE DONALD RUMSFELD CALLED A HIGH-LEVEL briefing at the Pentagon several weeks after the September 11 attacks, which included former secretaries of defense and state, national security advisers and congressional leadership. "It was called to discuss the plans for going to war in Afghanistan and toppling the Taliban," according to a former member of House leadership who attended. The attendee stated that as Secretary Rumsfeld began to describe the upcoming war, Zbigniew Brzezinski, national security adviser under Jimmy Carter, interrupted the meeting and told the group, "I hope we're not going to do the same chicken s— stuff like we did before, send some cruise missiles through a tent up a camel's a—."[1] Not surprisingly, William Cohen, secretary of defense under Clinton who was also an invited guest, did not appreciate the remark, and his anger became visually apparent.

George W. Bush was responding to the war on terror in a way that Clinton never did. In fact, before September 11, 2001, President Bush was undoing much of the damage Clinton had done to national security during his eight years in office. As pointed out in the previous chapter, Bush immediately reinstated the customary face-to-face meetings between himself and the CIA briefer. In response to one of those briefings, he requested a plan to eliminate Al Qaeda.

President Bush took immediate action to strengthen the military, with increased budgets and fundamental changes in deployment policy. In keeping with his campaign promise to revitalize the military, he also directed Defense Secretary Donald Rumsfeld to come up with pragmatic plans for deployment of a missile-defense system and to streamline and modernize the

B-1 bomber force.[2] And under President Bush's leadership, the FBI received funding for much-needed technology upgrades and budget increases to hire desperately needed special agents.

After September 11

In the days following 9/11, President Bush established the Office of Homeland Security in order to integrate all of America's vast resources to fight the war on terror. With congressional approval, the office was promptly elevated to a cabinet level department.

He took the battle to the terrorists' backyard by ordering the invasion of Afghanistan and toppling the Taliban regime, Osama bin Laden's ally and protector. This action put Bin Laden on the run and liberated nearly twenty-five million people from oppression and tyranny.

President Bush then built a coalition of forty-three countries committed to action in Iraq, to eliminate a grave danger to the Middle East and remove from power a tyrant who had funded, protected, and armed terrorists. In the process, the United States liberated over twenty-five million people from a brutal, murderous dictator, Saddam Hussein.

Through his bold and decisive actions, Bush persuaded nations like Pakistan to stop cooperating with terrorists and join the international community in fighting the war on terrorism and move toward a more open society. His firm actions also persuaded Libyan leader and terror sponsor Moammar Kadafi to renounce the pursuit of weapons of mass destruction and cooperate in the war on terror.

Under Bush's principled leadership, Congress passed, and he signed, the U.S. Patriot Act, which gives law enforcement the ability to combat terrorists with twenty-first-century technology. This law allows the Justice Department to use laws initially intended to fight organized crime and drug traffickers as a weapon against terrorism.

Bush also prompted Congress to pass the Aviation Security Act and the Enhanced Border Security and Visa Entry Reform Act in order to keep terrorists out of the country and protect our air travel system.

At the CIA, the John Deutch guidelines restricting recruitment were rescinded. The CIA is now able to operate effectively once again in the recruitment of sources and undercover operatives vital to the war on terror. The agency was also given "a blank check to wage covert warfare against al-Qaida," according to one analyst.[3]

For fiscal year 2003, Bush submitted "the first budget proposal ever submitted by a president that seeks to coordinate and prioritize the homeland security policy."[4] As promised in his 2003 State of the Union address, President Bush ordered the establishment of a Terrorist Threat Integration Center with the cooperation of the FBI, the CIA, and the Departments of Homeland Security and Defense. The Center reports directly to the director of Central Intelligence.

On the foreign policy front, the Bush administration is working to build a better relationship with Russia in order to stop the proliferation of weapons and gain cooperation in the war on terror. And on July 3, 2003, and September 18, 2003, the Bush State Department imposed sanctions on Chinese entities for providing weapons technology to Iran and elsewhere.[5]

Despite these bold initiatives, President Bush finds himself under attack from those who want to rewrite history and blame him for September 11, in order to distract from Bill Clinton's true legacy.

The Accusations

In early 2004, reports began to surface that Thomas H. Kean, chairman of the Presidential Commission on 9/11, was going to place a significant amount of blame for the attacks on the Bush administration. The report is not slated for release until late May 2004; nevertheless, inferences can be drawn from information obtained from prior investigative reports, news reports, and the backgrounds of key commission members.

The report will likely state that the CIA should have watch-listed Khalid al-Mihdhar and Nawaf al-Hazmi. The agency learned about these two terrorists in early 2000 when they attended an Al Qaeda leadership meeting in Malaysia. This important meeting got the attention of CIA operatives, but the intelligence gathered from it was never acted on. The CIA failed to watch-list these terrorists and failed to share their information with the FBI.[6]

Bush critics also contend that if the now-notorious Phoenix Memo, written on July 10, 2001, had been taken seriously and passed up the chain of command, rather than simply passed over by midlevel FBI management, 9/11 might have been averted. The memo, sent from the FBI field office in Phoenix, noted a trend of an "inordinate number of individuals of investigative interest" pursuing flight training. The FBI failed to take action. Specifically, there was a failure to communicate the memo's content to bureau specialists who could have analyzed it appropriately.[7]

Additionally, certain facts came to light shortly before the attacks, which critics say should have alerted officials that a terrorist plot was afoot. In August, "a closely held intelligence report for senior government officials included information that Bin Laden had wanted to conduct attacks in the United States since 1997." The report mentioned "that members of Al Qaeda, including some U.S. citizens, had resided in or traveled to the United States for years and that the group apparently maintained a support structure here" and cited "uncorroborated information obtained and disseminated in 1998 that Bin Laden wanted to hijack airplanes to gain the release of U.S.-held extremists." The report also referenced "FBI judgments about patterns of activity consistent with preparations for hijackings or other types of attacks; as well as information acquired in May 2001 that indicated a group of Bin Laden supporters was planning attacks in the United States with explosives."[8]

The "old" CIA and "old" FBI, critics say, had enough data to warn the FAA to institute new security measures. Neither agency ever took those steps, which might have prevented the attacks of September 11. Cockpit doors could have been reinforced to be more secure, and pilots could have been retrained so that they would not have cooperated with the hijackers. Previously, pilots were trained to cooperate with terrorists who threaten passengers and crewmembers. It was expected that the pilots would land the plane and the terrorists would make political statements and list their demands. Terrorists did not need to know how to fly planes in order to hijack them and analysts at both the CIA and FBI should have noticed the training pattern if, in fact, the two organizations had been sharing all of their intelligence data.

Finally, President Bush will be blamed for not ordering the military to get fighter aircraft into the air to shoot down civilian airplanes quickly enough to have saved the Pentagon.

Killing American Civilians

Of all the criticisms of George Bush and his administration for what happened on 9/11, perhaps the most reasonable is that he could have saved the 125 people killed in the attack on the Pentagon by ordering Air Force pilots to shoot down civilian jets that were heading toward potential targets. Forty minutes passed between the attack on the second World Trade Center tower and the attack on the Pentagon. There was almost an hour between the first World Trade Center attack and the attack on the Pentagon. As Bush critics tell it, the president had the time to give the military orders to intercept and destroy the hijacked civilian aircraft.

This assertion is simply not plausible. First, the president of the United States wasn't told we were under attack until the second plane hit. And second, when the second plane hit, it was not immediately clear that the plane that hit the Pentagon had been hijacked. Are we supposed to believe that, within forty minutes, the president should have decided for the first time in history to order the United States military to shoot down airplanes loaded with Americans over American soil without confirmation that it was indeed hijacked? The president had even less time to consider this extreme action since it would take precious minutes to scramble the jets for this horrific act.

As a former senior CIA operative told me, within those minutes, "the president could not have known to shoot down U.S. airliners with Americans on board." Nor had anything truly prepared President Bush beforehand for making such a momentous decision: "That's just twenty-twenty hindsight" the former CIA operative said. "Osama bin Laden was dangerous, and we should have known he was going to do something, but there was no actionable intelligence that I've ever seen or heard of. If Bin Laden had blown up a car bomb in a mall or near a government building maybe people could say 'you should have moved the perimeters back.' That's one thing, but no one had ever used an airplane. That argument is bulls—. There was no actionable intelligence, period."

According to veteran reporter Bill Sammon, Vice President Cheney discussed a possible shootdown order with the president soon after Air Force One took off at 9:57 A.M.[9] The military needed a direct order from the commander-in-chief before firing upon a civilian aircraft.

[H]e was being asked to make the most momentous decision of his life: whether U.S. fighter jets had the right to shoot down civilian airliners that were packed with innocent men, women, and children. Bush talked it over with Cheney. If he didn't give the order, another plane might slam into a building, killing countless people on the ground. On the other hand, if he did give the order, he might be signing the death warrant for hundreds of civilians aboard a commercial aircraft. Of course, they would die anyway if their plane slammed into a crowded building. But if the jetliner were shot down over an uninhabited area, at least no one on the ground would be killed.[10]

Bush gave the go ahead to shoot down any aircraft that could not otherwise be deterred from a suicide attack.[11] Obviously he made the right decision. But it was an unprecedented decision that had to be made amid a great deal of confusion and danger. To claim that Bush should have instantaneously ordered fighter pilots to shoot down a jet carrying hundreds of American civilians is simply preposterous. Can anyone imagine an American president giving an order that would kill hundreds of Americans without deliberate and serious consideration?

Al-Mihdhar and Al-Hazmi

The CIA learned about Khalid al-Mihdhar and Nawaf al-Hazmi and their connections to Al Qaeda during the Clinton administration. Remember from Chapter Three that the FBI had an informant in contact with three of the 9/11 hijackers, but because the CIA never watch-listed the terrorists, they gained entry into the country. Furthermore, the CIA did not inform the FBI of their known connection to Al Qaeda, so the FBI did not know to attempt to uncover the terrorists' plans. This communication failure at the CIA may have been vital to preventing the 9/11 attacks. It was under Clinton's watch that this information should have been communicated to the FBI. And it was under the Clinton administration that these two terrorists should have been placed on the watch list to be denied entry into the United States.

Of course, no one holds former President Clinton guilty for failing to read the minds of CIA operatives, nor is he the person tasked with giving the FBI the needed information. But Clinton is accountable, as argued in this book, because he demoralized, handcuffed, and neglected the CIA at the very time he was receiving threat assessments that should have brought about increased vigilance. By alienating the CIA's director and then picking replacements who were not devoted to the CIA's primary mission, Clinton frustrated those who wanted to do something about terrorism and national security, and he encouraged others who distracted the agency from its mission. It was *his* "old CIA" that was asleep at the switch in the war on terrorism.

Former President Clinton and several of his administration's top officials, including former Secretary of State Madeline Albright and former National Security Advisor Sandy Berger, will testify before the Commission that they warned the incoming administration of the dire threat posed by Al Qaeda. Dick Clarke, who served in the Bush administration for a period, after serving as Clinton's counterterrorism chief, is reported to be writing a tell-all book that echoes these accusations. Clarke left the Bush administration after being denied a plum job in the Homeland Security Department, and White House sources state Clarke is a self-centered egotist who is quick to take credit for achievements and even quicker to lay blame elsewhere for any failures. What's important to note is that each of these former officials played a key role in the intelligence failures that led to 9/11.

Clinton had eight full years to investigate and defeat Al Qaeda, eight full years to lead the CIA and FBI in dealing with these terrorist threats. Yet, Clinton defenders claim Bush should be held personally responsible for what the CIA and FBI failed to do even before he was in office.

The Phoenix Memo

When an agent in the Phoenix FBI field office sent a memo to the Radical Fundamentalist unit and the Osama bin Laden unit of the FBI in Washington on July 10, 2001, someone should have passed it on for analysis. But in the "old FBI," a combination of poor communication, political correctness, and poor middle management cast the memo aside. If the

Phoenix Memo represents a failure, it is a failure attributable to Clinton's policies, not those of the Bush administration.

Remember what former FBI Deputy Director Oliver "Buck" Revell said from his decades of experience: "The Phoenix Memo was bulls—! The agents were doing their job, and they did a fine job. However, they didn't open a case because of political correctness. They had explicit orders not to racially profile and if they had opened a case because a bunch of 'Arab students' were taking flying lessons, they would have been shut down immediately and their careers would have been hurt. The Arab community would have been in an uproar."

As I mentioned in the prior chapter, President Bush saw Al Qaeda as a serious threat, and he promptly put a team together to develop a plan to deal with the threat. But to expect the president to develop and fully implement a plan during his first eight months in office that included rewriting the eight politically correct years of Clinton polices is simply not plausible.

After the 9/11 attacks, these problems were exposed, and the Bush administration took the initiative to change the FBI to deal with important clues in a much more serious and expeditious manner to protect the American people. As John Ashcroft testified, "the new FBI, America's domestic counterterrorism force, fully integrates intelligence and law enforcement capabilities to protect American lives."[12] Under Bush's leadership, the Justice Department has been enabled to analyze threats and work with the intelligence community as never before. Ashcroft spoke of the indictment of Sami al-Arian and several other members of Palestinian Islamic Jihad as the result of an FBI investigation. Though the terrorist group was responsible for over a hundred murders,

> [p]rior to the passage of the Patriot Act, the prosecutors in this case did not have the ability to participate fully in this investigation that ultimately led to RICO and material support charges against Al-Arian and his associates.
>
> Today, Americans are safer because we have transformed the rules of engagement for investigating and prosecuting suspected terrorists within our borders.

- First, the passage of the Patriot Act in October 2001 allowed for information sharing between law enforcement and intelligence and allowed us to implement our new FISA guidelines;

- Second, on November 18, 2002, the Foreign Intelligence Surveillance Court of Review reversed the district level FISA court and upheld our new FISA guidelines for information sharing;

- Third, we have tasked the U.S. Attorney's offices to review all intelligence material that may provide the basis for criminal charges against terrorists and terrorist financiers.

As the FISA Court of Review noted: "Effective counterintelligence . . . requires the wholehearted cooperation of all the government's personnel who can be brought to the task. A standard which punishes such cooperation could well be thought dangerous to national security."

This dangerous standard existed until we reformed the law, rewrote our FISA procedures and directed prosecutors to change their practices.[13]

This sort of investigative work was not possible under the old Clinton rules, and could have, in fact, gotten an FBI agent in trouble.

Of course, none of this means that President Bush is relying primarily on law enforcement to wage war on terror. Rather, he is improving the ability of the FBI not only to prosecute cases but also to support the greater effort against terrorism by collecting information and protecting the country in ways the FBI failed to do in the 1990s.

The Office of the Inspector General in the Justice Department has worked tirelessly since 9/11 to improve the FBI's ability "to collect, analyze and disseminate intelligence and other information." Steps have been taken to make sure that nothing like the Phoenix Memo incident happens again, including the transfer of twenty-five CIA analysts to the FBI. The bureau also recruited a manager with experience in the CIA to oversee the training of FBI analysts. In his report, Inspector General Glenn Fine concludes that "Fundamental reform is underway at the FBI."[14]

To blame the Bush administration for the policies of his predecessor is simply an argument with no merit. Clinton had eight years to lead the FBI, in the face of increasing terrorist attacks. He permitted his relationship with the director, Louis Freeh, to be one of open hostility. As pointed out previously, Clinton and Freeh had no working relationship, and they viewed each other with contempt. It simply strains credulity to hold President Bush responsible for not fixing unknown problems in the first eight months of his administration.

Although the Phoenix Memo incident reveals serious problems with the old FBI that needed to be fixed, it is highly unlikely that an investigation of possible terrorists activities in Arizona that started on July 10, 2001, would have uncovered and stopped the 9/11 hijackers just sixty-two days later.

The inability of the FBI to cooperate with the CIA, or for the criminal and intelligence divisions within the FBI to cooperate with each other, were failures of Bill Clinton's leadership. The fact is, much of what was known in July and August 2001 was old news that had been off the radar for quite some time. There was no new information or actionable intelligence that would have changed anything at that late date. It is hard to make definitive statements about what could have happened had an investigation opened midsummer 2001. We do know, however, that if an investigation had begun in 1995 after the Paris subway bombings, it is far less likely that Osama bin Laden and his henchmen would have been around to conceive or implement the 9/11 attacks.

Protecting the Airlines

While it is true that there was information indicating that planes might be used as weapons, the Clinton administration had actively suppressed the details of the Terror 2000 report, which warned of the threat and the possible targeting of the Pentagon and the World Trade Center.

There were other warnings as well. In 1998, the FBI's chief pilot in Oklahoma City warned that an inordinate number of men from the Middle East were getting flight training in Oklahoma.[15] An FBI agent wrote a memo about the pilot's concerns, but the memo never made it beyond his superior. What makes Terror 2000 unique is that top officials within the

Clinton administration analyzed the report and consciously decided not to take the threat seriously.

By the time President Bush came into office the old information had been buried and there was no new information available. Even if the intelligence community had warned the FAA of the potential threat in late July or August, no one can seriously argue that the airlines could have retrofitted cockpit doors or retrained pilots about how to respond to hijackers that quickly. This time-consuming and costly procedure, embraced after 9/11, would have been fought by the airlines in the name of profit. Indeed, even in the wake of 9/11, it took much longer than two months to retrofit cockpit doors and implement other changes in aviation security.

The Truth about Bush and Clinton

President Bill Clinton never effectively dealt with Osama bin Laden and Al Qaeda. Rather than acting in the interests of national security, his actions repeatedly jeopardized national security and encouraged Bin Laden and other terrorists to continue their openly declared war against the United States. Not only did he repeatedly fail to strike at Bin Laden and refuse to follow through after promising action, he oversaw the decay of both the FBI and the CIA. Serious intelligence failures occurred in the FBI because Bill Clinton became alienated from its director, Louis Freeh; and serious intelligence failures occurred in the CIA because Bill Clinton ignored his first director, James Woolsey, and imposed political correctness on the agency. In both cases, the results were disastrous. Militarily, Clinton refused to take action or remain focused on the terrorist threat to national security. He constantly relied on ineffective law-enforcement methods rather than on intelligence and the military in dealing with Al Qaeda—not to mention his overriding risk aversion. According to a media source, late in the Clinton administration an unarmed UAV (Unmanned Aerial Vehicle) picked up an image of what intelligence experts believe was Osama bin Laden, but this information was never acted upon because of the proximity of the closest military assets and the Clinton administration's aversion to civilian casualties. Ironically, it was Woolsey's foresight and persistence in the face of Clinton's indifference that led to the development of the unmanned "Predator" drone that has been so effective in the war on terror in the post-Clinton era.

The fact is, our best opportunities to go after Bin Laden and track down his terror network occurred on Clinton's watch. From the bombing of the World Trade Center in 1993, the Paris Subway bombings in 1995, and the Millennium Bomber case in December 1999, Clinton and his administration were given repeated warnings that we were in a war, but they failed to acknowledge it. The issue was not simply failures in intelligence but failures by Bill Clinton personally and his administration. The Clinton administration had more than one chance to snatch Bin Laden, as well as gain detailed intelligence regarding Al Qaeda.[16]

The Sudanese government wanted to shed their associations with terrorism and give up Bin Laden in order to prove their sincerity. Sudanese businessman Mansoor Ijaz, a link between the Clintons and the Muslim community, saw this as an opportunity to support positive trends in the Muslim world. But Clinton didn't want to do anything so bold as to snatch Bin Laden, despite repeated appeals from Sudan. As Ijaz told the *Washington Times*, what happened "was the greatest U.S. foreign policy failure of the last half-century. It has affected hundreds of millions worldwide. Even if we get him now, who will be the next Bin Laden? There are many willing candidates standing in line. Islamic radicalism exists today because Clinton didn't dismantle Al Qaeda when he had the chance."[17]

Clinton defenders claim that the Sudanese were untrustworthy, but French Judge Jean-Louis Bruguière had successfully worked with the Sudanese government to get Carlos the Jackal. When the Clinton administration told the Sudanese to kick Bin Laden out of the country, they did so promptly—to Afghanistan.

During his first term, Clinton did not even meet in private with CIA Director James Woolsey, nor did he task Woolsey to take action in the wake of the first bombing of the World Trade Center. Clinton let the CIA be further weakened by the next director, John Deutch, and the moral crusades of Democrats in Congress. And to top it off, he pardoned Director Deutch for his crimes before leaving office. Clinton did nothing to solve the conflicts between the FBI and the CIA, and he watched the proliferation of weapons of mass destruction by China and Russia.

To add insult to injury, President Clinton gave amnesty to Puerto Rican terrorists. He ignored the attack on the U.S.S. *Cole* for the sake of deal-making with Palestinian terrorists in a desperate attempt to secure a legacy as a peacemaker. His administration stopped an IRS investigation and audit of Islamic charities while numerous political enemies were targeted with investigations and audits.

Prior to Bush taking office, terrorism was just not a priority. George W. Bush, on the other hand, accomplished more in his first eight months than Clinton had in eight years. He restored the personal daily intelligence briefing, he immediately resolved to strengthen America's military, and he personally asked for a plan to crush Al Qaeda. September 11, 2001, may have happened under Bush's watch, but it will always remain Clinton's legacy. There is no amount of spinning that could cause the 9/11 Commission report to get around this reality.

The Kean Commission

The Kean Commission must be viewed in the context of its makeup. There are five Republicans and five Democrats on the commission, and logic holds that it should be fair and balanced—nothing could be further from the truth. The Democrats are, for the most part, a very political, ideological, and ruthless group of Clinton supporters, while the Republicans are, for the most part, tepid centrists that lack extensive foreign policy experience.[18]

Jamie Gorelick was appointed by President Clinton as deputy attorney general under Janet Reno from 1994 to 1997. She is a known partisan for Bill Clinton and served as the Justice Department supervisor of Louis Freeh and the FBI.

Lee Hamilton is a former Democrat congressman from Indiana, known as a thoughtful but partisan member of Congress from 1965 until 1999.

Timothy Roemer is a former Democrat congressman from Indiana and a liberal activist who previously served as chief counsel to Senator DeConcini. Remember Senator DeConcini from Chapter Five? He led the opposition against Woolsey's budget requests. The senator must be held accountable for his actions during the nineties that supported Clinton's failed policies, and it would be nearly impossible for commission member Roemer to objectively criticise his old boss.

And then there is Richard Ben-Veniste. It was reported in the *New York Post* that Chaiman Kean met with Bill Clinton for dinner on February 24, 2003. The meeting is memorialized in the *Post* article, though an important detail is missing:

> Bill Clinton . . . finally had his first dinner at Rao's on Monday. The former Prez broke bread with New Jersey Sen. Jon Corzine and former Jersey Gov. (and current Homeland Security co-chair) Thomas Kean. At nearby tables were former Sen. Al D'Amato and Susan Lucci. Clinton seemed fascinated by the clubby camaraderie in the East Harlem eatery, delighted to meet bartender Nicky the Vest, and to hear the vocal stylings of owner Frank Pellegrino, who plays an FBI boss on "The Sopranos."[19]

What the newspaper fails to mention is that Richard Ben-Veniste was also at that dinner meeting with President Clinton.

Richard Ben-Veniste is one of the smartest and shrewdest lawyers in Washington, D.C., and one of Clinton's most ardent defenders. Ben-Veniste served as the Democrat chief counsel on the staff of the Senate Whitewater Committee, investigating the infamous Arkansas land deal. Throughout the investigation, Ben-Veniste saw no wrongdoing by Clinton and became a favorite of the Clinton White House.

Ben-Veniste's questioning of Resolution Trust investigator Jean Lewis during the Whitewater hearings vividly illustrates his partisan fervor and "ends justify the means" approach to protecting Bill Clinton. On November 29, 1995, Lewis testified before the Senate Whitewater Committee regarding her findings that led to a criminal investigation into Madison Guaranty Savings and Loan and President and Mrs. Clinton.

Lewis, a career employee with a spotless record, testified that her supervisors embarked in a "concerted effort to obstruct, hamper, and manipulate the Whitewater probe." This damaging testimony, however, was overshadowed by the heavy-handed tactics of Ben-Veniste, who used high-tech means to scour a computer disk that Lewis had given to the committee and "undeleted" a twenty-two-page personal letter dated February 5, 1992.

In the letter, Lewis was describing problems she was having with her seventeen-year-old stepson. In that context, she described how Clinton was not a good example for children and how he had repeatedly denied his relationship with Gennifer Flowers, calling him a "lying bastard." Ben-Veniste attempted to use this letter to undermine Lewis's damning testimony of the Clintons' involvement in the Whitewater case. During aggressive questioning, he drove Lewis's blood pressure up so high that she had to be taken by ambulance to the hospital.

Ben-Veniste's conduct prompted calls for an investigation by Lewis's attorney, Mark Levin of the Landmark Legal Foundation, and several Republican senators. Senators questioned Ben-Veniste's invasion of Lewis's privacy and his use of unethical means to reconstitute the deleted letter. Levin filed a complaint with the Senate Ethics Committee demanding an investigation into how Ben-Veniste had obtained a copy of Lewis's personal letter. Missouri Senator Kit Bond, a member of the committee, sent a letter demanding an investigation to Whitewater Committee Chairman Alphonse D'Amato.

Clearly, with Bill Clinton's poor record on terrorism, he needs supporters on the commission, and Richard Ben-Veniste fits that bill.

Conclusion

This book could not possibly include every event leading up to 9/11. Many things took place out of the public eye. But the events included are, by themselves, more than enough to prove that Osama bin Laden feverishly pursued his war against the United States throughout the 1990s, and that he was behind each of the significant attacks on the U.S. throughout the decade. The events and failed policies of the 90s present a pattern that culminated in the destruction of the Twin Towers. Each of the preceding terrorist strikes and corresponding intelligence failures occurred under the watch of Bill Clinton and those he appointed to power. Although the tragedy of September 11 caught us by surprise, the war had been going on for quite some time.

In issuing its report, the 9/11 Commission needs to stick to the facts of this case and review President Bush's State of the Union message on January 20, 2004:

I know that some people question if America is really in a war at all. They view terrorism more as a crime—a problem to be solved mainly with law enforcement and indictments. After the World Trade Center was first attacked in 1993, some of the guilty were indicted, tried, convicted and sent to prison. But the matter was not settled. The terrorists were still training and plotting in other nations, and drawing up more ambitious plans. After the chaos and carnage of September 11, it is not enough to serve our enemies with legal papers. The terrorists and their supporters declared war on the United States—and war is what they got.

SELECT BIBLIOGRAPHY

Albright, Madeleine. *Madame Secretary: A Memoir*. New York: Miramax, 2003.

Alexander, Yonah and Michael S. Swetam. *Osama bin Laden's al-Qaida: Profile of a Terrorist Network*. Ardsley, NY: Transnational, 2001.

Benjamin, Daniel and Steven Simon. *The Age of Sacred Terror*. New York: Random House, 2002, 2003.

Bergen, Peter L. *Holy War, Inc.: Inside the Secret World of Osama bin Laden*. New York: Free Press, 2001.

Bodansky, Yossef. *Bin Laden: The Man Who Declared War on America*. Rosseville, CA: Prima/Forum, 1999, 2000.

Bodansky, Yossef. *The High Cost of Peace: How Washington's Middle East Policy Left America Vulnerable to Terrorism*. Rosseville, CA: Prima/Forum, 2002.

Booth, Ken and Tim Dunne, eds. *Worlds in Collision: Terror and the Future of Global Order*. New York: Palgrave MacMillan, 2002.

Bossie, David N. and Floyd E. Brown. *Prince Albert: The Life and Lies of Al Gore*. Bellevue, WA: Merril Press, 2000.

Calrridge, Duane R. *A Spy For All Season: My Life in the CIA*. New York: Scribner, 1997.

Gilmore Commission. "Second Annual Report to the President and the Congress of the Advisory Panel to Assess Domestic Response Capabilities for Terrorism Involving Weapons of Mass Destruction: Toward a National Strategy for Combating Terrorism." Rand Corporation, 15 December 2000.

House Permanent Select Committee on Intelligence and the Senate Select Committee on Intelligence. "Joint Inquiry into Intelligence Community Activities before and after the Terrorist Attacks of September 11, 2001," December 2002.

Kessler, Ronal. *The Bureau: The Secret History of the FBI*. New York: St. Martin's Press, 2002.

Ledeen, Michael A. *The War Against the Terror Masters*. New York: St. Martin's Press, 2002.

Lowry, Rich. *Legacy: Paying the Price for the Clinton Years*. Washington, D.C.: Regnery, 2003.

Miller, John and Michael Stone with Chris Mitchell. *The Cell: Inside the 9/11 Plot, and Why the FBI and CIA Failed to Stop It*. New York: Hyperion, 2002.

Miniter, Richard. *Losing bin Laden: How Bill Clinton's Failures Unleashed Global Terror*. Washington, D.C.: Regnery, 2003.

SELECT BIBLIOGRAPHY

Patterson, Robert. *Dereliction of Duty: The Eye Witness Account of How Bill Clinton Compromised America's National Security.* Washington, D.C.: Regnery, 2003.

Revell, Oliver "Buck" and Dwight Williams. *A G-man's Journal.* New York: Pocket Star Books, 1998.

Ruddy, Christopher and Carl Limbacher, Jr., ed. *Catastrophe: Clinton's Role in America's Worst Disaster.* West Palm Beach, FL: NewsMax.com, 2002.

Sammon, Bill. *Fighting Back: The War on Terrorism—From Inside the Bush Whitehouse.* Washington, D.C.: Regnery, 2002.

Speaker's Advisory Group on Russia. "Russia's Road to Corruption: How the Clinton administration Exported Government Instead of Free Enterprise and Failed the Russian People." September 2000.

Timmerman, Kenneth R. *Preachers of Hate: Islam and the War on America.* New York: Crown Forum, 2003.

Woodward, Bob. *Bush At War.* New York: Simon & Schuster, 2002.

NOTES

CHAPTER 1: A Near Miss, or Missed Opportunity?

1. Hal Bernton, Mike Carter, David Heath, and James Neff, "The Crossing," part 12 of a special report, "The Terrorist Within," SeattleTimes.com, 23 June–7 July 2002. Available online at http://seattletimes.nwsource.com/news/nation-world/terrorist-within/.

2. According to a knowledgeable law-enforcement source familiar with the case.

3. Massimo Calabresi, "The Terror Countdown," *Time*, 20 December 1999.

4. "The Millennium Plot," *60 Minutes II*, CBSNews.com, 26 December 2001.

5. Bernton, et al., "The Terrorist Within," part 12.

6. Bernton, et al., "The Terrorist Within," part 12.

7. "The Millennium Plot," *60 Minutes II*.

8. Calabresi, "The Terror Countdown."

9. Daniel Benjamin and Steven Simon, *The Age of Sacred Terror: Radical Islam's War Against America* (New York: Random, 2003), 32.

10. Benjamin and Simon, *The Age of Sacred Terror,* 30–31.

11. "The Millennium Plot," *60 Minutes II*.

12. Benjamin and Simon, *The Age of Sacred Terror*, 32.

13. "The Millennium Plot," *60 Minutes II*.

14. John Miller, Michael Stone, and Chris Mitchell, *The Cell* (New York: Hyperion, 2002), 225.

15. Miller, et al, 225.

16. "The Millennium Plot," *60 Minutes II*.

17. Hal Bernton, Mike Carter, David Heath, and James Neff, "Joining Jihad," part 7 of a special report, "The Terrorist Within," SeattleTimes.com, 23 June–7 July 2002. Available online at http://seattletimes.nwsource.com/news/nation-world/terrorist-within/.

18. "False American Alarm on Mauritanian Bin Laden Buddy," *Middle East Times*, August 2000.

19. "Another Suspect Detained with Possible Links to Border Bomb Suspect," CNN.com, 28 January 2000.

20. "Ressam Pleads Not Guilty on Bomb Smuggling Charges," CNN.com, 27 January 2000.

21. "Secret Witness Sought in 9/11 Case." Iafrica.com, 4 Dec 2002; Toby Harnden and Sean O'Neill, "Death Penalty Faces '20th Hijacker,'" *Telegraph*, 12 December 2001.

22. Christopher Isham and Salim Jiwa, "Bin Laden Linked to Terror Suspects," ABCNews.com, 27 January 2001.

23. "The Millennium Plot," *60 Minutes II*.

24. "Ressam Pleads Not Guilty . . ."

25. Hal Bernton, Mike Carter, David Heath, and James Neff, "Going to Camp," and "A Bunch of Guys," parts 8 and 9 of a special report, "The Terrorist Within," SeattleTimes.com, 23 June–7 July 2002. Available online at http://seattletimes. nwsource.com/news/nation-world/terroristwithin/.

26. Ward Sanderson, "Bosnian Police Arrest Four Men, Including One Suspected of Terrorist Ties," *Stars & Stripes*, 27 July 2001.

27. According to an interview with a source very familiar with the case.

28. According to information contained in several court documents acquired from the Federal Court in Montreal, Canada, and other sources.

29. John V. Parachini, "The World Trade Center Bombers (1993)," *Toxic Terror: Assessing Terrorist Use of Chemical and Biological Weapons*, ed. Jonathan B. Tucker (Cambridge, MA: MIT Press, 2000), 185–206.

30. Benjamin and Simon, 162.

31. Benjamin and Simon, 163.

32. Hal Bernton, Mike Carter, David Heath, and James Neff, "It Takes a Thief," part 6 of a special report, "The Terrorist Within," SeattleTimes.com, 23 June–7 July 2002. Available online at http://seattletimes.nwsource.com/news/nation-world/terroristwithin/.

CHAPTER 2: Intelligence Failures

1. Hal Bernton, Mike Carter, David Heath, and James Neff, "The Crossing," part 12 of a special report, "The Terrorist Within," SeattleTimes.com, 23 June–7 July 2002. Available online at http://seattletimes.nwsource.com/news/nation-world/terroristwithin/.

2. Bruce Crumley, "Terror Takes the Stand," *Time Magazine Europe*, 14 October 2002; Peter Humi, "Bomb Explodes on Paris Subway," CNN.com, 17 October 1995.

3. Kelly Ryan, "From Milan to Madrid to Montreal: the Worldwide Web of Terror," CBC.ca, 14 December 2001.

4. Hal Bernton, Mike Carter, David Heath, and James Neff, "Terrorist Tracker," part 5 of a special report, "The Terrorist Within," 23 June–7 July 2002. Available online at http://seattletimes.nwsource.com/news/nation-world/terroristwithin/.

5. Ryan, "From Milan to Madrid to Montreal."

6. According to a "Memorandum of Facts" and related court documents obtained from the Federal Court in Montreal, Canada.

7. Bernton, et al., "The Terrorist Within," part 5.

8. Bernton, et al., "The Terrorist Within," part 5.

9. "Britain Hardens Its Stance on Fundamentalism," *The Age*, 22 January 2003.

10. Philip Johnston, "Hard-line Cleric Faces Expulsion from Finsbury Park Mosque," *Telegraph*, 17 January 2003.

11. Sean O'Neill, "Militant Cleric Had Links with Al-Qa'eda Chiefs, Says FBI Report," *Telegraph*, 25 June 2003.

12. C. Spencer Beggs, "London Students React to Rising Iraq Tension," *Observer*, 29 January 2003.

13. *Newsweek Online*, 16 April 2003.

14. Michel Isikoff and Mark Hosenball, "Who, and What, Does He Know?" *Newsweek*, 1 October 2002.

15. Bob Drogin, Josh Meyer, and Carol J. Williams, "2 Indonesians Seen as Key Link to Terrorists," *L.A. Times*, 28 November 2001.

16. Isikoff and Hosenball, "Who, and What, Does He Know?"

17. Isikoff and Hosenball, "Who, and What, Does He Know?"

18. Hal Bernton, Mike Carter, David Heath, and James Neff, "Joining Jihad," part 7 of a special report, "The Terrorist Within," SeattleTimes.com, 23 June–7 July 2002. Available online at http://seattletimes.nwsource.com/news/nation-world/terrorist-within/.

19. Hal Bernton, Mike Carter, David Heath, and James Neff, "A Bunch of Guys," part 9 of a special report, "The Terrorist Within," SeattleTimes.com, 23 June–7 July 2002. Available online at http://seattletimes.nwsource.com/news/nation-world/terroristwithin/.

20. Hal Bernton, Mike Carter, David Heath, and James Neff, "Going to Camp," part 8 of a special report "The Terrorist Within," SeattleTimes.com, 23 June–7 July 2002. Available online at http://seattletimes.nwsource.com/news/nation-world/terroristwithin/.

21. John Miller, Michael Stone, and Chris Mitchell, *The Cell*, (New York: Hyperion, 2002), 260.

22. Miller, et al., 260.

23. Miller, et al., 260.

24. James Risen and Eric Lichtblau, "C.I.A. Was Given Data on Hijacker Long Before 9/11," *New York Times*, 24 February 2004.

25. Hal Bernton, Mike Carter, David Heath, and James Neff, "Puzzle Pieces," part 15 of a special report, "The Terrorist Within," SeattleTimes.com, 23 June–7 July 2002. Available online at http://seattletimes.nwsource.com/news/nation-world/terrorist-within/.

26. Bernton, et al., "The Terrorist Within," part 15.

27. Bernton, et al., "The Terrorist Within," part 15. This contradicts the claim that the map was found in the car when he was arrested ("The Millennium Plot," *60 Minutes II*, CBSNews.com, 26 December 2001). According to the *Seattle Times* story, the FBI did not know the intended target until finding evidence in Canada.

28. Hal Bernton, Mike Carter, David Heath, and James Neff, "The Reckoning," part 16 of a special report, "The Terrorist Within," SeattleTimes.com, 23 June 23–7

July 2002. Available online at http://seattletimes.nwsource.com/news/nation-world/terroristwithin/.

29. Bernton, et al., "The Terrorist Within," part 16.

30. Craig Pyes, Josh Meyer, and William C. Rempel, "U.S. Sees New Terrorist Threat from N. Africa," *L.A. Times*, 8 July 2001.

31. Hal Bernton, Mike Carter, David Heath, and James Neff, "Nine Eleven," part 17 of a special report "The Terrorist Within," SeattleTimes.com, 23 June–7 July 2002. Available online at http://seattletimes.nwsource.com/news/nation-world/terroristwithin/.

32. Bernton, et al., "The Terrorist Within," part 17.

33. "Terror Suspect Trial Begins in Germany," *Deutsche Welle*, 26 June 2003. Available online at http://www.dw-world.de/english/0,3367,1430_A_900864,00.html. "Bin Laden 'Warned of Thousands Dead,'" BBC News, 27 November 2002.

CHAPTER 3: What You Don't Know Will Kill You

1. See Bill Gertz and Rowan Scarborough, "Inside the Ring: Notes from the Pentagon," *Washington Times*, 16 May 2003.

2. Peter Huess, "Former Administration Clueless," *Washington Times*, August 7, 2003.

3. Dick Morris, *Off with Their Heads: Traitors, Crooks & Obstructionists in American Politics, Media & Business* (New York: Regan Books, 2003).

4. Quoted by Chuck Noe, "Aide: Clinton Unleashed bin Laden," *NewsMax*, 5 December 2001.

5. Austin Bay, "What's Keeping Donald Rumsfeld up Late at Night?" Strategypage.com, 5 February 2001.

6. Bay, "Rumsfeld."

7. Bay, "Rumsfeld."

8. Michael Ledeen, *The War Against the Terror Masters* (New York: Saint Martin's Press, 2002), 115.

9. Ledeen, 116.

10. Richard Miniter, *Losing Bin Laden* (Washington DC: Regnery, 2003), 88.

11. Miniter, 88.

12. Leeden, 117.

13. L. Brent Bozell III, "Clinton's Intelligence Scandals," Creators Syndicate, 23 July 2003.

14. "A Total Lack of Intelligence," *Washington Times*, 3 September 2003.

15. *New York Times Magazine*, 23 July 2003.

16. *New York Times Magazine*, 23 July 2003.

17. *New York Times Magazine*, 23 July 2003.

18. Reuel Marc Gerecht, "The Counterterrorist Myth," *Atlantic Monthly*, July/August 2001.

19. For more on this topic, see Jayna Davis, *The Third Terrorist* (Nashville: WND Books, 2004).

CHAPTER 4: Deutch Treat

1. Thomas Powers, "The Trouble with the CIA," *New York Times Review of Books*, vol. 49, no. 1, 17 January 2002.
2. Powers, "The Trouble with the CIA."
3. Michael Ledeen, *The War Against the Terror Masters* (New York: Saint Martin's Press, 2002), 118.
4. Powers, "The Trouble with the CIA."
5. Powers, "The Trouble with the CIA."
6. Powers, "The Trouble with the CIA."
7. Powers, "The Trouble with the CIA."
8. Powers, "The Trouble with the CIA."
9. Ledeen, 121.
10. Ledeen, 121.
11. Vernon Loeb, "Panel Advocates Easing CIA Rules on Informants," *Washington Post*, 6 June 2000.
12. Loeb, "Panel Advocates."
13. Loeb, "Panel Advocates."
14. Loeb, "Panel Advocates."
15. AFIO, *Weekly Intelligence Notes*, 9 June 2000. Emphasis added.
16. "James Risen CIA Inquiry of Its Ex-Director Was Stalled at Top, Report Says," *New York Times*, 1 February 2000.
17. For example see, Jeff Gerth's "Under Scrutiny: Citibank's Handling of High-profile Foreigners' Accounts," *New York Times*, 27 July 1999, as well as "Citigroup Head Concedes Laundering Controls Were Poor," *New York Times*, 10 November 1999, and "Hearings Offer View into Private Banking," *New York Times*, 8 November 1999.
18. Ledeen, 118.
19. J. Michael Waller, "PC Security," *Insight on the News*, 28 October 2003.
20. Waller, "PC security."
21. Waller, "PC security."
22. Reed Irvine and Cliff Kincaid, "The CIA and Homosexuals," *Media Monitor*, Accuracy in Media, 23 October 2001.
23. J. Michael Waller, "Blinded Vigilance," *Insight on the News*, 15 October 2003.
24. Waller, "PC Security."
25. Waller, "PC Security."
26. Waller, "PC Security."
27. Waller, "PC Security."
28. Waller, "PC Security."
29. Waller, "PC Security."
30. Waller, "PC Security."

CHAPTER 5: Systemic Failures

1. The text of this report can be found at http://www.fas.org/irp/threat/commission.html.

2. Paul Sperry, "Leahy Blocked Key Antiterror Reforms," WorldNetDaily.com, 5 June 2002.

3. "Experts: A Variety of Intelligence Factors May Have Played a Role," CNN.com, 16 September 2001.

4. Sperry, "Leahy Blocked Key Antiterror Reforms."

5. See Paul Sperry, "Why FBI Missed Islamic Threat," WorldNetDaily.com, 25 July 2002.

6. Douglas Jehl, "CIA Nominee Wary of Budget Cuts," *New York Times*, 3 February 1993.

7. Jehl, "CIA Nominee Wary of Budget Cuts."

8. "World War IV" FrontPageMagazine.com, 22 November 2002.

9. Report of the U.S. Senate Select Committee on Intelligence and U.S. House Permanent Select Committee on Intelligence Together with Additional Views, "Joint Inquiry into Intelligence Community Activities before and after the Terrorist Attacks of September 11, 2001," December 2002.

10. "Joint Inquiry into Intelligence Community Activities," 264.

11. "Joint Inquiry into Intelligence Community Activities," 264.

12. "Joint Inquiry into Intelligence Community Activities," 264. President Bush's record will be dealt with in a later chapter.

13. "Joint Inquiry into Intelligence Community Activities," 265.

14. "Joint Inquiry into Intelligence Community Activities," 266.

15. "Joint Inquiry into Intelligence Community Activities," 216.

CHAPTER 6: Degrading the FBI

1. Siobhan Roth, "Khobar Towers: A Case of Futility," *Legal Times*, 17 September 2001.

2. In addition to an interview with the author, November 2003, Freeh sent me the text of his testimony before the Joint Intelligence Committee given on 8 October 2002.

3. John F. Harris and David A. Vise, "Relations Soured Over FBI's Role: For or Against Administration?" *Washington Post*, 10 January 2001, A01.

4. Harris and Vise, "Relations Soured."

5. Hearing on Current Implementation of the Independent Counsel Act before the House committee on Government Reform and Oversight, 105th Cong., 1st sess., 294-295 (1997); Ann Scott Tyson, "Turf wars ensnare plain-talking FBI chief," *Christian Science Monitor*, 1 October 1999.

6. Tyson, "Turf Wars."

7. Harris and Vise, "Relations Soured."

8. Harris and Vise, "Relations Soured."

9. Richard Lowry, *Legacy: Paying the Price for the Clinton Years* (Washington DC: Regnery, 2003), 198.

10. Interview with author, November 2003, and text of the former director's 8 October 2002 testimony before the Joint Intelligence Committee.

11. Freeh testimony before the Joint Intelligence Committee, 8 October 2002.

12. Freeh testimony, 8 October 2002.
13. Freeh testimony, 8 October 2002.

CHAPTER 7: Degrading the Military

1. See, "The Homosexual Exclusion Law vs. the Clinton 'Don't Ask, Don't Tell" Policy," Center for Military Readiness, 7 January 2002.
2. Bob Livingston, "Clinton's Defense Policy: Indefensible?" Heritage Lecture #466, Heritage Foundation, 1 September 1993.
3. Baker Spring, "Clinton's 'No-win' Defense Budget," Executive Memorandum #467, Heritage Foundation, 14 February 1997.
4. Spring, "Clinton's 'No-win.'"
5. Spring, "Clinton's 'No-win.'"
6. Spring, "Clinton's 'No-win.'"
7. James H. Anderson, Ph.D., "Putting Muscle in Clinton's Proposed Defense Hike," Backgrounder #1244, Heritage Foundation, 25 January 1999.
8. "Prepared Text of Clinton's State of the Union Speech," CNN.com, 19 January 1999.
9. "Prepared Text of Clinton's State of the Union Speech."
10. Lawrence T. DiRita, Baker Spring, and John Luddy, "Thumbs Down to the Bottom-up Review," Backgrounder #957, Heritage Foundation, 24 September 1993.
11. DiRita, et al., "Thumbs Down." Emphasis added.
12. DiRita, et al., "Thumbs Down."
13. DiRita, et al., "Thumbs Down."
14. DiRita, et al., "Thumbs Down."
15. DiRita, et al., "Thumbs Down."
16. DiRita, et al., "Thumbs Down."
17. Livingston, "Clinton's Defense Policy."
18. Livingston, "Clinton's Defense Policy."
19. Livingston, "Clinton's Defense Policy."
20. Livingston, "Clinton's Defense Policy."
21. Livingston, "Clinton's Defense Policy."
22. DiRita, et al., "Thumbs Down."
23. Margo MacFarland, "Nunn Warns That Outlay Problem in '95 Could Be Even Worse Than '94," *Inside the Navy*, 21 June 1993, cited in DiRita, et al., "Thumbs Down."
24. Livingston, "Clinton's Defense Policy."
25. DiRita, et al., "Thumbs Down."
26. DiRita, et al., "Thumbs Down."
27. Baker Spring, "Building an Army for the Post-Cold War Era," Backgrounder #956, Heritage Foundation, 24 September 1993.
28. DiRita, et al., "Thumbs Down."
29. DiRita, et al., "Thumbs Down."
30. DiRita, et al., "Thumbs Down."
31. DiRita, et al., "Thumbs Down."

32. DiRita, et al., "Thumbs Down."

33. Lawrence T. DiRita and Baker Spring, "Clinton Defense Increases: Good Start, but Not Enough," Backgrounder #399, Heritage Foundation, 12 December 1994.

34. DiRita and Spring, "Clinton Defense Increases."

35. DiRita and Spring, "Clinton Defense Increases."

36. Livingston, "Clinton's Defense Policy."

37. Livingston, "Clinton's Defense Policy."

38. Livingston, "Clinton's Defense Policy."

39. Livingston, "Clinton's Defense Policy."

40. Livingston, "Clinton's Defense Policy."

41. Defense Policy Points, United States Senate Republican Policy Committee, 11 February 1999.

42. Defense Policy Points.

43. Defense Policy Points.

44. Defense Policy Points.

45. Defense Policy Points.

46. Livingston, "Clinton's Defense Policy."

47. "At Rumsfeld Ceremony, Bush Promises to Beef Up Military," CNN.com, 26 January 2001.

CHAPTER 8: A Pattern of Failure

1. Byron York, "Clinton Has No Clothes: What 9/11 Revealed about the Ex-president," *National Review*, 17 December 2001.

2. Scot Lehigh, "While Clinton Slept," *Boston Globe*, 2 January 2002.

3. Lehigh, "While Clinton Slept."

4. Lehigh, "While Clinton Slept."

5. David N. Bossie and Christopher M. Gray, "Al Qaeda's Revenge: Its Methods and Nation-state Allies," *Citizens United*, vol. 2, issue 2. Available at www.citizensunited.org/al-qaeda.html.

6. Bossie and Gray, "Al Qaeda's Revenge."

7. "Out of Reach," *60 Minutes II,* CBSNEWS.com, 10 October 2001.

8. "Out of Reach," *60 Minutes II.*

9. "Shadow Warriors," CBSNews.com, 1 May 2002.

10. "Shadow Warriors," CBSNews.com.

11. "Shadow Warriors," CBSNews.com.

12. "Shadow Warriors," CBSNews.com.

13. J. Michael Waller, "A Visa for Castro's Terrorism Chief in Washington?" *Insight Magazine*, 24 September 1999.

14. Quoted in Waller, "A Visa for Castro's Terrorism Chief."

15. Waller, "A Visa for Castro's Terrorism Chief."

16. Waller, "A Visa for Castro's Terrorism Chief."

17. Waller, "A Visa for Castro's Terrorism Chief."

18. Waller, "A Visa for Castro's Terrorism Chief."

19. Waller, "A Visa for Castro's Terrorism Chief."

20. Waller, "A Visa for Castro's Terrorism Chief."

21. Waller, "A Visa for Castro's Terrorism Chief."

22. Jeff Jacoby, "An Unpardonable Offer," *Boston Globe*, 6 September 1999.

23. Jacoby, "An Unpardonable Offer."

24. Jacoby, "An Unpardonable Offer."

25. Jacoby, "An Unpardonable Offer."

26. Jacoby, "An Unpardonable Offer."

27. Jacoby, "An Unpardonable Offer."

28. Jacoby, "An Unpardonable Offer."

29. Jacoby, "An Unpardonable Offer."

30. Jacoby, "An Unpardonable Offer."

31. Louis Fisher, "The Law: When Presidential Power Backfires: Clinton's Use of Clemency"; *The FALN*, 1 September 2002. Available at http://www.puertorico-herald.org/issues/2002/vol6n38/LawPresPwrBkfir-en.shtml.

32. Fisher, "The Law."

33. Fisher, "The Law."

34. Neil A. Lewis, "Records Show Puerto Ricans Got U.S. Help with Clemency," *New York Times*, 21 October 1999.

35. Fisher, "The Law."

36. Fisher, "The Law."

37. Lewis, "Records Show Puerto Ricans Got U.S. Help."

38. Lewis, "Records Show Puerto Ricans Got U.S. Help."

39. Waller, "A Visa for Castro's Terrorism Chief."

40. "Terrorism: Islamic Clerics at Guantanamo," *Newsweek*, 6 October 2003.

41. Douglas Farah, "U.S. Says Activist Funded Terrorists," *Washington Post*, 1 October 2003, A06.

42. Rowan Scarborough and Steve Miller, "Airman Accused of Terror Spying," *Washington Times*, 24 September 2003.

43. Douglas Farah and John Mintz, "Islamic Activist Accused in Libyan Money Case," *Washington Post*, 30 September 2003. Emphasis added.

44. Jerry Seper, "Clinton White House Axed Terror-fund Probe," *Washington Times*, 2 April 2002.

45. Jennifer Barrett, "We Have Barely Scraped the Surface," *Newsweek*, 30 September 2003.

46. Barrett, "We Have Barely Scraped the Surface."

47. Barrett, "We Have Barely Scraped the Surface."

48. Barrett, "We Have Barely Scraped the Surface."

49. "Terrorism: Islamic Clerics at Guantanamo," *Newsweek*.

50. Michael Ledeen, *The War Against the Terror Masters* (New York: St Martin's Press, 2002), 91.

51. Carl Limbacher, "Judicial Watch: Clinton IRS Turned Blind Eye to Terrorists," NewsMax.com, 23 September 2001.

52. Carl Limbacher, "IRS Official to Judicial Watch: Clinton Enemies Were Audited," NewsMax.com, 23 April 2002.

53. Joseph Farah,"IRS Gestapo Strikes Again," WorldNetDaily, 24 August 2000.
54. "O'Reilly: Clintons Sicced IRS on Me," NewsMax.com, 24 September 2003.
55. Limbacher, "IRS Official to Judicial Watch."
56. Limbacher, "IRS Official to Judicial Watch."
57. Limbacher, "IRS Official to Judicial Watch."
58. Simon Reeve and Giles Foden, "A New Breed of Terror," *The Guardian*, 12 September 2001.
59. "Clinton Hushed Up Federal Report Warning of Hijack Attacks," NewsMax.com, 18 May 2002.
60. "Clinton Hushed Up Federal Report," NewsMax.com.
61. "Clinton Hushed Up Federal Report," NewsMax.com.
62. James A. Phillips, "Time for Arafat to Get Serious about Peace," Executive Memorandum #469, The Heritage Foundation, 27 February 1997.
63. Phillips, "Time for Arafat to Get Serious."
64. Phillips, "Time for Arafat to Get Serious."
65. James A. Phillips, "Middle East: Give Sharon a Chance," Press Room, Heritage Foundation, 26 February 2001.
66. Madeleine Albright, *Madame Secretary: A Memoir* (New York: Miramax, 2003), 313.
67. This 13 May 2002 interview can be found at http://www.jinsa.org/articles/print.html?documentid=1494.
68. Joseph Farah, "Was Clinton Pro-Taliban?" WorldNetDaily.com, 31 October 2001.
69. Farah, "Was Clinton Pro-Taliban?"
70. "Commemorating 9-11," Speech before the U.S. House of Representatives, 11 September 2002.
71. "Commemorating 9-11."

CHAPTER 9: Clinton's Silk Trail

1. As recently confirmed. Joby Warrick, "Nuclear Program in Iran Tied to Pakistan," MSNBC.com, 22 December 2003.
2. "Quid pro quo? A China Chronology," *Washington Times*, 22 May 1998.
3. "Export Controls: Some Controls over Missile-related Technology Exports to China Are Weak" (Letter Report, 17 April 1995), General Accounting Office/NSIAD-95-82). Available at www.fas.org/man/gao/gao9582.htm.
4. Murray Waas, "Clinton Administration Failed to Monitor China's Use of Missile-technology Exports," Salon.com, 29 May 1998.
5. "Quid pro quo?" *Washington Times*; John Minte, "To Loral's Schwartz, Donations Are about Fun, Not Favors," *Washington Post*, 18 March 1997.
6. See The Cox Report, chapter 1, page 59.
7. The Cox Report.
8. The Cox Report.
9. The Cox Report.
10. The Cox Report.

11. Jeff Gerth and David E. Sanger, "How China Won Rights to Launch Satellites for U.S., *New York Times*, 17 May 1998.

12. Tim Curry and Robert Windrew, "Time Line of Clinton China Decisions," MSNBC, 17 May 1998.

13. Investigation of Political Fundraising Improprieties and Possible Violations of Law, Interim Report, Sixth Report by the Committee on Government Reform and Oversight, 63, 1398.

14. "Quid pro quo?" *Washington Times*.

15. "Quid pro quo?" *Washington Times*.

16. "Quid pro quo?" *Washington Times*.

17. Investigation of Political Fundraising Improprieties, 1715.

18. Investigation of Political Fundraising Improprieties. The *Washington Times* rounds up to $300,000.

19. Investigation of Political Fundraising Improprieties, 1715.

20. Investigation of Political Fundraising Improprieties, 1716; *The Washington Times* reports on the picture.

21. Investigation of Political Fundraising Improprieties, 1673.

22. Investigation of Political Fundraising Improprieties, 1673.

23. Curry and Windrem, "Time Line of Clinton China Decisions."

24. Curry and Windrem, "Time Line of Clinton China Decisions."

25. "Quid pro quo?" *Washington Times*.

26. "Quid pro quo?" *Washington Times*.

27. "Quid pro quo?" *Washington Times*.

28. The Cox Report, chapter 9, page 51.

29. The Cox Report, chapter 9, page 51.

30. "Quid pro quo?" *Washington Times*.

31. "Quid pro quo?" *Washington Times*.

32. "Campaign Finance Key Player: John Huang," *WashingtonPost.com*, July 24, 1997.

33. "Quid pro quo?" *Washington Times*.

34. "Quid pro quo?" *Washington Times*.

35. "Technology Deals with China Harmed U.S. Security, House Committee Says," CNN.com, 31 December 1998.

36. "Technology Deals with China Harmed U.S. Security," CNN.com.

37. "Technology Deals with China Harmed U.S. Security," CNN.com.

38. "Technology Deals with China Harmed U.S. Security," CNN.com.

39. Bill Gertz, "No Warheads Secret after China Spying," *Washington Times*, 25 May 1999.

40. Gertz, "No Warheads Secret."

41. Daniel Benjamin and Steven Simon, *The Age of Sacred Terror: Radical Islam's War Against America* (New York: Random, 2003), 203.

42. Benjamin and Simon, 204.

43. Jeff Gerth, "China Buying U.S. Computers, Raising Fears of Enhanced Nuclear Weapons," *New York Times*, 10 June 1997.

44. Gerth, "China Buying U.S. Computers."

CHAPTER 10: Neglecting the Bear

1. U.S. House of Representatives Speaker's Advisory Group on Russia. Chairman Christopher Cox. "Russia's Road to Corruption; How the Clinton Administration Exported Government Instead of Free Enterprise and Failed the Russian People," chapter 9, page 119.
2. "Russia's Road to Corruption," chapter 9, page 119.
3. "Russia's Road to Corruption," chapter 9, page 120.
4. "Russia's Road to Corruption," chapter 11, page 155.
5. "Russia's Road to Corruption," chapter 6.
6. David Bossie and Floyd Brown , *Prince Albert: The Life and Lies of Al Gore* (Bellevue, WA: Merril Press, 2000), 117–121.
7. "Russia's Road to Corruption," chapter 9, page 117.
8. James Risen, "Gore Rejected C.I.A. Evidence of Russian Corruption," *New York Times*, 23 November 1998.
9. "Russia's Road to Corruption," chapter 9, page 117.
10. "Russia's Road to Corruption," chapter 9, page 117.
11. "Russia's Road to Corruption," chapter 9, page 118.
12. "Russia's Road to Corruption," chapter 9, page 119.
13. "Russia's Road to Corruption," chapter 9, page 118.
14. "Russia's Road to Corruption," chapter 9, page 113.
15. "Russia's Road to Corruption," chapter 9, page 113.
16. "Russia's Road to Corruption," chapter 9, page 113.
17. "Russia's Road to Corruption," chapter 9, page 113.
18. "Russia's Road to Corruption," chapter 9, page 114.
19. "Russia's Road to Corruption," chapter 9, page 114.
20. "Russia's Road to Corruption," chapter 9, page 114.
21. "Russia's Road to Corruption," chapter 9, page 114.
22. "Russia's Road to Corruption," chapter 9, page 114.
23. "Russia's Road to Corruption," chapter 9, page 114.
24. "Russia's Road to Corruption," chapter 9, page 114.
25. "Russia's Road to Corruption," chapter 9, page 113.
26. "Russia's Road to Corruption," chapter 9, page 113.
27. "Russia's Road to Corruption," chapter 9, page 113.
28. "Russia's Road to Corruption," chapter 9, page 114.
29. "Russia's Road to Corruption," chapter 9, page 116.
30. "Russia's Road to Corruption," chapter 9, page 116.
31. "Russia's Road to Corruption," chapter 9, page 116.
32. "Russia's Road to Corruption," chapter 9, page 116.
33. "Russia's Road to Corruption," chapter 9, page 116.
34. "Russia's Road to Corruption," chapter 9, page 117.
35. "Russia's Road to Corruption," chapter 9, page 116.
36. "Russia's Road to Corruption," chapter 9, page 117.
37. "Russia's Road to Corruption," chapter 11, page 151.
38. "Russia's Road to Corruption," chapter 11, page 151.

39. "Russia's Road to Corruption," chapter 11, page 151.

40. "Russia's Road to Corruption," chapter 11, page 156.

41. "Russia's Road to Corruption," chapter 11, page 156.

42. "Russia's Road to Corruption," chapter 11, page 149.

43. "Russia's Road to Corruption," chapter 11, page 155.

44. "Russia's Road to Corruption," chapter 11, page 155.

45. "Russia's Road to Corruption," chapter 11, page 158.

46. "Russia's Road to Corruption," chapter 11, page 158.

47. "Russia's Road to Corruption," chapter 11, page 158.

48. "Russia's Road to Corruption," chapter 11, page 158.

49. "Russia's Road to Corruption," chapter 11, page 162.

50. "Russia's Road to Corruption," chapter 11, page 161.

51. "Russia's Road to Corruption," chapter 11, page 161.

52. "Russia's Road to Corruption," chapter 11, page 161.

53. "Russia's Road to Corruption," chapter 9, page 123.

54. "Russia's Road to Corruption," chapter 9, page 119.

55. "Russia's Road to Corruption," chapter 9, page 119.

56. "Russia's Road to Corruption," chapter 9, page 122.

57. "Russia's Road to Corruption," chapter 9, page 122.

58. "Russia's Road to Corruption," chapter 9, page 122.

59. "Russia's Road to Corruption," chapter 9, page 122.

60. "Russia's Road to Corruption," chapter 9, page 124.

61. "Russia's Road to Corruption," chapter 9, page 124–125.

62. President George W. Bush, "Remarks by the President in Roundtable Interview with Foreign Press," Press Release, 17 July 2001.

CHAPTER 11: World Trade Center One

1. Dave Williams, "The Bombing of the World Trade Center in New York City," *International Criminal Police Review*, No. 469–471 (1998). Available at Interpol.com.

2. Dick Morris, "Why Clinton Slept," *New York Post*, 2 January 2002.

3. Morris, "Why Clinton Slept."

4. Morris, "Why Clinton Slept."

5. Williams, "The Bombing of the World Trade Center."

6. Williams, "The Bombing of the World Trade Center."

7. Williams, "The Bombing of the World Trade Center."

8. Williams, "The Bombing of the World Trade Center."

9. Williams, "The Bombing of the World Trade Center."

10. Williams, "The Bombing of the World Trade Center."

11. Williams, "The Bombing of the World Trade Center."

12. Williams, "The Bombing of the World Trade Center."

13. Williams, "The Bombing of the World Trade Center."

14. Williams, "The Bombing of the World Trade Center."

15. Williams, "The Bombing of the World Trade Center."

16. Daniel Benjamin and Steven Simon, *The Age of Sacred Terror: Radical Islam's War Against America* (New York: Random, 2003), 7.
17. Williams, "The Bombing of the World Trade Center."
18. Oliver Revell, "Law Enforcement Views Radical Islam: Protecting America," *The Middle East Quarterly*, March 1995.
19. Benjamin and Simon, 7.
20. Williams, "The Bombing of the World Trade Center."
21. "World Trade Center Bombing Suspect Apprehended in Pakistan," Department of Justice, 8 February 1995, available at http://www.usdoj.gov/opa/pr/Pre_96/February95/78.txt.
22. John V. Parachini, "The World Trade Center Bombers (1993)," *Toxic Terror: Assessing Terrorist Use of Chemical and Biological Weapons*, Jonathan B. Tucker ed., (Cambridge, MA: MIT Press, 2000), 185–206.
23. Benjamin and Simon, 22–23.
24. Benjamin and Simon, 23.
25. Simon Reeve and Giles Foden, "A New Breed of Terror," *The Guardian*, 12 September 2001.
26. Benjamin and Simon, 20; also, Laurie Mylroie, "The World Trade Center Bomb: Who is Ramzi Yousef? And Why It Matters," *The National Interest*, Winter 1995/96.
27. Benjamin and Simon, 20.
28. Benjamin and Simon, 21.
29. Parachini, "The World Trade Center Bombers," 185–206.
30. Benjamin and Simon, 25.
31. Benjamin and Simon, 25.
32. "World Trade Center Bombing Testimony Ends," CNN.com, 5 November 1997.
33. "World Trade Center Bombing Testimony Ends."
34. Mylroie, "The World Trade Center Bomb."
35. Mylroie, "The World Trade Center Bomb."
36. Mylroie, "The World Trade Center Bomb."
37. Mylroie, "The World Trade Center Bomb."
38. Morris, "Why Clinton Slept."
39. Morris, "Why Clinton Slept."
40. Morris, "Why Clinton Slept."
41. Dick Morris, "While Clinton Fiddled," *Wall Street Journal*, 5 February 2002.
42. "The First Hundred Days of the Administration of President Clinton," available online at http://www.ibiblio.org/pub/academic/political-science/whitehouse-papers/1993/Apr/The-First-100-Days-of-the-Administration-of-President-Clinton.htm.
43. "The First Hundred Days."
44. "The Damage Clinton Did," *Sunday Times*, 30 September 2001.
45. Morris, "Why Clinton Slept."
46. Benjamin and Simon, 219.
47. Benjamin and Simon, 226.
48. Mylroie, "The World Trade Center Bomb."

CHAPTER 12: The Somalia Massacre

1. Art Pine, "Missiles Strike Bases Linked to African Blasts," *Los Angeles Times*, 21 August 1998.
2. Ed Offley, "Who's Afraid of 'Black Hawk Down'?" *Defense Watch*, 22 March 2002; Paul Greenberg, "The Ghosts of Mogadishu," TownHall.com, 16 August 2002.
3. Bob Livingston, "Clinton's Defense Policy: Indefensible?" Heritage Lecture #466, The Heritage Foundation, 1 September 1993.
4. Livingston, "Clinton's Defense Policy."
5. Livingston, "Clinton's Defense Policy."
6. There are many descriptions of the events of October 3, 1993 available. For my purposes what follows is based primarily on the summary of Yossef Bodansky's *Bin Laden: the Man Who Declared War on America* (Roseville: Prima Forum, 1999, 2001), 84ff.
7. Larry E. Joyce, "Did My Son Have To Die?" *USA Today*, 20 October 1993.
8. Joyce, "Did My Son Have to Die?"
9. Broadcast on BBC on 3 October 1993. Available at http://news.bbc.co.uk/onthis-day/hi/dates/stories/october/4/newsid_2486000/2486909.
10. "Rangers to Exit Somalia," *Roanoke Times*, 20 October 1993.
11. "Rangers to Exit Somalia," *Roanoke Times*.
12. Among many general sources about the events, see the *Frontline* chronology at http://www.pbs.org/wgbh/pages/frontline/shows/ambush/etc/cron.html.
13. Art Pine, "U.S. Soldiers Killed, 24 Hurt During UN Sweep in Somalia," *Los Angeles Times*, 5 October 1993.
14. Bodansky, 89.
15. Bodansky, 89.
16. Bodansky, 89.
17. Daniel Benjamin and Steven Simon, *The Age of Sacred Terror: Radical Islam's War Against America* (New York: Random, 2003), 118.
18. Bodansky, 64–65.
19. Bodansky, 66.
20. Bodansky, 71.
21. Bodansky, 73.
22. Bodansky, 83.
23. Bodansky, 83–84.
24. Bodansky, 83–84.
25. Michael R. Gordon with John H. Cushman Jr., "Mission in Somalia; After Supporting Hunt for Aideed, U.S. Is Blaming UN for Losses," *New York Times*, 18 October 1993.
26. Gordon and Cushman, "Mission in Somalia."
27. Gordon and Cushman, "Mission in Somalia."
28. Gordon and Cushman, "Mission in Somalia."
29. Gordon and Cushman, "Mission in Somalia."
30. Gordon and Cushman, "Mission in Somalia."
31. Gordon and Cushman, "Mission in Somalia."

32. Gordon and Cushman, "Mission in Somalia."

33. Gordon and Cushman, "Mission in Somalia."

34. Gordon and Cushman, "Mission in Somalia."

35. Gordon and Cushman, "Mission in Somalia."

36. David H. Hackworth, "Hearing on Somalia: Excuses, Excuses," Defending America, www.hackworth.com, 17 May 1994.

37. Hackworth, "Hearing on Somalia."

38. Hackworth, "Hearing on Somalia."

39. Joyce, "Did My Son Have To Die?"

40. "'Black Hawk Down' Dad Bristles at Attempt To Blame Bush," NewsMax.com, 11 August 2002.

41. "Black Hawk Down' Dad," NewsMax.com.

42. "Black Hawk Down' Dad," NewsMax.com.

43. Paul Greenberg, "The Ghosts of Mogadishu," Townhall.com, 16 August 2002.

44. http://www.defenselink.mil/specials/secdef_histories/bios/aspin.htm.

45. http://www.defenselink.mil/specials/secdef_histories/bios/aspin.htm.

46. http://www.defenselink.mil/specials/secdef_histories/bios/aspin.htm.

47. Joyce, "Did My Son Have To Die?"

48. "Black Hawk Down' Dad," NewsMax.com.

49. Offley, "Who's Afraid of 'Black Hawk Down'?"

50. Rick Erickson, "Today We Revive the Fading Memory of the Tragedy at Mogadishu," GOPUSA.com, 3 October 2003.

51. "Clinton's Black Hawk History," *Wall Street Journal*, 6 August 2002.

52. "Clinton's Black Hawk History," *Wall Street Journal*.

53. "Bin Laden's Sole Post-September 11 TV Interview Aired," CNN.com, 31 January 2002.

54. Interview in May 1998 with ABC's John Miller; available at the Web site of the PBS show *Frontline* at http://www.pbs.org/wgbh/pages/frontline/shows/bin-laden/who/interview.html.

55. Bodansky, 89.

CHAPTER 13: Khobar Towers

1. Elsa Walsh, "Annals of Politics: Louis Freeh's Last Case," *The New Yorker*, 14 May 2001.

2. Yossef Bodansky, *Bin Laden: The Man Who Declared War on America* (Roseville: Prima Forum, 1999, 2001), 169.

3. "I Was Just Spun Around," CNN.com, 28 June 1996.

4. "I Was Just Spun Around."

5. Byron York, "Clinton Has No Clothes: What 9/11 Revealed about the Ex-president," *National Review*, 30 November 2001.

6. Walsh, "Annals of Politics."

7. Most reports only mention the number of Americans who died, but according to Yossef Bodansky there were others as well. Bodansky, 151.

8. Dan Eggen and Vernon Loeb, "U.S. Indicts 14 Suspects in Saudi Arabia Blast" *Washington Post*, 22 June 2001, A01.

9. "Massive Bomb Rocks U.S. Military Complex," CNN.com, 26 June 1996.

10. Bodansky, 151.

11. "General Didn't Tell Superiors about Saudi Reluctance," CNN.com, 2 July 1996.

12. Ken Booth and Tim Dunne, ed., "Desperately Seeking Bin Laden: The Intelligence Dimension of the War Against Terror," *Worlds in Collision: Terror and the Future of Global Order* (New York: Palgrave MacMillan, 2002), 61.

13. Emphasis added. This chilling interview took place in May 1998 with ABC's John Miller and is available at the Web site of the PBS show *Frontline* at http://www.pbs.org/wgbh/pages/frontline/shows/binladen/who/interview.html.

14. Barton Gellman, "U.S. Was Foiled Multiple Times in Efforts to Capture Bin Laden or Have Him Killed," *Washington Post,* 3 October 2001, A01.

15. Andrew Sullivan, "While Clinton Diddled," Salon.com, January 9, 2002.

16. Eggen and Loeb, "U.S. Indicts 14 Suspects."

17. Eggen and Loeb, "U.S. Indicts 14 Suspects."

18. Bodansky, 171.

19. Michael Ledeen, *The War Against the Terror Masters,* (New York: St. Martin's Press, 2002), 46.

20. David E. Kaplan, Nancy Bentrup, Chitra Ragavan, and Kevin Whitelaw, "Five Years Later, a Window on Terror," *U.S. News & World Report,* 2 July 2001, 24.

21. "Clinton Pays Tributes to Airmen Killed in Saudi Bombing," CNN.com, 30 June 1996.

22. Siobhan Roth, "Khobar Towers: A Case of Futility," *Legal Times,* 17 September 2001.

23. York, "Clinton Has No Clothes."

24. York, "Clinton Has No Clothes."

25. "Perry: Saudis Close to Naming Bombers," CNN.com, 2 August 1996.

26. "Saudis Allege Iran behind Bombing," CNN.com, 12 December 1996.

27. "Christopher Tours Saudi Bomb Wreckage," CNN.com, 26 June 1996.

28. "White House: Reports of Uncooperative Saudi Officials Are False," CNN.com, 2 November 1996.

29. "Reports of Uncooperative Saudi Officials Are False," CNN.com.

30. "Report: U.S. Gets New Info on Saudi Bomb," CNN.com, 6 December 1996.

31. "U.S. Gets New Info on Saudi Bomb," CNN.com.

32. "U.S. Gets New Info on Saudi Bomb," CNN.com.

33. "U.S. Gets New Info on Saudi Bomb," CNN.com.

34. Eggen and Loeb, "U.S. Indicts 14 Suspects."

35. Joe Klein, "Closework: Why We Couldn't See What Was Right in Front of Us," *New Yorker,* 1 October 2001.

36. For an example see Timothy Noah, "Freeh at Last?" Slate.com, 25 July 2003.

37. Walsh, "Annals of Politics."

38. Ambrose Evans-Pritchard, "'Victimized' FBI Chief Savages Meddling Clinton," *Sunday Telegraph,* 16 April 1996.

39. Walsh, "Annals of Politics."

40. Walsh, "Annals of Politics."

41. Walsh, "Annals of Politics."

42. Walsh, "Annals of Politics."

43. Walsh, "Annals of Politics."
44. Walsh, "Annals of Politics."
45. Walsh, "Annals of Politics."
46. Walsh, "Annals of Politics."
47. Report of the U.S. Senate Select Committee on Intelligence and U.S. House Permanent Select Committee on Intelligence, "Joint Inquiry into Intelligence Community Activities before and after the Terrorist Attacks of September 11, 2001," December 2002.
48. Walsh, "Annals of Politics."
49. Walsh, "Annals of Politics."
50. Walsh, "Annals of Politics."
51. Walsh, "Annals of Politics."
52. Walsh, "Annals of Politics."
53. Walsh, "Annals of Politics."
54. Walsh, "Annals of Politics."
55. Walsh, "Annals of Politics."
56. Roth, "Khobar Towers."
57. Roth, "Khobar Towers."
58. Roth, "Khobar Towers."
59. Eggen and Loeb, "U.S. Indicts 14 Suspects."
60. Eggen and Loeb, "U.S. Indicts 14 Suspects."
61. Roth, "Khobar Towers."
62. "Charges Dropped against Saudi Suspected in Khobar Bombing," CNN.com, 21 October 1997.
63. "Departed Khobar Bombing Suspect Arrives in Saudi Arabia," CNN.com, 11 October 1999.
64. Roth, "Khobar Towers."
65. Kaplan, et al., "Five Years Later," 24.
66. Kaplan, et al., "Five Years Later," 24.
67. Kaplan, et al., "Five Years Later," 24.
68. Kaplan, et al., "Five Years Later," 24.
69. Eggen and Loeb, "U.S. Indicts 14 Suspects."
70. Eggen and Loeb, "U.S. Indicts 14 Suspects."
71. Eggen and Loeb, "U.S. Indicts 14 Suspects."
72. David Horowitz, "The Left Should Look in the Mirror," History News Network, 17 May 2002: available at http://hnn.us/articles/printfriendly/740.html.
73. Sullivan, "While Clinton Diddled."
74. Sullivan, "While Clinton Diddled."
75. Sullivan, "While Clinton Diddled."
76. "Saudis Allege Iran behind Bombing," CNN.com, 12 December 1996.

CHAPTER 14: Embassy Bombings
1. Youssef Bodansky, *Bin Laden: The Man Who Declared War on America* (Roseville: Prima Forum, 1999, 2001), 231.

2. Wendy S. Ross and Jane A. Morse, "U.S. Investigates Bombings at Its Embassies in Kenya, Tanzania," United States Information Agency, August 7, 1998.

3. "DOD Update on Nairobi, Dar Es Salaam U.S. Embassy Bombings," United States Information Agency, 9 August 1998.

4. Daniel Benjamin & Steven Simon, *The Age of Sacred Terror: Radical Islam's War Against America* (New York: Random House, 2002, 2003), 258.

5. "DOD Update on Nairobi," United States Information Agency.

6. Statement by Secretary of State Madeleine K. Albright, U.S. Department of State, 7 August 1998. Available at http://usinfo.state.gov/topical/pol/terror/98080702.htm.

7. Remarks by the president, Office of the Press Secretary, The White House, 7 August 1998. Available at http://usinfo.state.gov/topical/pol/terror/98080704.htm.

8. Statement of the vice president on the bombings of U.S. embassies in Africa, Office of the Vice President, The White House, 7 August 1998. Available at http://usinfo.state.gov/topical/pol/terror/98080708.htm.

9. "Congressional Report," United States Information Agency, 7 August 1998.

10. Text of the president's announcement, United States Information Agency, 20 August 1998.

11. President's announcement, 20 August 1998.

12. Art Pine, "Missiles Strike Bases Linked to African Blasts," *Los Angeles Times*, 21 August 1998.

13. "A Quick Look at Reactions in Congress," CNN.com, 20 August 1998.

14. "A Quick Look at Reactions in Congress," CNN.com.

15. President's announcement, 20 August 1998.

16. "Poll: Most Americans Support Strikes against Terrorists," CNN.com, 23 August 1998.

17. "Protecting Embassies Difficult . . . and Probably Impossible," CNN.com, 10 August 1998.

18. "Protecting Embassies Difficult," CNN.com.

19. Transcript: Clinton Oval Office remarks on antiterrorist attacks, United States Information Agency, 20 August 1998, 5:30 P.M. EDT.

20. Transcript: Clinton Oval Office remarks on antiterrorist attacks.

21. Transcript: Clinton Oval Office remarks on antiterrorist attacks.

22. Transcript: Clinton Oval Office remarks on antiterrorist attacks.

23. Transcript: Clinton Oval Office remarks on antiterrorist attacks.

24. Pine, "Missiles Strike."

25. "Wag the Dog? Lewinsky Buried; Rock Crushed; Starr: Face of Nazi & a Persecutor," CyberAlert, 21 August 1998, vol. 3, no. 137.

26. "Wag the Dog?" CyberAlert.

27. Barton Gellman, "Iraq Hasn't Cooperated, Arms Inspector Reports; Finding Revives Prospect of Airstrikes," *Washington Post*, 16 December 1998.

28. Rowan Scarborough, "Did White House Orchestrate the Iraq 'Crisis'?" *Washington Times*, 20 December 1998.

29. Scarborough, "Did White House Orchestrate the Iraq 'Crisis'?"

30. Scarborough, "Did White House Orchestrate the Iraq 'Crisis'?"

31. Scarborough, "Did White House Orchestrate the Iraq 'Crisis'?"

32. Christopher Hitchens, "Most Dangerous Presidency: Weapons of Mass Distraction," FrontPageMag.com, 22 March 1999.

33. Hitchens, "Most Dangerous Presidency."

34. "Highlights from the House Impeachment Debate," CNN.com, 18 December 1998.

35. Hitchens, "Most Dangerous Presidency."

36. Hitchens, "Most Dangerous Presidency."

37. Hitchens, "Most Dangerous Presidency."

38. DOD News Briefing, Office of the Assistant Secretary of Defense (Public Affairs), 19 December 1998. Available at http://www.defenselink.mil/news/Dec1998/t12201998_t1219coh.html.

39. DOD News Briefing, 19 December 1998.

40. "Highlights from the House Impeachment Debate," 18 December 1998.

41. Hitchens, "Most Dangerous Presidency."

42. "World Reaction: China Condemns, Germany, Japan Back Use of Force," CNN.com, 17 December 1998.

43. "World Reaction," CNN.com.

44. Gellman, "Iraq Inspections."

45. "World Reaction," CNN.com.

46. Peter Finn, "End of Raids Spurs Conflicting Arab Reactions," *Washington Post*, 21 December 1998, A24.

47. Finn, "End of Raids Spurs Conflicting Arab Reactions."

48. Finn, "End of Raids Spurs Conflicting Arab Reactions."

49. "Transcript: President Clinton Explains Iraq Strike," CNN.com, 16 December 1998.

50. Bruce Sullivan, "'Wag the Dog' Haunts Clinton," CNS News, 17 December 1998.

51. "Let Wag the Dogs of War," *Washington Times*, 17 December 1998.

52. "Let Wag the Dogs of War," *Washington Times*.

53. "Let Wag the Dogs of War," *Washington Times*.

54. Judy Aita, "Bin Laden, Atef Indicted in U.S. Federal Court for African Bombings," United States Information Agency, 4 November 1998.

55. Aita, "Bin Laden, Atef Indicted."

56. Aita, "Bin Laden, Atef Indicted."

57. "Intelligence Analyst Warns Bin Laden Could Strike Anywhere." CNN.com, 26 June 1999.

58. "Intelligence Analyst."

59. "Intelligence Analyst."

60. Siobhan Roth, "Khobar Towers: A Case of Futility," *Legal Times*, 17 September 2001.

CHAPTER 15: The U.S.S. *Cole*

1. John Miller, Michael Stone, Chris Mitchell, *The Cell*, (New York: Hyperion, 2002), 228.

2. Miller, et al., 226.

3. See sidebar by Sascha Sagan, "About Yemen," in "6 Dead, Dozens Hurt in Attack on Navy Ship," ABCNews.com, 12 October 1999.

4. Sagan, "About Yemen."

5. Miller, et al., 229.

6. Miller, et al., 229.

7. "U.S. Vows to Find Terrorist Attackers of Navy Destroyer." CNN.com, 12 October 2000.

8. See Andrea Koppel, Eileen O'Connor, and Matthew Chance, "Clock Running Down for Clinton's Hopes for Mideast Deal," CNN.com, 6 January 2001.

9. "Clinton: 'We Will Find Who Was Responsible,'" Office of International Information Programs, U.S. Department of State, 12 October 12, 2000. Available at http://usinfo.state.gov/topical/pol/terror/00101205.htm.

10. Rich Lowry, *Legacy: Paying the Price for the Clinton Years* (Washington, DC: Regnery, 2003), 336.

11. "Lawmakers Decry Mideast Violence, Attack on U.S.S Cole," CNN.com, 12 October 2000.

12. "Lawmakers Decry Mideast Violence."

13. Byron York, "Clinton Has No Clothes: What 9/11 Revealed about the Ex-president," *National Review*, 17 December 2001.

14. Miller, et al., 235; "The Cole Bombing: Moving beyond 'the Usual Suspects,'" Press Room Commentary, Heritage Foundation, 1 December 2000, available at http://www.heritage.org/Press/Commentary/ed120100.cfm.

15. "The Cole Bombing," Heritage Foundation.

16. Michael Elliott, "Could 9/11 Have Been Prevented?" *Time*, 4 August 2002.

17. Richard Miniter, "Bill Clinton's Failure on Terrorism," *Washington Times*, 2 September 2003.

18. Elliott, "Could 9/11 Have Been Prevented?"

19. Elliott, "Could 9/11 Have Been Prevented?"

20. Miller, et al., 231.

21. See, PBS *Frontline's* story "The Man Who Knew Too Much" at www.pbs.org/wgbh/pages/frontline/shows/knew/john/yemen.html.

22. Miller, et al., 231.

23. Miller, et al., 236.

24. Elliott, "Could 9/11 Have Been Prevented?"

25. Miller, et al., 231–232.

26. Ewen MacAskill, "U.S. Sacks Its Woman in Baghdad," *The Guardian*, 12 May 2003

27. Elliott, "Could 9/11 Have Been Prevented?"

28. Susan Schmidt, "U.S. Charges Two Linked to Al Qaeda in Cole Bombing," *Washington Post*, May 15, 2003.

29. Schmidt, "U.S. Charges Two Linked to Al Qaeda."

30. Art Pine, "Missiles Strike Bases Linked to African Blasts," *Los Angeles Times*, 21 August 1998.

CHAPTER 16: Turning on a Dime

1. "Clinton Warned Bush of Bin Laden Threat," Reuters, 15 October 2003.

2. Statement of Samuel R. Berger, U.S. House of Representatives and U.S. Senate, Select Committees on Intelligence, Joint Hearing, 19 September 2002.

3. House Permanent Select Committee on Intelligence and the Senate Select Committee on Intelligence, "Joint Inquiry into Intelligence Community Activities before and after the Terrorist Attacks of September 11, 2001," December 2002, 218.

4. For background on the Hanssen case see http://www.cnn.com/SPE-CIALS/2001/hanssen/.

5. "Ashcroft Wants Probe into Security at Justice," CNN.com, 11 March 2001.

6. Michael Elliot, "Could 9/11 Have Been Prevented?" *Time*, 4 August 2002.

7. Austin Bay, "What's Keeping Donald Rumsfeld up Late at Night?" *On Point*, 5 February 2001.

8. "At Rumsfeld Ceremony, Bush Promises to Beef Up Military," CNN.com, 26 January 2001.

9. David Ensor, "Bush Prefers CIA Intelligence Briefings Face to Face," CNN.com, 18 January 2001.

10. Ensor, "Bush Prefers CIA Intelligence Briefings Face to Face."

11. See, for example, "Powell: U.S., Russia Not in 'Deep Thaw' After Expulsions," CNN.com, 23 March 2001, and "White House Plays Down Russia Expulsions," CNN.com, 23 March 2001.

12. "Bush Pledges Whatever It Takes to Defend Taiwan," CNN.com, 25 April 2001.

13. "Bush Holds Arafat Responsible for Ending Violence," CNN.com, 29 March 2001.

14. "Bush to Outline Missile Defense Plan in Speech," CNN.com, 26 April 2001.

15. Daniel Benjamin and Steven Simon, *The Age of Sacred Terror: Radical Islam's War Against America* (New York: Random House, 2002, 2003), 387.

16. Elliot, "Could 9/11 Have Been Prevented?"

17. Elliot, "Could 9/11 Have Been Prevented?"

18. Elliot, "Could 9/11 Have Been Prevented?"

19. George W. Bush, Remarks by the president to students and faculty at National Defense University, Press Release, 1 May 2001.

20. George W. Bush, "Notice: Continuation of Emergency with Respect to the Taliban," Press Release, 2 July 2001.

21. Bush, "Notice: Continuation of Emergency."

22. "Many Say U.S. Planned for Terror But Failed to Take Action," *New York Times*, 30 December 2001.

23. Elliot, "Could 9/11 Have Been Prevented?"

AFTERWORD : 9/11 Commission Report

1. Interview with an unnamed former member of House leadership, 19 December 2003.

2. Jack Spencer, "Why Secretary Rumsfeld's Plan to Modernize the B-1B Bomber

Force Is Necessary," Executive Memorandum #765, The Heritage Foundation, 10 August 2001.

3. John J. Lumpkin, "CIA Gets Big Spending Boost in President's Proposed Budget," Associated Press, 5 February 2002.

4. Michael Scardaville and Jack Spencer, "9/11 One Year Later: Progress and Promise," Backgrounder #1584, The Heritage Foundation, 10 September 2002.

5. John J. Tkacik, Jr., "Time for Washington to Take a Realistic Look at China Policy," Backgrounder #1717, The Heritage Foundation, 22 December 2003.

6. House Permanent Select Committee on Intelligence and the Senate Select Committee on Intelligence, "Joint Inquiry into Intelligence Community Activities before and after the Terrorist Attacks of September 11, 2001," December 2002, xii.

7. "Joint Inquiry into Intelligence Community Activities," xiii.

8. "Joint Inquiry into Intelligence Community Activities," 9.

9. Bill Sammon, *Fighting Back: The War on Terrorism—From Inside the Bush White House* (Washington, DC: Regnery, 2002), 102.

10. Sammon, 102.

11. For corroborating testimony, perhaps emphasizing Vice President Dick Cheney's insistence more than Sammon does, see Bob Woodward, *Bush At War* (New York: Simon & Schuster, 2002), 17–18.

12. Prepared Remarks of Attorney General John Ashcroft, Senate Judiciary Committee Hearing: "The Terrorist Threat: Working Together to Protect America," 4 March 2003.

13. Ashcroft, "The Terrorist Threat."

14. Jerry Seper, "FBI Cooperation Levels Seen Rising," *Washington Times*, 24 December 2003.

15. Nolan Clay, "1998 Terrorist Warning on Men Training at Oklahoma Airports," *Oklahoman*, 29 May 2002.

16. "Avoiding Clinton's Mistakes," *Washington Times*, 22 October 2003.

17. "Avoiding Clinton's Mistakes," *Washington Times*.

18. "9/11 Mischief," *Wall Street Journal*, 10 July 2003.

19. "About Time," *New York Post*, 27 Feb 2003, 10.

ACKNOWLEDGMENTS

I WISH TO ACKNOWLEDGE AND THANK THE MANY PEOPLE WHO helped make this book possible.

Mark Horne, who diligently helped with the research and writing of what turned out to be a hefty project.

Curt Despain, who came into this project late to help with research and revisions and grew to deal with organizing the chapters as well as displaying an incredible editing eye.

Court Michua, who possessed fantastic research skills and a keen sense for finding good stories.

Mike Boos, without whom I would have never gotten this book to press. His editing skill and pension for detail got me to the publisher on time.

My parents, Norman and Marie Bossie, whose love and support during this difficult year allowed me the time to write this book.

My father-in-law, Bill Blackwell, who came through for my wife and me at a very difficult time in our lives.

To my family and friends, who assisted Susan and me in bringing our son home again.

My editor at WND Books, Joel Miller, whose patience and good nature along with a sharp pen polished this complicated story.

My publisher, David Dunham, who stood by me from the original concept to the final product, you have my eternal thanks and gratitude.

Finally, thank you to all of the people who I cannot name but were instrumental in this endeavor.

INDEX

INDEX

INDEX

INDEX

Somalia, 75, 79, 146-60, 191
Soskovets, Oleg, 126
Soviet(s), 8, 19, 24-25, 44, 52, 101, 111, 122-31, 143, 151, 159, 160, 202
Sovremenny, 129
Speaker's Advisory Group on Russia, 122
Specter, Arlen, 183
spies, 20, 24-25, 33-34, 40, 86-87, 143
State Department, xvii, 8, 36, 43, 86-87, 94, 98, 101, 104-7, 110-11, 115-16, 143, 155, 199, 209
Stephanopoulos, George, 21, 83, 141, 184
Stethem, Robert Dean, xvii, 35-36, 84
Strategic and Defense Studies Center, 162
Strategic Defense Initiative (SDI), 68
Strategic Information Operations Center (SIOC), 61
Sudan, xvi, 5, 18, 82, 146, 150, 160, 163, 174, 179-82, 190-91, 217-18
Sullivan, Andrew, 143, 163, 176-77
Sullivan, Bruce, 190
"Supporters of Sharia", 10
Syria, 47, 92, 111, 119

Taliban, 10, 32, 101-2, 105, 196-97, 205, 207-8
Tanzania, 83, 191, 193
Task Force on Combating Terrorism, 87
Task Force Ranger, 147
Tehran, 150
Temple Mount, 100
Tenet, George, xvi-xvii, 12, 24, 32, 38, 40-43, 45-48, 55, 100, 123-24, 204-6
"Terror 2000", 97-98, 216
"Terrorism 101", 13
Terrorist Threat Integration Center, 209
Tet Offensive, 68
Third Ranger Batallion, 156
Tiananmen Square, 104, 107, 127
Time, 197, 203
Tokyo, 138
Torricelli, Robert, xvii, 32-33
Treasury Department, 39, 93
Turabi, 150
Turner, Stansfield, 20
Tutu, Bishop Desmond, 88
TWA Flight 800, 165
TWA Flight 847, xv, xvii, 36, 84

U. S. Patriot Act, 208
Ujaama, James, 10
UN Operation Restore Hope, 191
UN Security Council, 188
Unabomber, 52
United Nations Special Commission (UNSCOM), 186, 188-89
United Nations (UN), 79-80, 102, 140, 147-48, 152, 154-55, 188

U.S. Capitol, 10
U.S. Customs, xv, 1-2, 93, 107, 109
U.S. Embassy, 18, 32, 47-48, 52, 55, 83, 94, 105, 178-93, 198
U.S. House Permanent Select Committee on Intelligence, 54
U.S. Immigration Control, 1, 93
U.S. News & World Report, 164, 174
USA Today, 155
USA vs. Enaam, 39
U.S.S. *Cole*, xvii, 4, 18, 52, 82, 192, 194-99, 205, 218
U.S.S. *Sullivans*, 4

Velasquez, Nydia, 88
Verizon, 174
Visa Reform Act, 208
Vista Hotel, 133, 135
VX gas, 131

Waco (Texas), 59
Wag the Dog, 183-84, 186, 190
Wahhaj, Siraj, 92
Wall Street Journal, 158
Waller, J. Michael, 40-41, 86, 91
Wallop, Malcolm, 53
Walsh, Elsa, 168-69, 171-72
Wang Jun, 107
Wang Zen, 107
Warsaw Pact, 111
Washington Post, 40, 59, 93, 153, 167, 171, 175, 184-85, 188-89, 196, 199, 219
Washington Times, 17, 25, 92-93, 184, 190, 197, 217
Weekly Intelligence Notes, 37
Wen Ho Lee, 38
West Bank, 99-100
Western Journalism Center, 96
White, Mary Jo, 92, 192
White House Counsel, 29
Whitewater, ix, 64, 220
Whitewater Committee, Senate, 220
Williams, Dave, 134-35
Woolsey, James, xv-xvii, 13-14, 20-28, 30, 34, 41, 47, 52-54, 99-100, 143-45, 217-19
World Trade Center (WTC), xvii, 6, 12, 14, 18, 25, 40, 49-50, 52, 56, 58, 83, 92-94, 97-98, 133-46, 163, 166, 198-99, 211, 216-18, 221
WorldNetDaily, 101

Yee, James, 92
Yeltsin, Boris, 122, 124-25, 127, 131
Yemen, xvii, 4, 150-51, 174, 194, 198-99
York, Byron, 82, 165, 196
Yousef, Ramzi, xvii, 6, 50, 136-39, 141
Yugoslavia, 79

Zubaydah, Abu, 10, 205